COMMENTARIES ON
THE EPISTLE TO THE ROMANS

COMMENTARIES ON
THE EPISTLE TO THE ROMANS
1532 – 1542

T. H. L. PARKER

T. & T. CLARK LTD.
59 GEORGE STREET, EDINBURGH

Copyright © T. & T. Clark Ltd, 1986.
Typeset by Pennart Typesetting (Edinburgh) Ltd, Edinburgh,
corrected by C. R. Barber & Partners (Highlands) Ltd,
Fort William, Scotland,
printed and bound by Billing & Sons, Worcester,

for

T. & T. CLARK LTD, EDINBURGH.

First printed in the U.K. 1986.

British Library Cataloguing in Publication Data

Parker, T.H.L
    Commentaries on the Epistle to the Romans 1532-1542.—
    (Commentaries on the Epistle to the Romans)
    1. Bible. N.T. Romans—Commentaries
    I. Title II. Series
    227'.107   BS2665.3

    ISBN 0-567-09366-2

CONTENTS

Preface   vii

A Guide to References   xi

PART I   A Survey of the Authors and their Books   1

PART II   Romans 1.18–23
              Text and Exegesis
              Exposition   84

PART III   Romans 2.13–16
              Text and Exegesis
              Exposition   125

PART IV   Romans 3.20–28
              Text and Exegesis
              Exposition   142

CONCLUSION   201

Bibliography   210

Index   223

98806

PREFACE

Everyone knows that Luther and Calvin wrote commentaries on Romans. In the last few years those of Bucer and Melanchthon have become more widely known. Even Caietan and Sadoleto have begun to emerge from the shadows. But how many, even among students of the sixteenth century, have met with Guilliaud's *Collatio*, or Grimani's *Commentarii*, with Haresche's ill-named *Expositio tum dilucida, tum brevis*, or Titelmann's *Collationes*, or Gagney's *Epitome Paraphrastica*? Probably many of the names of the commentators are as little known to my readers as they were to me when I started on this investigation; and, as for their books, they have sat on the shelves these four hundred and fifty years, disturbed only by the cleaners, the cataloguers, and infrequent historians like Richard Simon and Eduard Reuss.

Whether they deserved a better fate it would be ungenerous to decide, but they nearly all enjoyed some success in their own day. Did not Gagney run to four editions or, at least, printings, and Titelmann to three? This suggests a steady demand. And apart from the success of individuals, the large number of commentaries written in the period of which we are speaking must argue not only an urge to write on Romans but also a sufficiently strong interest in the Epistle among the reading public to make the printing of so many commentaries worth-while as commercial ventures.

We may well be surprised at the large number. In 1529 Melanchthon's second commentary (the first had appeared in 1522) and the first edition of Titelmann were published. In 1532, besides Melanchthon's third commentary and Titelmann's second edition, came Caietan's work. The next year brought the first edition of Gagney's paraphrases. Sadoleto followed in 1535. In 1536 there were two new works, commentaries by Bucer and Haresche, with Bullinger's after them in 1537. New editions of Gagney came in 1538 and 1539, with Pellicanus also in the latter year. Two new

commentaries, by Melanchthon and Calvin, were published
in 1540, as well as the third edition of Titelmann. Finally, two
more new commentaries appeared in 1542, those by Grimani
and Guilliaud. After this, no new commentaries came out
before the Council of Trent. Thus, in those thirteen years, no
less than fourteen separate works on Romans were published.
Have so many ever been published in a comparable period in
any other century?

But perhaps this is a little misleading. Many were not
commentaries on Romans alone but formed part of a more
extended work. Thus, those of Caietan, Bullinger, Guilliaud,
and Pellican appeared as one section of commentaries on the
Epistles or on the whole New Testament. Bucer and Calvin
published theirs separately but both were intended as
first-fruits of at least the Pauline Epistles and therefore started
with Romans as the first in the Canon. Hence only
Melanchthon, Titelmann, Gagney, Haresche, Sadoleto, and
Grimani wrote commentaries on Romans by itself. The
interesting fact that, taking the commentaries as a whole, six
of the authors were Romanists and five Reformers, becomes
more remarkable when we narrow the number to those who
wrote only on Romans as a deliberate choice. Then we see
that there are five Romanists to one solitary Reformer.

Should we relate this fact to the current ecclesiastical
controversies? The "Lutherans" were preaching justification
by faith alone and were claiming that this was the teaching of
Scripture interpreted in its own light. What more natural than
that their opponents should defend themselves by attacking
them on their own ground? that they should write commentaries on Scripture to show that Scripture rightly understood
in the light of Church tradition, supported themselves? that
they should in particular take up the challenge of justification
by faith alone and demonstrate that the classic document for
that doctrine, the Epistle to the Romans, itself refuted the
novel teaching of the "Lutherans"? If we do draw this
inference, we must observe that, with one exception,
Sadoleto, it was done quite discreetly and politely. We do not
find the rabid polemic against the heretics that was to
embitter and enliven the pages of later writers like Soto and,

above all, Catharinus. One could read some of the Romanist commentaries without becoming aware from them that a furious conflict was raging within the Church.

Such an attitude, however, faithfully mirrors the period of the fifteen-thirties, when, despite the excommunications and the battle of books and the sporadic persecutions, hopes of reconciliation were still alive. The decade was sandwiched between the two sets of peace talks at Augsburg and Regensburg. Soto and Catharinus, on the other hand, were writing when dogmas had been determined at Trent and when therefore it had been made clear that the Reformers were heretics. Our present Romanist writers will disagree with the Reformers, perhaps, albeit tacitly, even deny their opinions, but the tenor of their writing is unpolemical. The same must also be said of the commentaries of the Reformers themselves. Calvin, indeed, is, in the later editions, sometimes sarcastic and bitter, but he is less sharp in this first edition. Melanchthon can be pugnacious on occasion, but usually only when he has been provoked. The others are mild and conciliatory when there is occasion to notice difference of opinion. Many on both sides, but especially the Reformers, who had the community feeling of the dispossessed, spoke overmuch of "us" in opposition to "them".

The Romanist – Reformer division does not unduly obtrude in these commentaries and, what is more, does not obscure other differences. Pellican and Calvin were both Reformers, but Calvin uses the Greek text, Pellican the Vulgate. Sadoleto and Haresche are both Romanists, but how different in approach and style the humanist Sadoleto from the scholastic Haresche! Melanchthon, Bucer, and Calvin are all Reformers, but there is a world of difference in their expository methods and compositions. Or, on theological grounds one must separate the semi-Pelagian Sadoleto from, for example, the Thomist Caietan and the Augustinian Calvin.

It is clear that, besides their not yet hardened ecclesiastical divisions, there were other differences between them, cutting across party lines, and equally interesting historically. This is not, therefore, a study of the disagreements between Romanists and reformed about the interpretation of the Epistle, but rather a survey of the commentaries and an investigation into some of the agreements and disagreements to be found in them. We shall get to know some authors whom most of us did not know before. We might decide that some of them are hardly worth knowing; but this would be a hasty judgment, for in his own way every one of the authors has something to be said for him. If he does not help us to understand Romans any better, he may help us to understand how a sixteenth century man looked at Romans. If we find Sadoleto's theology unattractive, we must appreciate his pretty device of method – was he the only one in the history of Romans to put his commentary in the form of a dialogue? Haresche is long-winded, Guilliaud no great shakes as a commentator, but the one, treading the path of Sorbonnic rectitude, continually surprises us by his scholastic ingenuity, the other, humbly acknowledging his limitations and handing on quotations from the acknowledged masters, has a certain deprecatory charm. When we come to Caietan and Bullinger, we come to good serious commentators in the common style, who are worth reading for the understanding of the Epistle. Melanchthon, using the "new" method, is, as always, a giant among theologians. But two of our authors stand out above the others. Calvin with his intense penetration into the mind of his subject and his single-minded objectivity; and Bucer, whose commentary must be considered as potentially the greatest in the pre-critical history of the interpretation of Romans. Whatever branch of the science of commentating we consider, textual, exegetical, historical, interpretative, Bucer is a master. Only his weakness in method, a weakness that extended to literary style and the organizing of his material, prevented his commentary holding its place as the *magisterium* on Romans. The fact that in the event it proved, at least in its entirety, virtually unreadable should not blind us to its excellence. The projected critical edition of Bucer's commentaries will, it is to be hoped, establish his position as one of the supreme Biblical commentators.

I have said that the aim of this present work is to examine

and compare these commentaries. We shall not, however, follow each one through the whole of the Epistle. This would take more time than I am able to allot to the task, far more than the reader could endure. We shall therefore confine ourselves to four topics. First, we will give a survey of each one in chronological order. Then we shall look at their treatment of Rom.1.18–23. This will lead us on to Rom.2.13, and finally to the important passage on justification, Rom.3.20–28. In each of these passages we shall first of all set out their exegesis of verses in detail and then turn to more general interpretation. The exegesis will be prefaced by the 1527 Erasmus Greek, and the 1527/28 Stephanus Vulgate, and Erasmus's Latin version, with the few variants indicated – merely to show how insignificant they are. This should not be taken as implying any opinion that these were the editions our authors – or indeed, any of them – used. They are merely the latest editions before 1532, our starting point. I have, somewhat reluctantly, omitted references to the paraphrases, which would seem to demand a different mode of treatment.

In conclusion, I wish to thank the University of Durham for granting me Sabbatical leave for the Epiphany and Easter Terms of 1981 in order to make a start on this work; I am also grateful to the President and Fellows of Queens' College, the Master and Fellows of Gonville and Caius College, and the Master and Fellows of Magdalene College, for permission to make use of their libraries.

A Guide to the References

As the books with which we are concerned are in different forms, some paginated, some foliated, some in single column, some in double, the references within the text are restricted, for simplicity's sake, to the figure only. The following information should make the references quite clear.

Bibles and New Testaments

Er[1] = the first edition of Erasmus' Greek N.T. The other editions are indicated with superscript[2,3,4,5].

Erasmi versio = Erasmus' Latin translation of the N.T., printed in double column with the Greek and therefore indicated by the same superscript numbers.

Erasmi Vulgata = the Vulgate text as given in Erasmus' N.T. of 1527.

Vulgata = the text of Stephanus' 1527/28 Biblia and collated with his Biblia of 1532.

Col = the Greek N.T. printed by Colinaeus in 1534.

Compl = Complutensian Polyglot of 1522, containing both the Greek and the Vulgate.

Commentaries

Bucer: paginated, double columns. Superscript [a] refers to the left hand column, superscript [b] to the right hand.

Bullinger: paginated; single column.

Caietan: foliated, single column; divided into sections labelled A – K. Hence, e.g., LII F = section F on fol. LII. It is, obviously, unnecessary to note recto and verso.

Calvin: references are to my edition (see Bibliography), with superscript line numberings.

Gagney: foliated; single column. Hence the customary superscript [r] and [v].

Grimani: foliated; single column. Hence as Gagney.

Guilliaud: paginated; single column.

Haresche: foliated; single column. Hence as Gagney.

Melanchthon: where two references are given, the first refers to 1532, the second to 1540/41; where only one reference, it is to 1540/41. Both are foliated; single column. Hence as Gagney.

Pellicanus: paginated; single column.

Sadoleto: because the first edition is a rare book, I have given references also to the more easily obtainable edition of 1738; 1535 references first; paginated, single column. The references of 1535 and 1536 coincide in the passages quoted.

PART ONE

A Survey of the Authors and their Books

1: 1532

The study of Romans in the sixteenth century may be said to begin with Lefèvre (1515) and Erasmus (1516) on the critical side and with Melanchthon on the methodological. No doubt Melanchthon received an initial impetus from Luther, both in general and also, if Professor Bizer is correct, from the actual study of Luther's 1515-16 lectures on the Epistle.[1] But this impetus was theological. Luther's lectures, which had kept to the old-fashioned form of *glossae* and *scholia*, could not help Melanchthon on method. Before he had met Luther, Melanchthon had learned from Aristotle, Cicero, and Rudolf Agricola the "new" method of rhetoric. His originality lay in applying this method to Romans.

He came back to the Epistle again and again throughout nearly the whole of his working life, now writing a new commentary, now revising an old one. The first came in 1522, a set of lectures published without his knowledge: *Annotations of Philip Melanchthon on the Epistles of Paul to the Romans and the Corinthians*. It had an immediate success, with a new edition the next January in Strasbourg and others in March, May, August, and September, as well as a German translation. After this period as a best-seller, the book pursued a more even course with an edition in February 1524 and the German translation again in 1527.

Melanchthon professed himself embarrassed by the publication of his notes, said, 'I never knew them', and wrote a new commentary, which appeared in 1529 under the title *Dispositio orationis on the Epistle of Paul to the Romans*.

---

[1] E. Bizer: Theologie der Verheissung. Studien zur theologischen Entwicklung des jungen Melanchthon (1519-1524) (Neukirchen, 1964), pp. 131f.

Dispositio orationis refers to Melanchthon's method of determining the main subjects in a document and arranging (disposing) them in an orderly fashion.[2] The *Dispositio*, although its career was less spectacular than that of the *Annotationes*, met with considerable success; there were two editions in 1529, two in 1530, and another, belatedly, in 1539.[3]

Not yet content, Melanchthon soon came to Romans again and brought out in 1532 *Commentaries on Paul's Epistle to the Romans, newly written, by Philip Melanchthon*. Again success crowned the effort, with fresh editions in 1532, 1533, and 1535. He then revised the book, so that it became *Commentaries on the Epistle of Paul to the Romans, revised in this year of 1540*. This appeared at Wittenberg in March, 1540, and at Strasbourg in the same month. After this, apart from *Theological Institutio on the Epistle of Paul to the Romans*, he left the Epistle alone for several years, returning to it at last in 1556 with his large-scale commentary, *Enarratio on the Epistle of Paul written to the Romans*, of which there were reprints in 1558 and 1561. It is the books of 1532 – 1540 with which we are now concerned.

Melanchthon's revision was so extensive that he left little unaltered – at least, in our sections. It was partly a redrafting and re-writing of the same material, and partly the inclusion of new material, sometimes as an addition, sometimes in substitution. Other passages are completely re-written, saying the same thing in different words. The revision is far more thorough than that which Calvin gave to his *Romans* between 1540 and 1556.

The lay-out is also re-ordered drastically, so as to make fewer and more general headings. Thus our first passage is set out in 1532 as follows:

---

[2] See P. Joachimsen: Loci Communes. Eine Untersuchung zur Geistesgeschichte des Humanismus und der Reformation. (Luther-Jahrbuch 1926, reprinted Amsterdam, 1966); N.W. Gilbert: Renaissance Concepts of Method (New York, 1960).

[3] Printed C.R. XV, 443-492 under the misleading title of *Annotationes*.

PROPOSITIONES.

The wrath of God is revealed from heaven on all ungodliness and unrighteousness of men.

Who suppress the truth in unrighteousness.

For as far as God can be known, he is known to them.

For the invisible things of him from the foundation of the world.

That they may be inexcusable.

They became vain.

They changed the glory of God.

Whereas 1540 has only:

For the wrath of God is revealed from heaven.

Who suppress the truth in unrighteousness.

For as far as God can be known, he is known to them.

Nine arguments for the existence of God.

They did not glorify God.

Yet 1540 covers all the same ground as 1532 and at greater length.

The *Argumentum* is revised even more thoroughly. In 1532 it is straightforward, with only the one sub-division (προλεγόμενα, On Justification). In 1540 it is both augmented and itemized. After an introductory passage of eight pages there follow:

The Sum of the teaching handed down in the writings of the prophets and apostles, on justification before God.

On the word "grace".

The difference between the Law and the Gospel.

Sin.

Justification.

Grace.

Testimonies of Scripture, that grace signifies gratuitous acceptance, etc.

Faith.

Testimonies, that faith signifies trust in mercy, etc.

Statements from the old writers.

On good works.

Testimonies, that sin remains in the saints.

Resolution of arguments which our adversaries oppose from Scripture.
Resolution of scholastic objections.

In substance (again I speak only of our sections) there seems little difference between the editions. It may be that 1540 takes up and develops more fully the references to the fathers and to sixteenth century philosophies. It may be that 1532 has a more pastoral tone, 1540 a more intellectual. But then, 1540 is also pastoral, and 1532 is far from being anti-intellectual.

Where Melanchthon is the subject, I have taken 1540 as definitive, since it makes the same points in a usually clearer and more distinct form. Where the same quotation occurs in 1532, even if not quite verbatim, a reference is also given to that edition. Sometimes a similar or a different opinion of 1532 is inserted as a footnote. We must, of course, always remember that contemporary references to Melanchthon before 1540, that is, before Calvin, Grimani and Guilliaud, will be to his first edition.

The edition of 1532 is a smallish book of 264 folios, with 25 lines to the page. As I have seen only a microfilm, I do not know the dimensions of the type-face. The work consists of an *Epistola nuncupatoria* (to Archbishop Albert of Magdeburg), an *Argumentum,* and the *Commentarii.* All is in italic except the Biblical text. The length is about 80,000 words.

The 1540 edition I have used was that printed at Wittenberg in January 1541 by the original printer, Clug. It has 278 folios and 25 lines to the page, with a type-face of 10.7 × 6.3 cm. The *Epistola nuncupatoria* (to Philip of Hesse) in roman, *Argumentum* and *Commentarii* in italic. Length about 135,000 words.

All Melanchthon's commentaries follow the same method. Modern commentaries, with few exceptions, work outwards from the text. They seek to understand the document by way of understanding its details and what they present to the reader is either the process by which they have arrived at their understanding or that process together with the understanding. This is not Melanchthon's way. What he presents to the reader is the understanding, with little or no mention of his investigations into the meaning of the text. This professor of Greek offers hardly any exegesis; all is interpretation. The attempt at understanding, however, does not end the commentator's search according to Melanchthon. He has then to go on to ask, 'Which are the most important subjects dealt with in this document?' The choice of these subjects or *loci*, to give them their classical name, is in no sense arbitrary; they are the actual subject matter of the document; these are what it is all about.

A qualification must be added at this point. Melanchthon's commentary does not consist only of a set of dogmatic essays on the various *loci* of Romans. It is also, and chiefly, a continuous exposition of the argument, sometimes following it in detail by sentences or even words, sometimes taking a whole paragraph in general. The exposition, even of single words, however, represents the final understanding of the Epistle as a whole applied to or brought out in a small part rather than the building up of the complete understanding from the detail.

Melanchthon explains Paul's argument as one that follows the prescriptions of rhetoric, as found in the classical rhetoricians, with whom, as himself the author of handbooks on rhetoric, he was well-acquainted.[4] Since a large part of the object of classical rhetoric was to train youths to plead cases in court, the address was conceived of as the conducting of a case – the whole is called *causa* (a case). The student is taught how to set out his initial explanation of the substance of his case (this is the *Argumentum*), how he is to lead into the case (the *Exordium*), how he is to present his first point of accusation or defence (the *Propositio*), and then how to come to the *status* of his case (a difficult word – basis, substance), and so on. This *schema* Melanchthon applies to Romans fairly strictly. Paul is seen as writing on behalf of the Gospel (his client!), addressing himself to the Roman Christians as a barrister before a court. Yet this is conceived as a literary

[4] De Rhetorica libri tres (1519); Institutiones Rhetoricae (1521); Elementorum Rhetorices libri duo (1542). *Rhetorices* in the last title is a Greek genitive singular in Latin script.

device; it is not integrated with the subject matter. Melanchthon's *Romans* is a model of the *mos novus*, the new style that came in with the Renaissance. But as such, we have also to observe that it has, on closer inspection, a remarkable smack of the old scholasticism about it. *Loci* are not much different from *scholia* and a strict imposition of the rules of rhetoric is not, after all, any less "scholastic" than a strict imposition of the rules of dialectic.

It is not difficult to account for the popularity of these commentaries. They were simply written, easy to understand even at a first reading, yet rich in ideas and repaying further study. The general reader was not lost in a forest of technical minutiae or abstruse reasoning, but led straight-forwardly and persuasively through subjects represented to him as of the closest relevance to his eternal welfare.

Not all specialist readers were so pleased, however. We find Erasmus writing to Boniface Amerbach on July 12, 1533, 'they are selling Philip Melanchthon's new commentary on the Epistle to the Romans here [Fribourg] . . . I confess that many things in it are very well. But there are several places that I mislike. Often he tortures the meaning. He rejects Origen and Augustine arrogantly. Not a few passages he leaves out altogether. I have read a few sections (*quaterniones*). He seems to have lighted upon the work of some schoolman or other, of which he [treats] the *argumentum*. The price of it is low' (PSA X, 244-5). But to Melanchthon himself he wrote on October 6, 1534 with the gratifying news that he had bought three copies of the commentary: 'one I sent to the Bishop of Augsburg, one to Sadoleto, Bishop of Carpentras; the third I kept for myself. What I shall think of it, I will perhaps indicate elsewhere.' (PSA XI, 44). And then to Sadoleto at the end of the month: 'I have sent you Melanchthon's commentary – but not for you to imitate! For he tortures Scripture more here than elsewhere; although, I grant you, a marvellous simplicity. However, the various opinions of many writers are mentioned in it, and I knew you would be prudent and gather from it anything that would help you to understand the mind of Paul' (PSA XI, 45). Whether Sadoleto made any use, other than a destructively critical, of Melanchthon's commentary would repay further study. Certainly it had a considerable influence on some of our other commentators, notably Bucer and Calvin.

In 1532 also appeared the last part of the Biblical commentaries of Thomas de Vio, Bishop of Gaeta and Cardinal of St Sixtus, commonly known, from his birthplace and see as Caietan or Cajetan (we will use the former). His Biblical work belongs to the last years of his life. His university lecturing on Lombard's *Sentences* and, above all, on Aquinas' *Summa Theologiae* had marked him out as the foremost scholastic theologian of his day. Whether his interpretation of Aquinas' doctrines and in particular of his concept of analogy are faithful to the originals is still a matter of debate, but of the magnitude of his Thomist influence on theology during his lifetime and posthumously in the Council of Trent and the post-Tridentine Roman Church there can be no question. It was the scholastic theologian who presided as Papal Legate over the famous examination of Luther at Augsburg in 1518. Five years later he gave himself up to full-time study and writing, and from then until his death in August 1534 published a series of Biblical commentaries.

He first applied his attention to the New Testament, beginning in 1525 with a small book which he called, perhaps half-humorously, *Ientacula novi testamenti*: in other words, 'New Testament Breakfasts' or 'First Tastes of the New Testament'. An apparently inappropriate title, for the book consisted of sixty-four rather scholastically executed little essays on notable or difficult verses. From this elementary start he went on to the Psalter (finished Easter 1527 and published at Venice in 1530) and then to the Gospels, Matthew (November 1527), Mark (December 1527), Luke (January 1528), and John (May 1528), as well as Acts (June 1529), published together at Venice, also in 1530. The commentaries on the Epistles, finished in August 1529 and published at Paris in 1532, brought his work on the New Testament to an end, for he was unable, he said, to interpret

Revelation according to the literal sense. Thereafter he wrote on the Old Testament. The commentary on the Pentateuch came out in 1531, that on Joshua etc. (written between June 1531 and July 1532) followed in 1533; Job, finished in March 1533, was published posthumously in 1535, while Proverbs, Ecclesiastes, and Isaiah 1–3 did not appear until 1542.

This incredible outburst of creative activity (even granting the probable help of secretaries and research assistants), with commentaries on practically all the New Testament and about half the Old, seems therefore to have been accomplished in not much more than ten years. It drew well-merited admiration from Sadoleto: 'in the midst of such turmoils, Caietan, you have focussed your mind completely on Holy Scripture and undertaken the interpretation of each Testament (*Instrumentum*) of our most holy Faith' (*Epist.*1.45ª). But we must not be so dazzled at the feat as to overlook its significance. Apart from Lefèvre and Erasmus, both Roman Catholics certainly, but both what is loosely called "humanist" and moreover both writing before the rise of Luther, Caietan was the first Romanist commentator of any stature in the sixteenth century. Sadoleto's final clause points us to a further conclusion. Within quite a short space of time Luther's position had developed from an attack on a particular doctrinal abuse to a general theological controversy. Luther had stated his conviction that the source and criterion of all dogmas is Holy Scripture. But Caietan knew well that, however much it has to be qualified, this was Catholic teaching, the teaching of his master St Thomas (e.g. *Summa Theologiae Qu.* 1,*Art.* 8, *Respondeo* and *Ad Secundum*). He showed himself too good a theologian to counter, like many of his obscurantist fellow-theologians, Bible with Church. It had to be shown that the Bible was on the side of the Roman Church and not of the Lutherans, who had made it the sole platform of their authority. He therefore set out on this remarkable programme of expounding the Catholic Scriptures.[5]

[5] This was also the view of Richard Simon: 'He was convinced that one could not solidly refute the new heresies without an exact knowledge of the literal sense of Scripture' (538ᵇ).

The commentary on Romans occupies fol.1-XLVIII^v (sig. AA-FF viii^v) of the 1532 edition of *The Epistles of Paul and other Apostles, corrected to the verity of the Greek and expounded according to the literal sense by the Most Reverend Lord, Lord Thomas de Vio* . . . The book is quite large, with a type-face of 25.3 × 15.2 cm. The type is roman, fifty-four lines to the page. Each folio is divided into sections; the recto A B C D E, the verso F G H I K; each section is of eleven lines, except E and K, which have ten.

The title is faithful to his intention and performance: 'amended according to the Greek', and 'expounded according to the literal sense'. His own text is the Vulgate, which he corrects by the Greek but without mention of the Greek word or phrase. His textual comments are usually expressed as an addendum to the running head: for example, '*In similitudinem. pro, in similitudine*' ('into the similitude – for, in the similitude' – l. 23). The former is the Vulgate reading, the latter the Latin translation of the Greek text. In the passages we are to scrutinize there will be little in the way of correction. In any case, he does not often go to the Greek to make an exegetical point but prefers to rely on the words of the Vulgate to bring out the same point. Where one of his contemporaries might have said, 'Note that Paul says φανερόν here, but ἀποκαλύπτεται in the previous verse. The former is a weaker word, expressing less than the revelation of grace', Caietan has 'He does not say *revelavit* . . . he says *manifestavit* (III H). Very occasionally he may use the phrase 'the Greek word . . .' but without quoting that word.

That his interpretation was according to the literal sense meant that he confined himself to this sense as a matter of policy. No doubt the policy was at least partly dictated by his intention of showing that the Bible was "Catholic" – not the Bible interpreted arbitrarily or fancifully, but the plain unvarnished letter of Scripture. He kept faithfully to his programme (of course, Romans does not lend itself to allegory or anagogy), and expounds in a literal and straight-forward manner. His most frequent formulae are the common-sensical *et est sensus* ("and the meaning is") and *id est*. He does not allow himself usually to be drawn into references to the Holy Spirit as the author of Scripture in the manner of Lefèvre or (rather differently) Calvin.

While not notable for profound insights or brilliant flashes of intuition, Caietan's commentary is eminently sober, sensible, and conservative. Yet there was no pleasing the Faculty of Theology in Paris, which issued a censorious open letter in 1534. They had, they said, expected great things from him in the way of refuting and suppressing the Lutheran plague. But behold a commentary on the Psalms where the text is not the Roman Psalter, a commentary on a New Testament text according to Erasmus and Faber (A2^r-2^v). Some had accused him of errors 'partly from the annotations of Erasmus and Faber, partly even from the books of Luther (which we do not ourselves believe)' (A2^v). A substantial list of his errors is given, but there is nothing specifically on *Romans*. Caietan's principal and pervasive sin was that he had placed the Vulgate version in subjection to the Hebrew and Greek. If the Faculty was hopelessly out of touch with the scholarship of the day and if Caietan saw that the use of that scholarship by theology was necessary, yet it was the spirit of the Faculty that was upheld at Trent. He was further censured by Catharinus in 1535 but again without direct reference to *Romans* apart from objections to the punctuation in Chapters 1 and 5. The Faculty approved of Catharinus' criticisms in 1545. And the matter was brought up again in 1547, when a fair trial was demanded. Unfortunately there is no record of the judgments of the commission. His commentaries, however, were never placed on the Index of the prohibited books.

They did not arouse great enthusiasm in the years to come. Richard Simon, who devoted a chapter to him and to Catharinus' censures, judged that he had bitten off more than he could chew, in that he possessed an insufficient command of the languages.[6] Walch probably speaks for most readers with his luke-warm 'His expositions are not to be despised'.[7] It is worth noting, however, (and we shall return to the point later) that a book was written in 1891 by R.C.Jenkins

---

[6] 'il a entrepris un ouvrage qui étoit au dessus de ses forces' (538^b).

[7] Walchii Bibliotheca Theologica Selecta. . .IV, 427.

suggesting that Caietan's *Romans* was the basis for the Anglican Thirty-nine Articles.[8]

The third work on Romans belonging to this year was a paraphrase by Francis Titelmann, of whom little seems to be known. According to the *Dictionnaire de Biographie Chrétienne* he was born at Hasselt, in the district of Liège, about the year 1498. He became a Recollect, or member of a particular Franciscan group, at Louvain, and a Capuchin in 1535. He wrote commentaries on all the epistles, on Job, the Canticles, Matthew, and John. He also attacked Erasmus in print. He died 'en odeur de sainteté', says the *Dictionnaire*, on September 12, 1537. John Bale, in his inaccurate list of the commentaries on the Apocalypse, names Titelmann as one of the authors.[9]

We can learn a little more about him from the title-pages of his two books on Romans. The former, published in May, 1529, runs: *Five Collations on the Epistle of the blessed Apostle Paul to the Romans, in which are most diligently treated and explained the more difficult passages in the Epistle, especially those which seem to have something of difficulty from the Greek, so that the significance (emphasis) of the Greek words may easily be grasped by those who know no Greek, and at the same time the ecclesiastical Latin edition of the New Testament is rationally defended – and that from the authority of the old interpreters and other best approved fathers, both Latin and Greek.* We see therefore that he knew some Greek, and that he accorded a certain authority, or, at least, priority, to the Greek text, but that he was loyal to the Vulgate; that he was a friar minor, which we already knew; that he was a *praelector*, or lecturer on Holy Scripture at Louvain (and we may therefore not improbably infer that his books had their origin in his lectures); that he was a godly, or at least, a pious man, for, where other authors dedicated books to friends or patrons, he dedicated his to God (*To the Supreme and First and Uncreated Truth Who, ever unbegotten, begets the Coeternal to Himself, let*

---

[8] R.C. Jenkins: Pre-Tridentine Doctrine (London, 1891), 70-72.
[9] Select Works, Parker Society (Cambridge, 1849), 258.

this work be vowed and dedicated), and included in the prefatory matter *Praises to the Omnipotent and most high Lord, the Giver of all good things,* and ended with *Psalm of Wonder, Praise, and Thanksgiving on the Handmaid of the Lord, the daughter of Jerusalem, redeemed from a lost race.* From the book itself we learn that he was opposed to the Renaissance authors on the Bible, since the book is directed passage by passage against the opinions of Valla, Faber, and Erasmus. Erasmus expressed his irritation in a letter to one Pero Mexia: 'There is at Louvain a certain Titelmann. . . a little more learnèd in the Scriptures than your man, and also more modest, although prodigious in his boasting and most impudent loquaciousness' (PSA VIII.406). The thing rankled and he even wrote a reply: *On the Collations, a recent work of a certain old-age-pensioner-lecturer* (gerontodidascali). Elsewhere he called him 'κακ elmannus [bad man], a youth over-confident and of unbridled impudence'[10] (PSA VIII.342).

The Prologue to the *Collatio* shows more fully his position on the Greek and the Vulgate. He admits the priority of the Greek New Testament, but censures the *moderni* who wish to correct the Latin by the Greek, because the Greek is *non satis emendata neque satis bonae fidei*, presumably meaning that none of the (printed?) Greek texts extant is well enough edited and therefore sufficiently trustworthy (sig.b7^r). For evidence he points to the disagreement between different *codices* (copies?) and the greater variation between Greek texts than between Latin (sig.b7^r). 'Nevertheless, we by no means reprehend the comparison of the Latin texts with the Greek, whatever they may in fact be like, but strongly accept its usefulness' (sig.c5^v); chiefly because Greek is a richer language and will often say in one word what Latin can express only in several. He goes a little further, permitting additions from the Greek or reference to the Greek on doubtful points, but only on the authority of 'the commentaries of interpreters' (that is, no doubt, *approved* interpreters) or of 'the decisions of the most approved fathers'(sig.c6^v). Titelmann shows us that not

---

[10] The jokes on his age are lost on us. He seems to have been in his thirties, and therefore neither a youth nor a pensioner.

every teacher in the trilingual college of Louvain was an enlightened scholar.

The *Elucidatio* of May, 1532 has quite a different character: *An Elucidation on all the Apostolic Epistles, the fourteen Pauline and the seven Canonical, together with the text added in the margin and so conveniently arranged that each particle of the text is set over against its elucidation; [the text] according to the truth of the old Vulgate edition (veteris et vulgatae aeditionis); with arguments added (which can stand in place of epitomies) embracing summarily the whole substance of the Epistles, according to the order of individual chapters; by Brother Francis Titelmann* . . . Romans is given in sig. A8ᵛ-F6ʳ (there are no page numberings). On the outer part of each page, taking up about a quarter of the space, is the Vulgate text in roman, the remaining three-quarters of the page being occupied by the *Elucidatio*, or Paraphrase. The type-face measures 12.5 × 8.7 cm.

According to the title page, this is the third edition; but I have not been able to find a first or second. It was reprinted in 1540, after Titelmann's death, with the printer's commendation: 'You will find here many things, Reader, ferreted out which hitherto no-one has touched on, many things explained which up to this day have seemed very obscure.'

Titelmann's preface *Ad lectorem Praemonitio*, advice to the reader on how to use his book, certainly shows that he thought about what he was trying to do: 'If you want to gather fruit from our *Elucidationes*, Christian reader, you should observe the following order. First, read and read again the text you wish to understand, even if you do not understand it. Then, when you have considered simply the words of the text and have impressed it lightly on your mind, turn to the *Elucidatio* and read it by itself attentively, without reference to the text; just dwell on the simple reading until you have fully understood its force and sense, so far as you can. Next, compare the words of the text with the sense of the *Elucidatio*. When you have weighed exactly how the *Elucidatio* grasps what the text says and on the other hand how the text says in such and such words what the *Elucidatio* has in other words, you must also consider what may be found within the text, how much may be added to the understanding above the words of the text. All this will be easily indicated by the division of the texts and their distribution into individual parts' (sig. A3ᵛ).

Also this year were published new editions of Theophylact and Aquinas.

2: 1533

Heinrich Bullinger's commentary on Romans was published within two years of his succeeding to Zwingli's position as leader of the Church in Zürich. It must therefore have been commenced at least soon after, if not before, that momentous change in his life. Although still a fairly young man he had already written commentaries on Hebrews and I John and was within two or three years to cover all the Epistles, with a collected edition in 1537. The first edition I have discovered for *Revelation* is 1557. All these works (except perhaps *Revelation*, of which I see but two) ran through several editions. Neither Romans nor the art of exposition was new to him in 1533, however, for he had lectured on the Pauline epistles between 1525 and 1527 when he was lecturer at the Cistercian monastery in Kappel. These lectures remain, unpublished, as manuscripts in the library in Zürich.

He came to his reformed position (merely with the guidance of books, if his *Diarium* is a reliable account) by the time he was seventeen. The way it happened was ordinary enough, sensible enough; yet no-one else, surely, took the same course unaided. His theology course at conservative Cologne was almost confined to Lombard's *Sentences* and Gratian's *Decretum*. But he used them as, so to say, telescopes which showed him a wide tract of distant land, the church fathers; for they are both packed with quotations from the fathers. Not content with theologians at second hand, he read more widely, as the *Diarium* narrates: 'the first patristic work I came across was St Chrysostom's homilies on Matthew. I read it and saw that the fathers followed a very different method in sacred subjects from Lombard and Gratian. Next I sipped at some writings of Ambrose and Origen and

Augustine. In the meanwhile I was studying Luther's books *de captivitate Babylonica, de libertate christiana, assertio articulorum de bonis operibus*, and so on. I observed that Luther came closer to the theology of the fathers than the schoolmen. I observed also that, whereas the schoolmen deferred to the opinions of the fathers, the fathers themselves deferred to the opinions of the two Testaments. I therefore obtained a New Testament. I read Matthew's Gospel and what Jerome wrote on it. I went on to read the other books in the New Testament . . . Then there came into my hands the first edition of Philip Melanchthon's *Loci communes*, which delighted me. In the end, I devoted myself mainly to the Holy Scriptures. These things happened and exercised me night and day in the years 1521 and 1522' (*Diarium* 6).

Despite the popularity of his commentaries (which may perhaps be ascribed to other causes than their inherent excellence) Bullinger must be regarded as a commentator whose theory and intentions surpassed his performance, even when he had faithfully put his methods into practice. I speak now only of his *Romans*; it may be that this is not true of other commentaries; nor do I forget that he was one of the three commentators praised by Calvin in his letter to Grynaeus. But his accounts of the art or science of interpreting and expounding Scripture in the preface to the collected epistles, *Christiano Lectori*, in the dedication to Berthold Haller of Bern, and in the *Ratio studiorum*, are certainly among the best and fullest statements of the sixteenth century evangelical position. It is with his theory that we are for the moment concerned.

His starting point in the preface was the unhappy state of Biblical studies: 'Canonical Scripture lies neglected and in its stead human inventions are accepted, which century after century have been increasingly cultivated and foisted on the Church as next door to divine oracles. This was done more moderately in the centuries from Augustine up to Bede and Rabanus. Then Scripture was held in honour; and it was also translated more diligently. But after that time appeared Gratian and Lombard, those compilers of the old authors. They doubtless acted without evil intent, but they nevertheless did great harm to the truth of Scripture and good authors when they made a patchwork of *sententiae* of the chief heads of our religion out of the ecclesiastical authors. These were received the more readily by theologians, since there was a greater scarcity of good books. For the authors which escaped the flames of the Barbarian and Gothic invasion certainly either lay hid in monastery libraries, accessible to few, or were copied by scribes with great labour and at greater expense. For that divine art which is called Printing was not then invented. And so they regarded [the compilations] as a treasure-house where they could find the best and choicest statements of the ancients about our religion. The result was that they took little account of reading the authors themselves. Certainly less regard was paid to the Scriptures, save that Lyra and Carrensis attempted some things on the line of the old writers. There were others, however, who devoted themselves, not to expounding Scripture but to explaining Lombard's *Sentences*. Who could stand up and merely recite all the names of those who have commented on the Master's fourth book? There were others who composed vast *Partes, Summae,* and *Tractatus* out of these compilers and commentaries . . . The more learned and industrious treated thorny questions out of Scotus or Thomas and brought out certain subtleties from Aristotle . . . But why go on? What it came to in the end was that you could find pastors of the people who knew no Gospel beyond what was in their *Postilla* or their missal, as they call them. In fact, there would not be found thirty among three hundred who would have read their Bible regularly (*ordinarie Biblia legerint*). No wonder that there are some who cannot even recite the list of the Canonical Books!' (aaa2^v–aaa3^r).

This call to leave commentaries and come to the Bible might seem to be cutting the throat of the commentary in which it was made. But Bullinger had already seen this point and was willing for his commentary to stand under the same judgment as all others, if it was holding readers back from Scripture instead of leading them into it. He indicates more precisely the sort of works he had in mind: 'I have never been able to approve either the over-prolix commentaries which call one away from Scripture and detain one in the muddy and all too human pools or the studies of those who spend their whole time in wrapping everything up in commentaries and touch on Scripture itself only rarely or perfunctorily' (aaa3^v). On the other hand, 'I always hate the captiousness of those who learned what they did learn from the commentaries of good men and yet damn all commentators *en masse* as useless theological pests' (aaa3^v).

Commentaries should be written, first, to promote the glory of Christ, and then to help others to understand the Scriptures; and these, he avows, are his motives in writing (aaa3^v). They have therefore only a limited value and should be relinquished as soon as they have led the reader to the goal. 'If commentaries on Scripture are written with a real desire to help, they should be regarded as indications or pointers (*index*), as the statues of Mercury were way-marks, left behind as soon as you had reached your destination. Those who desire the truth wish to penetrate into the genuine sense of Holy Scripture and to have the enjoyment of it. Because these things seem hard at the first approach, those who are a bit more experienced erect commentaries as way-marks – but just so that you may enjoy and cleave to Scripture alone and leave the commentaries once you have become familiar with them' (aaa3^r). And again: 'those commentaries are best which smooth the way to the Scriptures and do not drag us away from Scripture and push us into useless and perplexed questions' (aaa3^v).

Therefore, 'I have written, not regulations, but commentaries, which are to be thought over, not taken at once as certain or divine oracles. For I frankly confess that nothing human is alien to men, and there is nothing so human as to err and be deceived. I also frankly confess that only canonical Scripture inspired by the Holy Spirit is the unique, certain, and absolute rule of truth, right living and right judging, which neither errs itself nor leads anyone into error, and that by it are to be weighed and sifted all the writings, sayings, and deeds of all men' (aaa2^r).

Cognate with the authority of Scripture, which makes it 'the unique, certain, and absolute' criterion, is its self-interpretation (for who can understand the mind of the Divine Spirit who inspired it save that same Spirit?). But this self-interpretation is dependent on its being read in the right way, that is, in the light of the sum of its own message. We note that Bullinger expresses the *analogia fidei* more broadly as *charitatis fideique regula*, the rule of love and faith: 'I freely avow that the interpretation of Holy Scripture is to be sought from itself alone, so that it may itself be the interpreter, under the direction of the rule of love and faith. From which sort of interpretation, because the holy fathers did not depart, I not only receive them as interpreters of Scripture but venerate them as beloved instruments of God' (aaa3ʳ).

Bullinger set down the art and method of Biblical exposition in the prefatory matter to his commentaries and in the *Ratio studiorum*, a work based on a similar preface of Erasmus, the *Methodus*. The *Ratio* itself treats of the theory of commentating, the *Preface* is a prospectus of the method he intends to adopt, and the *Dedication* is in the nature of an apologia for the method.

The first necessity, according to the *Ratio*, is inward and spiritual. If scripture comes from God, as indeed it does, it cannot be understood by one who is opposed to God or careless of him, but only by one whose heart is devoted to God, whose mind is purged of all stain and whose life is free from all impurity. The commentator's first task is therefore to pray: to pray that God 'will implant in him a love of righteousness and uprightness and drive out all iniquity from him' (22ᵛ). Such a man will show reverence towards the book he is expounding.

The second necessity is that he shall know how to set about understanding his document. Without a clearly defined method he may work hard 'and yet lose all his time and labour' (26ᵛ). Clearly, the first step in understanding is to know the language in which it is written, and indeed, to possess a skill in languages in general. This involves hard work, as he himself knows. He had once thought such endeavour to be beyond his powers, 'but my reverend teacher Conrad Pellican, beyond praise for his piety and learning, a great Hebrew scholar, persuaded me that nothing is hard to one who loves' (27^v).

Next the *scopus* of the document must be determined, its purpose, its sum and substance. The initial enquiry here is to discover the *scopus* of Scripture as a whole, so as to employ it for the understanding of the portion under consideration. 'There is no doubt that all the Scriptural books possess a certain common *scopus* (29^v). This is the Covenant between God and ourselves: 'The unique *scopus* common to all the sacred books is the Testament of the Lord' (30^r).

It is also necessary to follow the general rules of rhetoric when expounding Scripture. As with Melanchthon, so also with Bullinger, we must bear in mind that he is thinking of the arts of reading and writing, not of forensic pleading. The first rule is a careful attention to the context. But context, it is clear for Bullinger, is a complex term. It may include analogy, 'which is a proportion and certain similitude of things. Analogy cannot be applied to any passage but only to those places which can rightly and truly be proved to be genuine inferences' (32^r). The sense of a word may vary in different books; its use in a particular context should therefore be determined linguistically and lexicographically (a task demanding wide reading in many authors) and by the context itself.

The second rule is that the "circumstances" of a passage should be noted and followed; that is, the reason why something was said, the occasion on which it was said, its timing, the way in which it was said, and so on. After this must come a lexicographical and comparative study of the passage – where the words are used elsewhere and in what sense, and in what other places the ideas expressed occur. Finally comes the injunction that the *status* must not be neglected. And here Bullinger quotes from Rudolf Agricola, that 'the *status* is our term for the *summa*, the head, the point at issue, on which the subject especially hinges, concerning which it especially debates, and on which all the arguments depend' (34^v). Bullinger therefore concludes: 'First and above all we must enquire what the author is trying to say, what he is teaching, what he is proving, what disproving, what is his

purpose and occasion in writing and what arguments he is
using' (35^r). He continues with a passage on the use of
allegoria, but in this there is no need for us to follow him.

The *Preface* explains Bullinger's *modus scribendi* in some
detail: 'First, I have striven after brevity all through the work.
And even if I have been forced not infrequently to write at
greater length, yet I have taken care and trouble to aim at an
active brevity. For I did not want the reader whom I was
preparing for the reading of Scripture to be burdened,
involved, imprisoned, or held overmuch by my expositions.
Secondly, I have taken the utmost care to quote faithfully
the Apostle's own words.[11] In this respect I have chiefly
followed the edition of D. Erasmus of Rotterdam of blessed
memory.[12] Yet I have, so far as my meagre ability permitted,
several times compared it [=Erasmus' Latin version?] with
the original Greek – as often, that is to say, as the Greek
seemed clearer or plainer. I have indicated where a word
seems rather unusual or obscure, and I have explained those
which are more involved. Also, so far as I could, I have
smoothed out and filled in any bumps and pot-holes in the
language. I have noted if any Hebraisms occur. Thirdly, I
have shown the thread of the argument, the *scopus* of what is
being treated, the inter-relationship of statements and reasonings, to what everything should be referred, what they
prove, or what they aim at. And at the same time I have by
these methods investigated and (by the grace which the Lord
has given me) made plain the sense of the Apostles' words.
For I have seen that this is the chief thing the scholars of our
age seek in interpretations of the holy writings. I have,
however, deliberately not dealt with the *loci communes*, but
only drawn attention to the more important ones. The things
which seem alien and irrelevant to us I have, so to say, taken
over and related to our own culture and age and thus made
our own. Quite often I have attacked heresies, errors, and

[11] Apostles' in the plural, since this preface relates to all the N.T.
Epistles.

[12] Erasmus died on July 11-12, 1536. This edition of the commentary
was published in March, 1537, when his death was still fresh in
Bullinger's mind.

abuses . . . Moreover, for the explaining of these things I have used, as you see, a simple and uncultivated style, for I have no taste for finery and ornamentation. I think it is enough if one's thoughts are really expressed in easy language. For language is instituted and acquired to explain what is conceived in the mind' (aaa4^{r-v}). He adds that he has borrowed not a little from the older and more modern authors and that he gives references so that he cannot be accused of misrepresentation. He is not using them because he relies on their authority but because, since they are used against the Reformers, the adversaries may see 'that the things we say are not novel, not heretical, but ancient and orthodox' (aaa4^{v}).

Brevity; literalness; faithfulness to the original; attention to the context; making the ancient Scriptures relevant to a new age; the correction of error – these are the virtues of a commentator according to Bullinger.

The *Dedication* dwells on two points. The first concerns the clarity of Scripture, an idea which Luther had asserted against Erasmus in *de servo arbitio* and which became a common Reformation principle. Bullinger's starting point is not empirical, that anyone reading the Bible can understand it, but theological, that God is the author of Scripture and that God's nature precludes obscurity. If Scripture is obscure to us, the fault lies with our spiritual dulness and our faulty method of reading: 'It cannot be that anything obscure could proceed from God, who is truth and the clearest light. All obscurity and difficulty in divine things comes from us, that is, from our dulness, and then from our neglecting of the idioms and figures (*schematum*), and finally, from not observing the context of the passage' (1). This is what causes bad exposition. The Epistle to the Romans is a case in point, 'for once in the school of Christians it was thought that there was no better way to expound the power of the Gospel than concisely, simply, and purely, and clearly rather than copiously, yet when once the opinion that it was difficult was acquired, some ceased to read it and did not believe it possible that anyone could understand it aright' (1). 'But this obscurity and despair [of ever understanding], in a thing most clear, was something men inflicted on themselves by their own dulness, laziness, and neglect' (1). 'You cry out that our author [Paul] is thorny and obscure (*spinosus*); but it is your feet that have the thorns, not the passage' (1). No, Paul 'is a good writer (*docte*) and clear – but he did write in his own idiomatic style' (1).

The second main point in the *Dedication* is a defence of the application of the classical and Renaissance rhetorical method to the understanding of Scripture. They accuse us, says Bullinger, of rhetoricizing and grammaticizing in Scripture, where it is out of place, 'wherever, after having heeded the context and examined the kinds of speech that were used, we interpret and expound the Scriptures by the common way of speaking . . . For they despise simplicity and in a perverse sort of way think that no-one is a good theologian who does not tear up what is said into many and diverse senses and involve the whole thing incredibly . . . They say that we rhetoricize in Scripture and search out the laws of oratory (*oratum canones*), and that it is all τὸν ἐν φακῇ μύρον (labour in vain). But these superstitious people fail to see that the method and usage of speaking is not to be sought for from rhetorical precepts, but the precepts from the carefully observed natural manner of speaking. If they once saw that, they would soon understand that those who keep to the context in Scripture are not observing rigid regulations but the native manner of speaking, without which no-one can be familiar and easy with authors, whether secular or sacred . . . What we seek is not fine-sounding decorations, the eloquence of a Demosthenes or a Tully, but a pure and clear simplicity, which is not at all different from the common but pure way of speaking'(1).

It is disappointing to have to record that Bullinger's reach exceeded his grasp. His commentary is undoubtedly among the best in our group, but it falls short of Bucer in profundity and thoroughness, of Melanchthon in clarity, and of Calvin in penetration. When Calvin commended him, it must surely have been for his theory rather than his practice.

The earliest edition I have been able to see is that of 1537. It consists of commentaries on all the Epistles, the Pauline and the Canonical in separate parts with their own pagination. *Romans* occupies pp. 3–121 of this large volume – type-face 22.2 × 13.2 cm. and 52 lines to the page. The preface *Ad Lectorem*, the *Index*, and the *Dedicatio* (to Berthold Haller of Bern) are in roman of varying sizes, the *Argumentum* in italic, and the *Commentarius* in roman. The recto page headings indicate Bullinger's divisions – *Inscriptio*, *Expositio*, *Status Epistolae*, *De Peccato*, *De Iustitia*, etc.

Johannes Gagnaeius or Jean Gagney[13] (both his Latin and French names were spelt in a variety of ways) published his *Epitome Paraphrastica* in 1533. He had taken his doctorate at Paris in the previous year and continued in that university for the rest of his life. In his arts course there, many years earlier, he had studied under Pierre Danès, the royal professor of Greek, who also taught Calvin in the early fifteen-thirties. Gagney himself, at the time he became Rector of the University in 1531, was said to be learnèd in Hebrew, Greek and Latin. His studies did not lead him, however, to any position of considerable emolument, for, although he applied to the university for a benefice every year from 1521 to 1532, he was apparently unsuccessful. But, as Virgil has it, that which none of the gods had dared to offer, lo! the lapse of time brought unasked. But perhaps not quite unasked. A poem he wrote on the death of the Dauphin in 1536 attracted the regard of the King and that grateful monarch rewarded him with many marks of favour during the next few years – chaplain to the King, three abbacies, a parish, a canonry in Paris, and librarian to the King. Rather more than Milton got for *Paradise Lost*. In 1546 Gagney became Chancellor of the University and as such was one of the ring-leaders in persecuting Robert Estienne; but he was dead by the time that that great printer fled to Geneva. He himself had ambitions in the printing line, setting up a press in his own house and printing a few works commercially. But the venture was not a success and was no doubt the main reason for his dying in

[13] For many of the biographical facts on Gagney I am indebted to J.K. Farge: *Biographical Register of Paris Doctors of Theology 1500-1536* (Toronto, 1980), 177-183.

debt. The paraphrase was not his only work on Romans. He
edited Primasius' commentary in 1537 and translated it into
French for an edition of 1540. In the meantime, in 1538, he
brought out his own *Scholia* on Romans, which we will look
at when we come to that year.

The *Epitome Paraphrastica* is a small book of 88 folios, with
a type-face of 12.5 × 7 cm. It is printed thoughout in italics
except that the names *Christus* and *Iesus Christus* appear in
roman capitals. Greek words are printed in Greek script. In
places the text is corrupt, no doubt from the fault of the
printer. The contents are: a preface to the reader, addressed
from his college of Navarre in Paris, the argument of the
Epistle, a list of errata, and the paraphrase itself. In the preface
he tells us of the circumstances of the birth of his book. For
long he had remained hidden, then 'we put out our head like a
new-born chick from the shell' (1ᵛ). In other words, he
undertook to expound Romans in a course of college lectures.
But he did this only at the urging of others, for he was
himself modestly unwilling. However, his 'uncle and Maece-
nas' Du Moulin, 'doctor of theology and most worthy cantor
of the sacred chapel in the royal palace', (and, we may add,
one of the Parisian hammers of the heretics), stirred him up to
attempt the task. And so, 'I explore Origen, I read
Chrysostom and Theophylact, I carefully examine Ambrose
and Augustine, Jerome I embrace; I compare the Greeks with
the Latins, and if I find in Paul anything they have omitted, I
look it up in commentaries. And so whereas we had before
lived a secluded life, we came out in public, and lectured at
the Collège de Navarre on the Epistle to the Romans, which
we finished by God's help at Easter. Would that the lectures
had been as learned and felicitous as their hearers!' (1ᵛ-2ʳ).
These lectures, which were critical of Erasmus and which
made use of Titelmann's *Collatio* of 1529[14], were no doubt the
basis of both his *Epitome* and also his *Scholia*.

The title *Epitome Paraphrastica*, if it is intended to denote
something of an abridgement of Romans, is a misnomer; the

---

[14] Or Titelmann's *Elucidationes* of 1532? See PSA X, 220-222.
Epist. 2807.

paraphrase is a good deal longer than the original, as, indeed, it should be. On the whole it is a readable enough version, usually keeping to the point of the Epistle, although sometimes slipping in something of Gagney's own. In its theological conservatism it is a typical production of Paris in the fifteen-thirties; but the marks of his humanist training are plain to see in, for example, his choice of words, in his use of Greek, and in his occasional quoting of the classics. The *Epitome* itself is better than a reading of the preface to the reader and the *Argumentum* leads us to expect. After the autobiography we have given above, he goes on to indulge in a long, long bemoaning of the difficulty of writing commentaries. This obsession with difficulty he continues in the *Argumentum*, where the first thing he does is to quote the reference in II Peter to 'the many hard things' in St Paul – 'and this one to the Romans' he grumbles, 'is the most difficult of all' (3ᵛ).

In **1534** there appeared only a reprint of the works of Ambrose, among which were the "Ambrosiaster" commentaries.

3: 1535

Jacopo Sadoleto's *Tres Libri Commentariorum* on Romans is one of the most interesting as well as most perplexing among those that we are considering. Interesting for the originality of its form and for its independent approach – or, at least, for the author's intention to take an individual line. Perplexing, in that the doctrinal expression of that individual line admits of more than one interpretation; was he a Pelagian, as Richard Simon asserted and as perhaps the Roman authorities also thought, or was he at one with Bucer, as M. Bernard Roussel has recently decided?

It would be difficult to understand the significance of this work apart from the events of Sadoleto's life. The all-important fact was his ability to write Latin of the sort of elegance that was admired at the time. This qualification won him, together with his friend Bembo, the post of secretary to Pope Leo X, a post in which his chief task was the framing and writing of official Papal letters – many of those dealing with the Luther affair after 1517 are of his composition. In such spare time as this ecclesiastical civil service work allowed him, he wrote books in the genre that the later nineteenth century would have classified as *belles lettres*, but which won the highest praise from his contemporaries – books in homage of philosophy, a poem on the newly discovered Laocoön, and the like.

Ten years of Curial life were enough for him, however. He wanted more time to call his own, more time for writing. The opportunity lay in his hands from 1517, when the Pope crowned his previous gifts of eight benefices, two canonries, and two pensions with the award of the bishopric of Carpentras. Carpentras, a city about fifty miles north of Marseilles, was no great prize, either financially or as a sphere of influence, but it did offer that chance of independent leisure so highly prized by the humanists. In 1523, therefore, after the death of Leo and when it became clear that the new Pope, Adrian VI, was not going to offer him employment, Sadoleto began to reside in his diocese. But Adrian's lease of the Vatican had all too short a date and in the following year Clement VII recalled Sadoleto to Rome and new secretarial duties. There he stayed until the sack of Rome was seen to be imminent in 1527. After this he resided in Carpentras and turned his attention to the care of his diocese and to the exposition of Holy Scripture. In the mid fifteen-thirties he was drawn into what was to prove to be the initial stages of the Counter-Reformation.

His main work on the Bible was the commentary on Romans. This he began to write in about 1530, having already expounded one or two psalms. It may be that he mentioned in too many letters to too many people not only that he was writing the commentary but that he believed himself to have discovered the true meaning of Romans. Thus to Giberti, Bishop of Verona, on October 27, 1531: 'I am writing my commentary on the Epistle to the Romans and I am treating this hard and difficult task in such a way that in it I am striving chiefly to offer you what I promised a long time ago – to make the many obscure and ambiguous statements in this Epistle more clear' (Op.om.I,68ᵃ⁻ᵇ). It seems that Giberti in reply sent him a copy of Chrysostom on Romans. To Erasmus he wrote more cautiously, however: 'I am writing up my commentary on the Epistle to the Romans. A difficult task, if there ever was one, as you yourself know and as I am learning . . . The subject is difficult. I write badly and slowly. What is more, I am finding numbers of new interpretations. To know if they are good or not (for I am not sufficiently self-confident) I would like to turn to the judgment of men like yourself (supposing any others exist!), above all, to your own judgment' (PSA X.21). Erasmus a little later asked Amerbach, in a letter we have already quoted (p.6) to send a copy of Melanchthon's *Commentarius* to Sadoleto, but at the same time to warn him to separate the gold from the dross (PSA X.245). Apparently Amerbach failed to comply, so that, as we have also seen, Erasmus himself sent both the commentary and the warning. It is probable, therefore, that Sadoleto had read the 1532 Commentary.

In this way some considerable interest in anticipation was aroused among the *cognoscenti*. This fine Latinist, this poet, was writing an original and profound work on the greatest and most sublimely difficult of the Apostle's letters. Sadoleto finished his commentary in 1533, although not, apparently, in the final draft, for he wrote to Erasmus on June 9: 'I have finished my commentary on the first Epistle of Paul (with what labour and midnight oil I cannot put into words – you yourself know well enough the obscurity of this famous letter) and have decided to stop at this point, calm and fresh, and to start revising and paying more attention to the restatement' (PSA X.234).

His wish to have the work published by Froben was disappointed and it was the press of Gryphius at Lyons which brought it out in 1535.

As soon as it was out, however, or possibly even before

publication, Sadoleto was astounded to hear that it had been censured by the Faculty of Theology at Paris – on what grounds we do not know. Worse was to follow. Badia, the Master of the Sacred Palace in Rome, did not merely censure the book but banned it and ordered that it be withdrawn from publication. His reasons were two: first, that it had not referred to the schoolmen and secondly, that on justification prevenient grace had been neglected. This was a severe blow to Sadoleto, expecting the praise due to an innovator. It is clear, as we read both his letters and the book itself, that he did not really see what all the fuss was about. Had he not, as a bishop of the Catholic Church, written a godly and learnèd commentary, aimed at elucidating the mysteries of the Apostle, written in good Latin and containing most fierce condemnation of the Lutherans? When he sent the manuscript to Paris in 1534 he had asked that the examiners should be good classical scholars, as if this was the standard by which he wished the book to be judged. Not unnaturally, in view of the blow to his *amour propre* and to his episcopal authority, he wrote very angry letters to Rome. He was particularly touched to the quick by the imputation of theological incompetence, for he had not studied theology at a university but was self-taught: 'I do not deny there is ignorance in me but say only that if those who go to Paris to study theology get doctor's degrees in six years, I, who have studied it continually at Carpentras for eight, cannot be so ill endowed by nature as not to derive some profit from it; and even if I have not studied Durandus, Capreolus, and Occam, I have studied the Bible, St Paul, Augustine, Ambrose, Chrysostom, and those most worthy doctors who are the pillars of true knowledge' (Ep.II.300).

The theological substance of the commentary and criticisms of it must be reserved until we come to deal with Romans 3.20seq. And the whole story itself is too long to be recounted here. We can read it in R.M. Douglas: *Jacopo Sadoleto*, pp. 86–91. All that concerns us now is that he agreed to supply in a new edition the deficiencies of which Badia complained. This came out in 1536. But according to Douglas, the revision was confined to the enlarging of some passages and there were no deletions. The most extensive addition, moreover, was omitted in later editions.[15]

Another strange turn in this story, and one which must have annoyed Sadoleto almost as much as the censure and ban, came when Bucer claimed, or seemed to claim, and whether sincerely or politically, that Sadoleto's doctrine on justification was one with that of the Reformers. This also is a matter whose discussion we must defer until Rom.3.20seq.

But now we return to the book itself. There is no preface to the reader and the *Epistola Dedicatoria* addressed to King Francis I tells us nothing about Sadoleto's views on the expositor's task or the circumstances of the writing. But the opening to Book I has some pious thoughts, perhaps culled from Erasmus: 'Humility is the first and chief gift, without which we cannot have knowledge of divine things. He who would penetrate to the understanding of them must believe. But none does that easily who trusts in himself' (7-8; 2). He continues in this strain for some time, emphasizing the need for faith, and at the same time comparing commentating with the other arts, and incidentally betraying that at least a large part of his reason for writing was artistic. From faith comes charity: 'It is charity which faith especially contains. Charity nourishes faith and increases hope in it; and when we are dismissed from this mortal body and taken to the heavenly and immortal life, this alone is ever true to us and a perpetual friend' (8; 3).

It is a natural step from charity to unity, and another from

[15] There is some confusion on the amount of revision carried into subsequent editions. B. Roussel (Martin Bucer et Jacques Sadolet, 513 n.18): 'A second edition at Lyons in 1536 offers a minimum of corrections and additions: in particular, an addition on the theme of free-will. The minor corrections disappeared in the later editions of Venice and Modena'. But R.M.Douglas: 'The most important of these changes, which appears only in the second and in none of the later editions, is a two-page insertion in which Sadoleto elaborated the interpretation of merit and the beginnings of salvation in his discussion of Romans 8.29-31. Later in the same book he introduced a brief reference to the action of prevenient grace and the disabling effects of sin in the section on Romans 9.7–26' (Jacopo Sadoleto (1477–1547), Humanist and Reformer. (Cambridge, Mass., 1959) 91).

unity to the Reformers. 'Since these things are so, since there is so much honour before God in faith and humility, so much power of brotherly conjunction with all, that the whole economy of the blessed life and of knowledge and of the reception of hope is especially placed and determined in them [it?], what are we to say of this new breed of heretics who have suddenly arisen and are trying with their dissensions to tear asunder not just one part but the whole body of the Church? They have gone on from slander and hatred of personalities to open enmity; and, unable to keep even within these limits, have been carried away by the onrush of wrath and tried to pluck up and completely destroy, not only many most salutary laws and customs rightly ordained by the Church, but also not a few central points of the Christian Faith. May God send a spirit of humility into their hearts, that they may bethink themselves and understand that they are not consulting brotherly love and that to disturb peace and unity in the Church and to break unity comes not from God' (8-9; 4).

He continues at great length with anti-Reformation polemic, accusing the Reformers of claiming license to sin unchecked. Thus: 'They say that they are reclaiming Christian liberty which has been suppressed and taken away by the traditions of men (as they call them) and by many impositions. But it is easy to see that this is not an attempt to be spiritually free but to serve sin' (9; 4). They write commentaries on Holy Scripture instead of studying the fathers, because Scripture is more obscure and so they can twist it to fit their own ideas. To counteract such falsification is why he himself has written the present commentary: 'they have insolently and arrogantly rejected the most holy and ancient doctors, who wrote so clearly about this [the whole mystery of redemption and the divine purpose for our salvation], and they fall back on those who, on account of the sublimity of their thoughts and the secrets of the counsel of God, spoke more concisely and obscurely, in order that so they might find refuge in these hiding places and might wrest the words to their own meaning. Because of all this it seemed good to us to expound carefully (so far as it shall be given us by God) the blessed Apostle Paul's Epistle to the Romans (which these men, with their dark and hidden meanings, make into subterfuges for their malice); a book so full of divine thoughts that it seems scarcely possible for the human mind to enter into its understanding, and so effective for showing the mystery of the Cross that whoever grasps it rightly and more fully cannot, it seems to us, doubt of the Catholic Faith' (10; 7).

Here, at any rate, is a clear and unambiguous statement of his motive in writing the commentary – to show that Romans, rightly understood, supports the Roman Catholics and therefore to refute the Reformers. And "rightly understood" means according to the new insights that Sadoleto so frequently said he had been vouchsafed and which were the result of his attempting to steer a middle course between Pelagius and Augustine.

He goes on, in the passage we are quoting, to relate the story of the origin of the commentary. He puts the work into the form of discussions, mainly between himself and his brother Julius (who died in 1521), but broadened in Book III into a wider circle of humanist protagonists. Presumably he did this with classical precedents, and most notably Plato, in mind; but it had an actual, and not merely an artistic, value in that it enabled him to raise and answer difficulties gracefully. He would not have realized that this was only the old scholastic method of *quaestio* and *responsio* in an elegant and imaginative form. But we may let him tell the story in his own words: 'This exposition of ours is not a new production but the fresh remembrance of an old conversation we had when I was in Rome, my brother Julius Sadoleto and I. He was very learned in Greek and Latin and had no equal in the finest arts, especially in the knowledge of philosophy, in which he far surpassed his elders. He very often talked with me about Holy Scripture, either enquiring from me or himself discussing the matter most subtly . . . But to come to the matter itself. When I was in Rome, during the Feast of Pentecost I was one day in my very pleasant and luxuriant gardens on the Quirinal Hill, near the high path. The heat of the day was increasing, for summer was coming on, and I sat

down in the shade. I had with me a volume of Paul's letters in
Greek and I was very engrossed in reading it when my
brother Julius came unexpectedly to me. As soon as we had
greeted one another, he said ". . .Now, what author have
you got there?" ' (11; 8). They fell to talking about Romans.
Julius remarked that this was well-met, for he had collected
certain verses in the Epistle that he would like James's
opinion on. So ' "since we are at leisure and it is a feast day",
he said, "nothing would please me better than for you to go
through the Epistle with me and interpret it completely . . .
For, although many of the most learned and holy men have
written on it, and that at great length, there still remains in
our minds a certain hesitation that something great and
divine, which we have not yet sufficiently grasped, seems to
lie hidden in it" ' (11; 9). James accedes to the request, and his
commentary is the outcome. It is not, however, he says,
from the Greek book he had with him, but from the Latin
(12; 9).

It is in a letter written to Contarini on Nov. 26, 1535 that
Sadoleto most fully opened his mind on the writing of the
commentary. 'I had taken up the exposition of this Epistle of
Paul and was for a long time involved with the commentaries
of many interpreters; but I did not seem to get what I wanted,
so as to enter fully into the Apostle's meaning. I greatly
approved their talent, their learning, their piety. And yet
there was a certain *je ne sais quoi* hidden and concealed in Paul
which they did not seem quite to reach. I therefore pursued
another method of study and investigation – by reading Paul
himself. I pondered and searched out in every direction, to
my utmost limit and working away interminably. So I
soldiered on a long time and diligently until I thought I had
arrived at his inner meaning. Whether I was right or mistaken
is irrelevant; I speak merely of how it seemed to me. When I
judged that I had reached those secret insights *(arcanas
quasdam illius sententias)*, especially those dealing with godliness and the knowledge of the Christian mystery, I did not
consider it consonant with Christian charity to keep that
which is light hidden any longer. And so I embarked on the
writing of the commentary. In it I attempted to open and

make clear something which had been particularly obscure to
me and which I had previously received in faith and on credit
but which seemed not understood rationally – that is, the
mystery of the death and cross of Christ. I tried to explain the
causes and reasons why it was necessary and requisite for our
salvation that Christ should come into the world; and that as
he died, so we should die with him; and that in him there
exists not only an example of how we should live our lives
but also the mystery of our life and salvation. And in this
argument I made Paul's ideas self-consistent (as it seems to
me) and followed the words themselves. But that I was more
sparing than I should have been in explaining the prevenient
grace of God, I acknowledge to have been a mistake, since
this is your opinion. But all the same, I did follow the manner
of expounding in the old Latin and Greek writers without
departing from Paul's declared argument. You yourself
know how rarely this is mentioned specifically by Chrysostom on this Epistle, and not much by Theophylact and
Euthymius, who, I find, took over many of the opinions of
Basil and Chrysostom in expounding Paul's Epistles.
Ambrose also does not very often advert to it. I believe that it
seemed to them sufficient to refer everything in general to the
grace of God, since this was very frequently found in Holy
Scripture. In particular, they were not involved in a
controversy which would compel them to make such a slight
distinction in this matter – which was necessary for Augustine who was waging a holy and salutary war against
Pelagius. Nevertheless, in those places where Paul gave me
occasion, I so spoke of the Holy Spirit as to attribute both the
beginnings and endings of all Christian virtues to him. This is
what I do in the words where Paul says that 'the love of God
is shed abroad in our hearts by the Holy Spirit who is given to
us' [Rom.5.1]. I vehemently desire you to read and ponder
this verse. In my exposition I have tried to set before the eyes
of all, not only that all things are done in us by the Holy
Spirit, but how they are done, and how we truly have the
Holy Spirit within us . . . I have, it is true, not used the terms
"prevenient" and "subsequent" grace; but the meaning is the
same to my mind. But on the weakness of our nature,

derived from Adam unto sin and death I say much in the place where Paul speaks of the same thing in regard to Adam and the sin derived from him to all the human race' (Ep. II.344-7). He will, he goes on, insert in a new edition of his book a passage 'by which all this matter may be declared briefly, yet aptly and sufficiently' (Ep. II.347). He does not think it Pelagianism, he says, 'if we retain something of our own in the initial stages' (Ep. II.348). This last thought he expresses in different words in another letter to Contarini: 'If I disagree with Augustine, it does not mean that I am differing from the Catholic Church' (Ep. II.393).

The first edition I have seen only in photocopies and therefore cannot describe precisely. It seems to correspond very closely to the second, which is printed in roman throughout, the Biblical text in a rather larger type. The type-face measures 23.7 × 14 cm.; there are fifty-four lines to the page; and two hundred and thirty-one pages.

This year also saw the publication of the fifth edition of Erasmus's *Novum Testamentum* and *Annotationes* and, in December, of an edition of Peter Lombard, reprinted also in 1536 or 1537. The *Annotationes*, first published as a part of the *editio princeps* of the Greek New Testament in 1516, had been revised more than once and was now revised by the author for the last time. There is no need to enter as fully into a description of this book as with most of our other authors. It will be sufficient to say that the annotations are almost entirely linguistic and exegetical; there is little in the way of theological exposition. This is why, although he will frequently appear in the exegetical portions of this book, he is never given a section to himself in the expositions. That he influenced most of the other writers is certainly true, but more probably from the fourth edition of 1527 than from this of 1535.

4: 1536

Two new commentaries appeared in 1536. The first, in March, was by Martin Bucer. It crushed into insignificance all but two or three of our other works and its influence was for a few years immense. For this reason, and because its contents will be little known save to students of Bucer[16], we must describe it in closer detail.

In contrast to Calvin's steady working through the Epistles in their canonical order, Bucer's procedure was somewhat haphazard. He had published commentaries on the Synoptic Gospels in 1527;[17] but then, instead of proceeding to John, he wrote his first commentary on Ephesians. The commentary on all four Gospels followed in 1530.[18] About three years later he began work on Romans. Bullinger wrote to him on October 28, 1534: 'I am writing on some of the Pauline Epistles and hear that you are labouring at the same task. What precisely you are doing, I do not know, except that you are publishing something on Paul's Romans. If that is so, I should like to read it'.[19] In the following January Bucer replied with a glimpse into one of his chief preoccupations: 'In my Enarrations on the Gospels I erred [in not citing the Church fathers]; but it was less of will than of necessity. For I had not the time to survey everything. I am now writing, when I have the leisure, on Paul's Epistles; and here I am carefully doing what there I could not. I am working hard to show the consent of the Church throughout all ages'.[20]

He intended *Romans* as the first of a series on all the Pauline Epistles, as the title page shows: *Metaphrases and Continual Enarrations on the Epistles of St. Paul. . .Volume I. Containing the* Metaphrasis *and* Enarratio[21] *on the Epistle to the Romans.* He wrote this vast work in two years[22] and seems to have

[16] I do not forget the excellent collection of *loci*, many from *Romans*, in Common Places of Martin Bucer, translated and edited by D.F. Wright (Sutton Courtenay Press, 1972). But this does not include the other elements in this many-sided commentary.

[17] Enarrationum in Evangelia Matthaei, Marci & Lucae, libri duo. . . (Strasbourg).

[18] Enarrationes perpetuae in sacra quattor evangelia (Strasbourg).

[19] J.V. Pollet: Martin Bucer – Etudes sur la correspondance avec de nombreux textes inédits (Paris, 1958, 1962), II.301 n.4.

[20] Pollet: *Ibid*.

[21] *Enarratio* = exposition.

[22] T.Schiess: Briefwechsel der Brüder Ambrosius und Thomas Blaurer 1509 – 68 (Freiburg, 1908ff.) I, 482.

finished it only as the book went to press.[23] It was dedicated to Thomas Cranmer, and from a subsequent letter from Bucer to him we learn that in 1538 Bucer still intended to continue the series. Cranmer had given him advice on the writing of these commentaries. He replied that he would try to put it into effect 'in the remaining Epistles'; but 'I have been harassed by so many journeyings since the publication of the first edition [= volume], and have been so struggling with a painful disease which has very much weakened my brain for these two years past, that I have been unable in the meantime to write anything upon the Apostle. This winter I hope to be allowed to return to this work'.[24] But *Romans* remained as the only volume until the second *Ephesians* joined it posthumously in 1562.

Earlier in the same letter Bucer had apologized for the short-comings in his *Romans*: 'I was moreover in circumstances of the greatest disquiet and obliged to hurry everything most prodigiously while I was writing my commentary on Romans. So I am well aware that there are innumerable defects in that work which even the most indulgent partiality must necessarily condemn'.[25] The outspoken complaints against Bucer's prolixity and disorder were many. But when we examine the book more closely, we find that the first charge is only partly justified. The first three chapters take up one hundred and eighty-two pages (41^a-222^b), whereas the last thirteen have only two hundred and eighty-five (223^a-507^b). Indeed, if we split it up still finer, we can see Bucer giving less and less space to his material:

Chapters				
1 – 3	182 pp.	(= 60 pages per chapter)
4 – 8	152 pp.	(= 30 " " ")
9 – 11	79 pp.	(= 26 " " ")
12 – 13	42½pp.	(= 21 " " ")
14 – 16	10½pp.	(= 3½ " " ")

[23] Arbenz and Wartman: Die Vadiansche Briefsammlung der Stadt-bibliothek St. Gallen (1892ff.) V,312; qu. H. Eells: Martin Bucer (New Haven and London, 1931), 196 and 472.

[24] Original Letters, Parker Society (Cambridge, 1847), II, 523.

[25] Original Letters, II, 522.

The reason for the inordinate length in the first part of the book lay in its character. Here is no simple arrangement of a continuous explanation of the verses or of selected passages. Bucer had a mind teeming with ideas, ever eager to investigate a problem by means of fresh methods. The critical would, with Luther, call him a chatterbox; the friendly, with Calvin, would speak of the rich fertility of his genius, pouring out his ideas as they came to him. For the commentary on Romans is not one book but many, pressed together and not infrequently running over into confusion. Here are to be found within one binding a metaphrase of the Epistles, a theological commentary for scholars, a critical and linguistic commentary, a simple commentary for the un-learnèd, and a set of essays on the theology of the Epistle – five books in one. Hence the title:

Metaphrasis and continuous Enarratio on the Epistles of St. Paul the Apostle, in which all the arguments, the sentences and words are individually examined carefully and rather fully, according to the authority of Holy Scipture and the faith of the Catholic Church past and present. Forty-two conciliations and decisions of apparent contradictions of places in Scripture and of the chief controversies in religious doctrine today. . .Volume I. Containing the Metaphrasis and Enarratio on the Epistle to the Romans, in which, as the Apostle treated the principal places of the whole of theology most exactly and fully, so in this volume is explained the greatest part of the whole, not only of Pauline, but also of universal holy Philosophy.

The book runs to five hundred and seven pages in double column, with sixty lines to a column. The type is roman throughout and the type-face measures 22.7 × 13 cm.

In a preface Bucer explains in detail the methods he intends to adopt. First, the word *Metaphrasis* demands elucidation. 'A rather free translation' is how he puts it, and we may accept that without going into the dictionary definition. But why he relates it to Hebraisms is less easy to see: 'a rather free translation or even conversion in certain places where he uses either Hebraisms or personal idiosyncrasies, especially in those which from my own daily experience seem to be unknown to public teachers. Even the holy fathers themselves failed, from ignorance of the Hebrew tongue, to understand a lot of the Pauline language' (Sig.iiii^v).

To enquire into the identity of the Greek text or texts from which Bucer made his metaphrase would lead us astray from our purpose; and it is idle to guess in matters textual. The lack of significant differences between the printed editions of the New Testament up to 1534-36 in the passages we shall consider make, in any case, such an enquiry otiose.

Bucer divided the commentary into three books and the books into *Sectiones* (it must be remembered that verse divisions lay yet in the future). His criterion for making the divisions is briefly described in the preface as 'new propositions or proofs' (Sig.iiii^v); that is, where St Paul begins a new subject or new proof or an enquiry. For example, Book I and its *Sectiones* are equivalent to the verses of Chapter I, as follows: Section I, v.1; II, vv.2-6; III, v.7; IV, vv.8-13; V,vv.14-17; VI, vv.18-20; VII, vv.21-23; VIII, vv.24-27; IX, vv.28-32.

After the *Metaphrasis* will follow, says Bucer, the *Expositio*. The explanation of his intention here is far from clear in its details. What emerges with certainty is that the *Expositio* concerns only the general argument of its *Sectio*. The discussion of words and phrases will come under another category, and for the present he will be occupied with the broad scope of the meaning of the passage in its context: 'In the *Expositio* I have tried in a continuous thread of explanation to indicate what the Apostle advances, and for what occasion, and also for what purpose; and then by what arguments and by what sort of arrangements and propositions (*enunciatis*) he proves what he has advanced. And since the Apostle, whenever he teaches, always writes the words of God, than which nothing could be more indubitable, I have taken care ἀναλύειν [to resolve] the arguments, so that it might be clear that in the argument also there is ἀξίωμα ἀμεσον, καὶ τὶς ἐννοία ἡ πρώτη [a definite principle and a certain primary idea], that is, the proposition (*enunciatio*) and the *notio*, which are present in the ulterior proof, and therefore the argument may be made known to the saints through itself' (Sig.iiii^v).

This last obscure sentence will be understood in the light of what follows. Bucer is now speaking theologically; that is, he is no longer considering the interpretation of Romans by means of general methods applicable to any piece of writing, but in terms of revelation. Because these are the words of God, they are understood by the light of faith. And the light of faith has a certainty not possessed by the light of reason. The argument of Romans, he is therefore saying, is self-authenticating; it is 'made known to the saints through itself'. For he continues: 'Inasmuch as sacred doctrine treats of what should be believed, and believed because God spoke it, demonstrations in theology are of primary certainty and are so much the more superior to those in other disciplines as the light of faith, by which we may see the principles of theology, is more certain than the light of the intellect, by which may be seen the principles of the other disciplines. Thus our demonstrations refer the first cause of everything to the word of God since the ἀποδείξις [demonstration] of disciplines subsists in the causes that are in the things themselves' (Sig.iiii^v). And this being so, he says a little later, 'none is able to arrive at the perception of the full truth except the regenerate; for before this men are destitute of the light of faith' (iiii^v–v^r).

The *Interpretationes*, on the other hand, are more closely allied to the other disciplines, for here 'I have set out to explain the native sense of the individual sentences and words of Paul' (v^r). The "native sense", *germanus sensus*, should be taken merely as "what the passage or word means". It should not be pressed too strictly as the *sensus literalis*. (Indeed, we may say in passing that the four "senses", so beloved of the text books, are not much in evidence in the commentaries of our period, at any rate in any schematized form). The *Interpretationes*, then, will consist of literary and linguistic notes on individual points that need elucidating.

After this come the *Observationes*, the shorter, undetailed explanations for the less learnèd. A laudable aim, but Bucer has to advertise them with his most learnèd foreword: 'In the *Observationes* I have aimed at setting out a *sylvulam* for the less learnèd. So that, from Paul's limited dogmas and precepts (limited from the complex of things, persons, times, and other περιστάσεων [circumstances], and which are called ὑποθέσεις [hypotheses], we may ascend more easily and surely ἀναγώγῃ [by inference?] to θέσεις [theses], that is, to the infinite dogmas and precepts, which are not bound to persons, places, and times' (vʳ). I take it that this piece of Holofernesian prose means that Bucer aims at leading these readers from the simplicity of the elementary to the profundities of the sublime. The *Observationes* are not a running commentary but brief essays on central texts.

This, therefore, was Bucer's prospectus for his Pauline commentaries. Since his work is so little known to any but specialists, it will be useful if we here give a complete plan of his Romans.

We must note, however, that before he comes to the first Section, he includes twelve essays (adding up to some thirty thousand words in Latin) which he calls *Prefaces to the* Enarratio *of the Epistles of St. Paul the Apostle, both in general, and in particular of what is written in Romans, by which the reader is provided with a pathway for understanding aright the doctrine of the Apostle.* These are: *On its merits; On the order of the Epistles and their dates; On the order of the Epistles as they are commonly divided according to their importance and argument; The principal* quaestio *in this Epistle, and the general head to which everything must be referred; The argument of the Epistle and the explication which the Apostle works out in individual chapters; What the Fathers thought on the* quaestio *of the Epistle and its case; The sum of the first reason by which he argues the principal* quaestio; *In what signification St. Paul uses the words "To be justified" and "Justification"; What Paul means by the words "Faith" and "To believe"; What Paul means by "Law" and "The works of the Law"; Whether there is in philosophy something that accords with Paul's teaching; Whether St.Paul keeps to the rules of rhetoric* (artem dicendi).

Metaphrasis of Rom.1–3 (41ᵃ–44ᵇ)

    Enarratio of Sectio I. Paul the servant etc. (45ᵃ–49ᵃ)

        Interpretatio:

            The name "Paul" (45ᵃ⁻ᵇ)

            The servant of Jesus Christ (45ᵇ–46ᵃ)

Called to be an apostle (46ᵃ-47ᵃ)
Selected to the Gospel of Christ (47ᵃ⁻ᵇ)
Of the Gospel of God (47ᵇ-48ᵃ)
Observatio I. On the name "Paul" (48ᵃ⁻ᵇ)
           II. The servant of the Lord (48ᵇ)
          III. On the word "called" (48ᵇ-49ᵃ)
           IV. On divine election (49ᵃ)
            V. The workmanship of the Holy Spirit
               (49ᵃ)

Enarratio of Sectio II. [No text] (49ᵃ seq)
  Interpretatio [Rom. 1.2-6] (49ᵃ-57ᵃ)
  Quaestio: What a Christian man should think about
    the Incarnation of the Word, that is, the reason
    why our Lord Jesus Christ, the Son of God, was
    born of the seed of David according to the flesh, he
    who was the Word which was in the beginning
    and by whom all things were made. (57ᵃ-61ᵃ)
  Observatio I. Which was promised afore (61ᵃ)
             II. Concerning his Son, made of the
                 seed of David (61ᵃ)
            III. Declared to be the Son in power
                 (61ᵃ⁻ᵇ)
             IV. Through whom we have received
                 grace (61ᵇ)
              V. Unto obedience of faith (61ᵇ-62ᵃ)
             VI. In all the Gentiles (62ᵃ)
            VII. For his name's sake (62ᵃ⁻ᵇ)
           VIII. Among whom you also (62ᵇ)

Enarratio of Sectio III. To all who are in Rome etc.
                (63ᵃ seq)
  Interpretatio [Rom. 1.7] (63ᵃ-65ᵃ)
  Observatio I.   [No text] (65ᵃ⁻ᵇ)
             II.   "   "   (65ᵇ-66ᵃ)
            III.   "   "   (66ᵃ⁻ᵇ)

Enarratio of Sectio IV. First I give thanks etc. (66ᵇ seq)
  Expositio (66ᵇ)

Interpretatio [Rom. 1.8-13] (66^b-72^a)
Observatio I. First I give thanks (72^{a-b})
        II. God is my witness (72^b)
        III. Whom I serve in my spirit (72^b)
        IV. That without ceasing I make mention of you (72^b-73^a)
        V. If by any means I may have (73^{a-b})
        VI. That I may impart some spiritual gift (73^b)
        VII. For I have often purposed, but was prevented (73^b-74^a)

Enarratio of Sectio V. To the Greeks and the barbarians, etc. (74^{a}seq)
Expositio (74^a-75^a)
Interpretatio [Rom. 1.14-17] (75^a-81^a)
Observatio I. To the Greeks and the barbarians (81^{a-b})
        II. It is the power of God (81^b)
        III. In it the righteousness of God is revealed (81^b-82^a)

Enarratio of Sectio VI. Now indeed the wrath of God, etc. (82^{a}seq)
Expositio (82^{a-b})
Interpretatio [Rom. 1.18-20] (82^b-86^b)
Conciliatio of places in Scripture which sometimes attribute, sometimes deny, knowledge of God to the ungodly (86^b-88^a)
Observatio I. The wrath of God is revealed from heaven (88^a)
        II. Who hold down the truth in unrighteousness (88^a)
        III. God manifested to them (88^b)
        IV. By the creature of the world (89^a)
        V. That they may be inexcusable (89^a)

Enarratio of Sectio VII. Because that they knew God (89^a seq)

Expositio (89^a-90^a)

Interpretatio [Rom.1.21-23] (90^a-96^b)

Quaestio: Can there be a Christian use of images? (97^a-100^a)

Observatio I. Because when they knew God (100^a)

II. Or gave thanks (100^a)

III. But became vain (100^{a-b})

IV. And changed the glory of God (100^b)

V. Wherefore God gave them up (100^b)

VI. Who changed the truth (100^b-101^a)

Enarratio of Sectio VIII. Wherefore, I say, God gave them up (101^a seq)

Expositio (101^a)

Interpretatio [Rom. 1.24-27] (101^a-103^a)

Observatio I. He gave them up to vile passions (103^a)

II. They changed the use of nature (103^a)

III. Working filthiness (103^{a-b})

Enarratio of Sectio IX. As they did not judge it good (103^b seq)

Expositio (103^b)

Interpretatio [Rom. 1.28-32] (103^b-106^b)

Observatio I. As they did not judge it good (106^b)

II. Filled with all unrighteousness (106^b)

III. Who when they knew the justice of God (106^b-107^a)

Chapter 2

Enarratio of Sectio I. Therefore there remains to thee (107^a seq)

Expositio (107^a-108^a)

Interpretatio [Rom. 2.1-4] (108^a-109^b)

Observatio I. Wherefore thou art inexcusable, o man that judgest (109^b-110^a)

II. We know that the judgment of God is according to righteousness (110^a)

III. Or despisest thou? (110^a)

Enarratio of Sectio II. But heapest up to thyself
(110^{a}seq)

Expositio (110^b)

Interpretatio [Rom.2.5-10] (110^b-120^b)

Observatio I. But heapest up to thyself (120^b-121^a)

          II. To those who in well doing (121^a)

        III. Who seek things glorious and honest (121^a)

        IV. But to those who act with contention (121^{a-b})

         V. Affliction, distress (121^b)

        VI. To the Jew first (121^b)

Enarratio of Sectio III. For there is no respect of persons
(121^{b}seq)

Expositio (121^b-122^a)

Interpretatio [Rom. 2.11-16] (122^{a}seq)

Conciliatio of this, that God does not accept the person; and, What is promised to the children of those who do well, for the sake of the godliness of their parents. (126^a-129^b)

Conciliatio II, of this, Those who do the Law are justified; with this, None are justified by the works of the Law. (129^b-130^b)

Observatio I. For there is no respect of persons (130^b-131^a)

        II. For if the Gentiles which by nature (131^{a-b})

        III. When God shall judge the secrets of men (131^b)

        IV. According to my Gospel (131^b-132^a)

Enarratio of Sectio IV. Thou, therefore, that callest thyself a Jew, etc. (132^{a}seq)

Expositio (132^a-133^a)

Interpretatio [Rom. 2.17-24] (133^a-136^b)

Observatio I. Behold, thou art called a Jew (136^b-137^a)

        II. Thou art confident that thou art (137^{a-b})

III. For through them my name is blasphemed (137^b)

Enarratio of Sectio V. Circumcision indeed profiteth (137^b seq)
Expositio (137^b-138^a)
Interpretatio [Rom. 2.25-29] (138^a-144^a)
Observatio I. For circumcision profiteth if thou keep the law (144^a)
II. But if thou art a transgressor of the law (144^{a-b})
III. But thou who by the letter and circumcision art a transgressor of the law (144^b)
IV. For he is not a Jew which is one outwardly (144^b-145^a)

Chapter 3

Enarratio of Sectio I. What advantage then hath the Jew? (145^{a}seq)
Expositio (145^a-146^a)
Interpretatio [Rom. 3.1-4] (146^a-150^b)
Quaestio: Of what sort and of what use are ceremonies in the Church of God? (150^b-164^b)
Observatio I. What advantage hath the Jew? (164^b-165^a)
II. Much in every way (165^{a-b})
III. Let God be true (165^b-166^a)
IV. That thou mightest be known to be just in thy words (166^a)

Enarratio of Sectio II. But if our unrighteousness (166^{a}seq)
Expositio (166^a-168^b)
Interpretatio [Rom. 3.5-8] (168^b-170^a)
Observatio I. But if our unrighteousness (170^a)
II. For how shall God judge the world? (170^{a-b})

III. Which indeed they condemn justly (170^b)

Enarratio of Sectio III. What then? are we better than the Jews? (170^b seq)
Expositio (170^b–172^a)
Interpretatio [Rom. 3.9–19] (172^a–175^b)
Observatio I. What then? are we better? (175^b)
II. There is none righteous, no not one (175^b–176^a)
III. We know that whatsoever the law says (176^a)

Enarratio of Sectio IV. Therefore by the works of the law (176^{a}seq)
Expositio (176^a–179^a)
Interpretatio [Rom. 3.20–26] (179^a–185^a)
Quaestio: Whether true righteousness, which is of the heart, first began to be proclaimed and revealed after Christ was glorified, or whether it also existed before among the people of Israel? (185^a–192^b)
Quaestio II. In what way the Law and the prophets testified of the righteousness to be revealed at the time when Christ was exalted (192^b–199^a)
Observatio I. Therefore by the works of the law (199^a)
II. By the law is the knowledge of sin (199^{a-b})
III. The righteousness of God by the faith of Jesus Christ (199^b–200^a)
IV. But they are made righteous freely (200^a)
V. That they might set forth and show his righteousness (200^a)

Enarratio of Sectio V. Where then is glorying? (200^{a}seq)

Expositio (200^a–201^b)

Interpretatio [Rom. 3.27-31] (201^b-203^a)

Conciliatio: By the law of works glorying is not excluded; and, By the law is the knowledge of sin (203^{a-b})

Conciliatio of this present statement, 'Therefore we abrogate the law by faith'; and what is said in II Cor. 3, 'what remains is much more glorious' (203^b-206^a)

Observatio I. Where then is glorying? (206^a)

II. A man is justified by faith apart from the works of the law (206^{a-b})

III. Yes, of the Gentiles (206^b)

To the Reader (206^b-207^b)

End of Book I of the Enarrations on the Epistles of St. Paul the Apostle.

The Second Book of Enarrations on the Epistle of St. Paul to the Romans.

To Christian Readers, grace and peace.[26] (209)

Metaphrasis of Rom.4 (210^a-211^a)

Summary of the chapter (211^{a-b})

Enarratio of Sectio I. What shall we say then? (211^{b}seq)

Expositio (211^b-213^b)

Interpretatio [Rom. 4.1-8] (213^b-217^a)

Conciliatio of these statements: 'The law of faith excludes boasting', and 'believing, he hath whereof to glory before God' (217^a-218^a)

Conciliatio II of 'Who believes him who justifies the ungodly', and what we read in Ex.23, 'I will not justify the ungodly' (218^{a-b})

Observatio I. What then shall we say our father Abraham (218^b)

II. For what saith the Scripture? (218^b)

---

[26] Bucer says that he will deal with Chapters 4–8 as a unit; 'in them there are proofs of the second order, by which the Apostle confirms as fully as possible that we receive from our heavenly Father absolution of sins, adoption as sons and heirs and therefore eternal life, only by faith in our Lord Jesus Christ and by no works of the Law, nor any other works at all, not even by the work and merit of faith' (209).

III. To him that believeth in him that justifieth the ungodly (218^{b})

IV. Faith is imputed for righteousness (219^{a})

Enarratio of Sectio II. Belongs, then, this blessedness to the circumcision (219^{a}seq)

Expositio (219^{a-b})

Interpretatio [Rom. 4.9-12] (219^{b}-222^{a})

Observatio I. Belongs this happiness to the circumcision (222^{a-b})

II. He received the sign of circumcision (222^{b})

III. In that he was the father of all who believe (222^{b})

Enarratio of Sectio III. For the promise was not to Abraham or his seed (222^{b} seq)

Expositio (222^{b}-224^{a})

Interpretatio [Rom. 4.13-18] (224^{a}-227^{b})

Conciliatio (227^{b})

Observatio I. The promise is not by the law (227^{b})

II. That he should be heir of the world (227^{b}-228^{a})

III. For the law works wrath (228^{a-b})

IV. Therefore it is of faith, that it might be by grace (228^{b})

V. Not to that only which is of the law (228^{b})

Enarratio of Sectio IV. And being not weak in faith (228^{b}seq)

Expositio (229^{a-b})

Interpretatio [Rom. 4.19-25] (229^{b}-232^{a})

Observatio I. For being not weak in faith (232^{a-b})

II. He doubted not of the promise of God (232^{b}-233^{a})

III. That God was able (233^{a-b})

IV. To those believing on him who raised Jesus (233^b)

End of Chapter 4.

Metaphrasis of Rom.5 (234^{a-b})
Summary of the chapter (235^a-236^a)
Enarratio of Sectio I. Being therefore justified by faith (236^{a}seq)
Expositio (236^a-237^a)
Interpretatio [Rom. 5.1-5] (237^a-240^a)
Conciliatio of the places in which Scripture says that the saints complain of their afflictions in deep bitterness of mind; with the present place, where Paul affirms that the saints glory in afflictions, that is, rejoice greatly and boast of them (240^a-244^a)
Observatio I. We have peace towards God (244^b)
II. Knowing that affliction (244^b-245^a)
III. Patience worketh probation (245^{a-b})

Enarratio of Sectio II. Christ in due time (245^{b}seq)
Expositio (245^b-246^a)
Interpretatio [Rom. 5.6-11] (246^a-248^b)
Conciliatio of this, that Paul here numbers sinners and the impious as enemies of God; with what, writing to the Galatians, he mentions he said to Peter, 'we are by nature Jews and not sinners of the Gentiles'. Again, with what he glories to the Philippians, that he lived blameless in the law (248^b-249^b)
Observatio I. When we were yet weak (250^a)
II. [no text] (250^{a-b})
III. We were reconciled (250^b)
IV. We also glory in God (251^a)

Enarratio of Sectio III. Wherefore, as through one (251^{a}seq)
Expositio (251^a-252^a)

Interpretatio [Rom. 5.12-14] (252^a-257^a)

Conciliatio of what St. John wrote in his Epistle, chapter 3, 'The devil sins from the beginning' (which agrees with what we read in Wisdom 2, 'By the envy of the devil sin entered into the world'); with the present statement, 'By one man sin entered' (257^{a-b})

Observatio I. As by one man sin (257^b-258^a)

        II. And by sin death (258^{a-b})

       III. But sin is not imputed where there is no law (258^b)

Enarratio of Sectio IV. But not as the fall of sin (258^{b}seq)

Expositio (258^b-259^a)

Interpretatio [Rom. 5.15-17] (259^a-262^a)

Observatio I. Not as the blessing (that is, χάρισμα) (262^a)

      II. For if by the fall of one many died (262^a)

     III. The gift of righteousness by Jesus Christ (262^a)

Enarratio of Sectio V. (262^{a}seq)

Expositio (262^a-263^a)

Interpretatio [Rom. 5.18-21] (263^a-267^a)

Quaestio: What is original sin? and what is its power? (267^a-274^b)

Observatio I. In all men unto condemnation (274^b-275^a)

      II. As by the disobedience of one (275^{a-b})

     III. But the law entered that sin (275^b)

    IV. When sin gained a kingdom (275^b)

End of Chapter 5.

Metaphrasis of Rom. 6-8 (276^a-279^b)

Summary of the things which are contained in these chapters (280^a-282^a)

Enarratio of Sectio I. What shall we say then? (282ᵃseq)
  Expositio (282ᵃ-283ᵇ)
  Interpretatio [Rom. 6.1-11] (283ᵇ-297ᵇ)
  Observatio I. If we are dead to sin (297ᵇ)
              II. By baptism therefore we are buried
                  with him (297ᵇ)

Enarratio of Sectio II. Let not sin reign therefore
                  (297ᵇseq)
  Expositio (297ᵇ-298ᵇ)
  Interpretatio [Rom. 6.12-14] (298ᵇ-300ᵃ)
  Observatio I. Let not sin reign therefore (300ᵃ⁻ᵇ)
              II. That ye should obey it (300ᵇ)
              III. Instruments of unrighteousness
                  (300ᵇ)

Enarratio of Sectio III. What then, you will say, shall we
                  sin? (300ᵇseq)
  Expositio (300ᵇ-301ᵃ)
  Interpretatio [Rom. 6.15-18] (301ᵃ-302ᵃ)
  Observatio I. What then? shall we sin? (302ᵃ⁻ᵇ)
              II. Or do you not know? (302ᵇ)
              III. Unto obedience (302ᵇ)
              IV. That form of doctrine which was
                  delivered unto you (302ᵇ)

Enarratio of Sectio IV. I speak after the manner of men
                  (302ᵇseq)
  Expositio (302ᵇ-303ᵃ)
  Interpretatio [Rom. 6.19-23] (303ᵃ-305ᵃ)
  Observatio I. I speak after the manner of men
                  (305ᵃ)
              II. Of iniquity unto iniquity (305ᵃ⁻ᵇ)
              III. Of which you are now ashamed
                  (305ᵇ)

Chapter 7.
  Enarratio of Sectio I. Or are you ignorant, brethren?
                  (305ᵇseq)

Expositio (305^b-306^b)

Interpretatio [Rom. 7.1-6] (306^b-309^b)

Conciliatio of these places on the Law (309^b-312^b)

Observatio I. Or are you ignorant, brethren? (312^b)

          II. And so you are dead (312^b-313^a)

         III. That you might be joined to the other (313^a)

Enarratio of Sectio II. What shall we say then? (313^{a}seq)

Expositio (313^a-314^a)

Interpretatio [Rom. 7.7-12] (314^a-317^b)

Conciliatio of Paul and Moses in this, that Paul quotes the last sentence of the Decalogue as simply, 'Thou shalt not covet', but Moses has 'Thou shalt not covet thy neighbour's wife, thou shalt not covet his house, etc.' (317^b-319^b)

Observatio I. I had not known sin except by the law (319^b)

         II. For I had not known coveting (319^b)

        III. But sin took occasion from the commandment (319^b-320^a)

        IV. And at the coming of the commandment, sin revived (320^a)

Enarratio of Sectio III. Therefore what is good (320^{a}seq)

Expositio (320^a-321^a)

Interpretatio [Rom. 7.13-20] (321^a-323^b)

Quaestio: How do these agree: We wish to do what is good, but do not do it; We do evil, yet do not wish to, and hate it. Both to do and not to do evil. For the Apostle affirms both. (323^b-327^a)

Observatio I. But I am carnal (327^a)

         II. But now it is not I that do it (327^a)

Enarratio of Sectio IV. I find then a law (327^{a}seq)

Expositio (327^a-328^a)

Interpretatio [Rom. 7.20-25] (328^a-329^b)

Observatio   I. I find then a law (329^b-330^a)

Enarratio of Chapter 8. Therefore there is no condemnation (330[a]seq)
    Expositio (330[a]-331[a])
    Interpretatio [Rom. 8.1-8] (331[a]-333[a])
    Observatio I. Who walk not according to the flesh
                (333[a])
             II. The preoccupation of the flesh is
                death (333[a])
           III. Of the Spirit, life and peace (333[a])

Enarratio of Sectio II. But you do not live according to
the lusts of the flesh (333[a]seq)
    Expositio (333[a]-335[a])
    Interpretatio [Rom. 8.9-17] (335[a]-339[a])
    Observatio I. But if any man have not the Spirit of
                Christ (339[a])
             II. If the Spirit of him who raised Christ
                (339[a])
           III. You have received the Spirit of adop-
                tion (339[a])

Enarratio of Sectio III. For we reckon (339[a]seq)
    Expositio (339[a-b])
    Interpretatio [Rom. 8.18-23] (340[a]-343[a])
    Quaestio: Whether all things are to be renewed when
    man is restored to incorruption and immortality
    (343[a]-346[a])
    Observatio I. And so we reckon (346[a])
             II. For whatsoever things were created
                (346[a])
           III. Because they shall also be freed (346[a])

Enarratio of Sectio IV. We are saved by hope (346[a]seq)
    Expositio (346[a]-347[b])
    Interpretatio [Rom. 8.24-27] (347[b]-351[b])
    Observatio I. But hope that is seen (351[b])
             II. For what we pray for (351[b])
           III. Who searches the hearts (351[b])

Enarratio of Sectio V. But we know that for those that love God (351^{b}seq)

    Expositio (351^b-353^b)

    Interpretatio [Rom. 8.28-34] (353^b-358^a)

    Quaestio: On predestination, what it is, to what end we should consider it, and whether it takes away free-will (358^a-361^a)

    Quaestio II. Whether it belongs to Christ alone to intercede for us to the Father, or whether this is also the office of the saints (361^a-362^a)

    Observatio I. We know that for those that love God (362^a)

           II. Who are the called according to his purpose (362^{a-b})

          III. That they may be conformed to the image of his Son (362^b)

          IV. That he might be the first born (362^b)

          V. But whom he predetermined (362^b)

          VI. If God be for us (362^b)

          VII. Who spared not his own Son (363^a)

          VIII. Who shall bring accusation against God's elect? (363^a)

Enarratio of Sectio VI. Who shall exclude us from the love of God? (363^{a}seq)

    Expositio (363^a-364^b)

    Interpretatio [Rom. 8.35-39] (364^b-369^b)

    Observatio I. Who shall separate us? (369^b)

          II. Like sheep to the slaughter (369^b)

          III. I am persuaded (369^b)

    Peroratio: On justification by the faith of Christ alone, as in the Apostle thus far; and, A refutation of calumnies, etc. (370^a-373^b)

    A last word on the Second Book of Enarrations on the Epistle of St. Paul to the Romans.

    To the Christian Reader, greetings in Christ.[27] (374)

[27] 'I had intended to end the Second Book of our Enarrations here, since the Apostle's secondary proofs, by which the Apostle confirms that faith alone justifies, ends at this place. But since the *locus* which the

Metaphrasis of Chapters 9-11. (375^a-378^b)
Summa of the things contained in these three chapters (378^a-380^b)

Enarratio of Sectio I. I say the truth through Christ (380^{b}seq)
   Expositio (380^b-381^b)
   Interpretatio [Rom. 9.1-5] (381^b-385^b)
   Observatio I. I say the truth through Christ (385^b)
          II. For I could wish myself to be anathema (385^b)
         III. My kinsmen according to the flesh (385^b-386^a)
         IV. Who are Israelites (386^a)

Enarratio of Sectio II. But it cannot be that the Word should be destroyed (386^{a}seq)
   [Expositio] (386^a-387^a)
   Interpretatio [Rom. 9.6-13] (387^a-388^b)
   Observatio I. For it cannot be (388^b)
         II. For not all who are of Israel (388^b-389^a)
        III. The elder shall serve the younger (389^a)

Enarratio of Sectio III. What shall we say then? (389^{a}seq)
   Expositio (389^a-391^a)
   Interpretatio [Rom. 9.14-21] (391^a-395^b)
   Conciliatio of these statements: 'Whom God will, he hardens', and 'God will have all men to be saved'; and what things agree with both. (395^b-400^a)
   Quaestio: On free-will; whether man is endowed with free-will; and for what it avails. (400^a-404^a)

Apostle treats in the following three chapters, on the temporary rejection of the Jews, on the calling of the Gentiles, and on the taking up of the Jews again, contains much that makes for the same thing, I have preferred to add the narration of this *locus* to the first as an addition to crown the whole' (374).

Observatio I. I will have mercy on whom I will
              have mercy (404^a)
          II. It is not of him that willeth (404^{a-b})
          III. O man, who art thou? (404^b)
          IV. Shall the thing formed say to him
              that formed it? (404^b)

Enarratio of Sectio IV. If God endured (405^{a}seq)
    Expositio (405^{a-b})
    Interpretatio [Rom. 9.22-29] (406^a-409^b)
    Observatio I. That he might make his power
                  known (409^b)
              II. He endured in much kindness (409^b)
              III. In the vessel of mercy (409^b-410^a)
              IV. I will call them that were not my
                  people (410^a)
              V. If the number of the sons of Israel
                  (410^a)

Enarratio of Sectio V. What shall we say then? (410^{a}seq)
    Expositio (410^a-411^a)
    Interpretatio [Rom. 9.30-33] (411^a-412^a)
    Observatio I. The Gentiles which have not pursued
                  righteousness (412^a)
              II. But Israel, following after the law
                  (412^{a-b})
              III. Stumbled on the stone (412^b)

Enarratio of Chapter 10 [Sectio I]. Brethren, my heart's
                  wish (412^{b}seq)
    Expositio (412^b-414^b)
    Interpretatio [Rom. 10.1-11] (414^b-418^b)
    Observatio I. Brethren, my heart's wish (418^b)
              II. But not according to knowledge
                  (418^b-419^a)
              III. Christ the end of the law (419^a)
              IV. Say not in your heart (419^a)
              V. That God raised him (419^{a-b})

Enarratio of Sectio II. For there is no difference
                  (419^{b}seq)

Expositio (419^b-420^a)

Interpretatio [Rom. 10.12-17] (420^a-421^b)

Observatio I. The same Lord is rich unto all (421^b-422^a)

            II. How should they believe in him of whom they have not heard? (422^{a-b})

           III. How shall they preach, except they be sent? (422^b-423^a)

Enarratio of Sectio III. But I say, did they not hear? (423^{a}seq)

Expositio (423^a)

Interpretatio [Rom. 10.18-21] (423^a-425^a)

Observatio I. Their sound is gone out into every land (425^{a-b})

            II. I will provoke to envy (425^b-426^a)

           III. I was found by them that sought me not (426^a)

Enarratio of Chapter 11 [Sectio I]. I say then, has God cast off his people? (426^{b}seq)

Expositio (426^b-427^a)

Interpretatio [Rom. 11.1-6] (427^a-428^a)

Observatio I. I also am an Israelite (428^b)

            II. He objects to God against Israel (428^b)

           III. I have left to me (428^b)

Enarratio of Sectio II. What then? What Israel sought (428^{b}seq)

Expositio (428^b-429^a)

Interpretatio [Rom. 11.7-10] (428^a-430^b)

Observatio I. The election has obtained (430^b-431^a)

            II. But the rest were blinded (431^{a-b})

           III. God gave them a spirit of remorse (*compunctionis*) (431^b)

           IV. Let their tables (431^b)

Enarratio of Sectio III [and IV]. I say, then, have they
                                    stumbled? (431^{b}seq)

> Expositio (431^b-434^a)
> Interpretatio [Rom. 11.11-24] (434^a-440^a)
> Conciliatio of those places in which all mortal men,
> even Jews, are declared to be wild olive trees by
> nature, that is sterile of true righteousness, because
> they are children of wrath: with those places in
> which the Jews are called the cultivated olive by
> nature, that is, fertile in godliness, and only the
> Gentiles wild olive trees (440^a-442^a)
> > Observatio I. But by their fall salvation is come to
> >   the Gentiles (442^a)
> >   II. If the first fruits are holy (442^a)
> >   III. But if thou art the wild olive tree
> >   (442^a)
> >   IV. Boast not, but fear (442^{a-b})

Enarratio of Sectio IV [= V]. For I would not have you
                                    ignorant, brethren (442^{b}seq)

> Expositio (442^b-443^b)
> Interpretatio [Rom. 11.25-32] (444^a-448^a)
> Observatio I. And thus all Israel shall be saved
>   (448^{a-b})
>   II. For this is my covenant with them
>   (448^b)
>   III. According to the gospel, enemies
>   (448^b-449^a)
>   IV. The gifts of God are without repent-
>   ance (449^a)
>   V. God hath concluded all (449^a)

Enarratio of Sectio V [= VI]. O the depth and the
                                    breadth (449^{a}seq)

> Expositio (449^a-450^b)
> Interpretatio [Rom. 11.33-36] (450^b-451^a)
> Observatio I. O the profound goodness (451^a)
>   II. How unsearchable (451^{a-b})
>   III. Who first gave to him? (451^b)

Peroratio (451^b-452^b)
The end of the second book.

The Third Book of Enarrations on the Epistle of St. Paul
to the Romans. (454seq)
To the reader (454)
Metaphrasis of Chapters 12 and 13 (455^a-456^b)
    Summa of the things in these two chapters (456^a-457^b)

Ennaratio of Chapter 12 [Sectio I]. I exhort you therefore (457^b seq)

    Expositio (457^b-458^b)
    Interpretatio [Rom. 12.1-2] (458^b-460^b)
    Observationes [no texts; one paragraph] (460^b)

Enarratio of Sectio II. For I tell you, by the gift
(460^{b}seq)
    Expositio (460^b-461^b)
    Interpretatio [Rom. 12.3-8] (461^b-465^a)
    Observationes [no texts]; (465^{a-b})

Enarratio of Sectio III. Let love be without dissimula-
tion (465^{b}seq)
    Expositio [Rom. 12.9-13] (465^b-467^b)
    [no Interpretatio]
    Observationes [no texts] (468^a)

Enarratio of Sectio IV. Bless them which persecute you
(468^{a}seq)
    Expositio (468^a-469^b)
    Interpretatio [Rom. 12.14-20] (469^b-473^a)
    Conciliatio of these, that Paul here forbids altogether
      the cursing of enemies; and yet he himself, as also
      the Prophets and the holy Psalms, solemnly cursed
      his enemies. (473^a-474^b)
    Another Conciliatio, of these, that here we are
      commanded to give food and drink to our
      enemies; and yet that the Apostle forbids them to

take food with the manifestly wicked who wish to be held as brethren. I Cor. 5 and II Thess. And John the Elder forbids him who brings alien doctrine to be received into a house or even to be greeted. (475^{a-b})

Quaestio: Whether it is lawful for Christians to appeal to the public authority in order to dispel injury; and, if this is not granted, whether he may use his own power in the matter, that is, whether it is lawful in a Christian place to repel force by force. (475^{b}-476^{b})

Observationes [no texts] (476^{b}-477^{a})

Enarratio of Chapter 13 [Sectio I]. Whosoever enjoys the present life (477^{a}seq)
Expositio (477^{a}-479^{a})
Interpretatio [Rom. 13.1-7] (479^{a}-482^{b})
Quaestio: Whether the power which wields the sword on earth is supreme, to whom whoever lives ought to be subject (482^{b}-492^{a})
Observationes [no texts] (492^{a})

Enarratio of Sectio II. Owe no man anything (492^{a}seq)
Expositio (492^{a}-493^{a})
Interpretatio [Rom. 13.8-10] (493^{a-b})
Observationes [no texts] (493^{b}-494^{a})

Enarratio of Sectio III. And this, since we know (494^{a}seq)
Expositio (494^{a})
Interpretatio [Rom. 13.11-14] (494^{a}-496^{a})
Observationes [no texts] (496^{a})

Metaphrasis of Chapters 14-16 (496^{a}-497^{b})
Summa of these chapters (497^{a}-500^{a})[28]

---

[28] These figures are not incorrect. The *Metaphrasis* is not set out in columns and the *Summa* is.

Enarratio of Chapter 14 [Sectio I]. Him that is
                                weak in faith (500[a]seq)
 Expositio (500[b]-502[a])
 Interpretatio [Rom. 14.1-13a] (502[a]-503[a])
 Observationes [no texts] (503[a])

Enarratio of Sectio II. But rather judge this (503[a]seq)
 Expositio [Rom. 14.13b-23] (503[a]-504[b])
 Interpretatio is put in the Expositio (504[b])

Enarratio of Chapter 15 [Sectio I]. But we ought
                                (504[b]seq)
 Expositio [Rom. 15.1-7] (504[b]-505[b])
 Interpretationes, as far as time allows, are placed in
 the Expositio (505[b])

Enarratio of Sectio II. But I say that Jesus Christ
                                (505[b]seq)
 Expositio [Rom 15.8-13] (505[b]-506[a])

Enarratio of Sectio III. But I am persuaded (506[a-b])
 [no Expositio, Interpretatio, or Observationes]

Enarratio of Sectio IV. Now I have no place (506[b]seq)
 [no Expositio, Interpretatio, or Observationes]

Enarratio of Chapter 16. (506[b]-507[b])
 [no Metaphrasis, Expositio, Interpretatio, or Obser-
 vationes]

Peroratio (507[b])

The End.

By going steadily through this outline and noting the
subjects singled out by Bucer and the space he allotted to the
parts of his commentary, the reader should have a good
general view of it and something of an insight into Bucer's

virtues and faults as a commentator. The final *Peroratio*
apologizes for his skimpy treatment of the end of the Epistle:
'There are certainly many things in these last three chapters
worthy of fuller and more careful treatment; but the Lord has
at this turn not granted me sufficient time for it. Yet the
earlier matters have been treated so fully that they ought to
shed some light on these' (507[b]). But, looking forward to the
other Pauline commentaries he was never to write, he
promises that he will include in them the matters here
neglected.

Not much is known about Philibert Haresche[29], the writer
of the next commentary, which came four or five months
later. He was born in Paris, attended that university,
proceeded licentiate in theology in January, 1526 without
distinguishing himself (he was placed fourteenth in a class of
twenty-four. In 1532 Gagney was second and Guilliaud third
in a class of twenty-eight), and took his doctorate in
December of that year. He belonged to the order of
Augustinian Hermits and became prior of their Paris convent
in 1526. Some years later he was made inquisitor-general of
France.

The title of his commentary on Romans,[30] which came out
in July 1536, however, is packed with information: *A Clear
and Short Exposition of the Epistle of St. Paul to the Romans, with
definitions of difficult words, and a note on differing interpretations*
(diuersarum acceptionum); *authorities from the Old Testament,
either in the Septuagint translation or the original* (veritatis)
*Hebrew, both of which the Apostle sometimes follows. Thus it will
be plain to you that everyone must gather fruit in abundance from it.
The author is Brother Philibert Haresche of the Augustinian
convent in Paris, Doctor of Theology in the Faculty of Paris, and
Parisian by birth.*

The type-face measures 12.8 × 6.5 cm. and the whole is
printed in roman characters. In spite of its small format, it is a

---

[29] For Haresche, see Farge: Biographical register, 231-2.

[30] According to Farge, Haresche also published in 1536 *Commentarii
breves* on Romans. But I think this must refer to the *Expositio*, for I can
find no mention of it in library catalogues.

longish book, with 337 folios, in other words, 674 pages.
After the title page follows the Dedication, dated August 14,
1536, and addressed 'from your Augustinian convent in
Paris', to Gabriel Venetus the "Pastor" of the Augustinian
Hermits (sig. ℂᵛ). Now either this date or that in the
colophon (July 1536 as the completion of printing) is wrong.
It is possible that the dedication should be dated in 1535, that
printing was delayed for a reason we will conjecture, and
that, when the printer came to set the date of the Dedication,
he inadvertently substituted the current year. We know that
the *Expositio* was examined and approved by three members
of the Faculty of Theology in 1535.[31] Their permission to
print, followed by that of 'M.le Prévost de Paris', comes on
sig. ℂ iiʳ. It is not at all improbable that these two censoring
bodies held up publication until 1536. If so, it could hardly be
that the Faculty at least could have been offended by the
dogmas expressed in the book, but more probably that they
were suspicious of the advertised use of the Septuagint and
Hebrew, with its implied denigration of the Vulgate.
However that may be, I think we may take it that the
Expositio was finished before or by August 1535.

After the permissions to print come an alphabetical index, a
preface, a list of errata, and then the *Expositio* itself.

We learn, then, from the Title (apart from the biographical
details, which we have already mentioned) three intentions of
the author: that he will define "difficult words", that he will
annotate differing interpretations, and that he will refer the
reader, in the many Old Testament citations occurring in
Romans, to the Greek and Hebrew originals. We note
without surprise that there is no mention of correcting the
Vulgate of the New Testament by the Greek. It would be
tempting to surmise that an original version of the commentary had done just that and had therefore run into trouble
with the Faculty; but the whole tenor of the book shows this
to be unlikely.

In the Dedication he informs the prior, and through him
the readers, that his intention to write a commentary on

[31] Farge: *Op. cit.*, 23.

Romans was no new thought. St. Paul's words, "Take heed to reading, exhortation, and teaching; do not neglect the grace which is in thee", acted as a stimulus. But why this pointed particularly to Romans, he does not say. He was deterred by what he saw as the difficulty of its style and the profundity of its thought. Nevertheless, he seems to have taken the difficulties as a challenge and to have used them as the foundation of his method. 'And so, that the reader might have a clearer understanding of the text, I have included descriptions, definitions, and marginal variant readings of words under the title of *Notulae*. These are followed in turn by a literal exposition of the text, in which there is omitted the elucidation of no saying and in which I have made plain the Septuagint and the Hebrew when the Apostle adduces authorities from the Old Testament' (℃ᵛ).

When we come to the *Expositio*, however, we find it does not match with the prospectus. Even the *Notulae*, instead of being the at least moderately humanistic annotations that we might expect at this date, are in fact brief dogmatic notes, akin to the *Glossa interlinearia*. And the "literal exposition" is very definitely a scholastic theological commentary which shows the author as the thorough conservative he was. Yet there is no anti-Reformation polemic in the parts I have read. He writes as if he had not so much as heard that there was any Reformation, pursuing his own quiet, convinced, often tortuous way, the well-trodden way of later medieval Christianity. He says nothing new or fresh, but he says the old with untroubled conviction. His own thinking is superficial and his style simple. For whom was he writing? One would have thought that his fellow-theologians and even students would have known it all already. And indeed, the Preface is, in contrast to the *Expositio*, so elementary and naïve that it is hard to see why he included it. He tells us what a letter is and mentions briefly the circumstances of Romans. He tells us what an apostle was and what *divus* means. He explains the name "Paul". Finally he tells us that the task of an apostle was to administer the sacraments and to feed the people with word and teaching; Paul certainly did the latter, and we know he did the former because he says so in

II Corinthians. This could hardly have been intended to silence Luther for ever. Perhaps he was writing for himself and for his brethren in the convent, to confirm them and himself in the faith in which they had been brought up.

5: 1537

Several reprints or new editions were published in 1537. A second or third edition of Bullinger in March, a third of Theophylact, the second of Lombard, and Gagney's edition of Primasius. Besides these there appeared at Basel in September the interesting compilation by John Lonicer. The title page explains the work sufficiently: *Succinct Exegesis of a certain old Greek theologian on the Epistle of St Paul to the Romans, taken from the Greek Interpreters of Holy Scripture: that is, from Theodoret, Gennadius, Isidore, John Chrysostom, Cyril, Oecumenius, Severianus, Gregory Nazianzen, Photinus, Basil, Titus* [of Bostra] *against the Manichees, Methodius in his sermon on the Resurrection, Dionysius of Alexandria.* It was, in fact, a sort of reversion to the early medieval method of glosses.

Nor, in this year, must we overlook Bonadus, who offered a verse paraphrase of the Pauline epistles: *The Divine Epistles of St Paul, Apostle to the Gentiles and Doctor of the Church of Jesus Christ, translated as a paraphrase for the Orphic lyre, by Francis Bonadus, presbyter of Angers.* The gist of his *Apologetica oratio* is 'Why should verse be addressed only to pagan gods and written only on secular subjects and not on the truths of the New Testament?' The work consists of a prose argument on each chapter, followed by the verse paraphrase. Bonadus was a man full of words, and strange words at that, a real humanist, whose prose style reminds one strongly of Spenser's Gabriel Harvey. It is unfortunate that the limits we have set ourselves exclude his paraphrase, for it is certainly of some interest in its historical context.[32]

[32] For a little more on Bonadus, see K. Hagen: Hebrews Commenting from Erasmus to Bèze 1516–1598 (Tübingen, 1981), 35.

6: 1538

In the March of 1538 Jean Gagney published another book on Romans, this time in a set of *scholia* on all the Pauline epistles. *The Epistles of the Apostle St Paul illustrated with very short and simple* scholia *by Jean Gagney.* . . .. The Epistle to the Romans occupies fol. 1^r-26^r of this book, which uses several types; the Dedicatory Epistle and Argument are in italic, the Biblical text roman, the running heads Gothic, and the *scholia* themselves a smaller roman. There is also sometimes a Greek word. The type-face measures 11.2 × 6.7cm.

The Dedicatory Epistle (to Cardinal Ioannes à Lothingaria[33]) contains information about the origin of this book. Some months before, Gagney had begun to deliver lectures on Paul to the Cardinal (and presumably a few of his household). But the lectures were continually interrupted by 'a crowd of importunate courtiers'. The Cardinal then forbade any entry to his presence before the end of the lecture. This, however, seems to have been ineffectual, and at last Gagney decided the best thing to do would be to write his lectures for the Cardinal to read, but he would not write full length commentaries, which often produced more darkness than light on account of their fulness and diversity. 'On the other hand, nothing helps the understanding of the epistles more than brief and lucid *scholia*' (Sig. Aii^v). But again the thought of the difficulty and obscurity of Scripture daunts him: 'But when I considered the spirit and nature of the Holy Scriptures and their multiple and inexhaustible interpretation, and especially the rugged epistles of Paul which I had read so often, the hiatuses with their long inversions, the unresolved *anapodota*, the inaccessibilities and dead ends amid such depth of meaning, it seemed as if I should need, not simply the divining power of the Python of Apollo, but the divine spirit of Paul himself ' (Sig. Aii^v). And this gives him the opportunity to refute the heretics: 'Hence I cannot but wonder at the impudence of those men who have the spirit, not of Paul (that is, of peace and quiet), but of schism and dissension, and

---

[33] Jean de Lorraine was the uncle of the regents of France, Francis and Charles, the latter of whom had succeeded to Jean's cardinalate.

who, disregarding interpeters and the commentaries of godly and learnèd men (which they are accustomed to cavil at), impudently claim that they are keeping to Paul's mind, as if they were sublimely caught up with Paul and admitted to the sight of inscrutable secrets of divine wisdom and alone have understanding of Paul's writings which, having forsaken all other interpretations, they explain by their own judgment – nay, they feign there is no need of explanation, as if in this matter it were the easiest and clearest of things' (Sig.Aii^v–Aiii^v). The inevitable quotation of II Pet.3.16 follows at once.

7: 1539

The only new commentary on Romans to appear in 1539 came out in August from the Froschauer press in Zürich. As it was the work of one of the now lesser known Reformers, we must give the more space to the author.

Conrad Pellican[34] (his so to say Renaissance name; he was born Kürstner) had been born as long ago as 1478. At quite an early age he came under humanist influence, which over the years crystallized into an Erasmianism. For some ten years he was a Franciscan, as a plain monk and as a teacher of theology. That he started to learn Hebrew as early as 1499 makes him something of a pioneer; that he wrote the first Hebrew grammar by a Christian establishes the claim. It was while he taught theology in Basel, that strongly humanist city, that he moved from Erasmianism into "Lutheranism". In 1526 he became professor of Greek and Hebrew at the *Prophezei*, the theological college in Zürich.[35] He still held that office when the seventh volume of his commentaries appeared in 1539.

Between 1532 and 1539 Pellican published commentaries on the whole Bible, five volumes on the Old Testament and the Apocrypha, two on the New Testament. As one of the

[34] Christoph Zürcher: Konrad Pellikans Wirken in Zürich 1526–1556 (Zürcher Beiträge zur Reformationsgeschichte Bd. 4 Zürich, 1975) 88.

[35] For the *Prophezei* see G.R. Potter: Zwingli (Cambridge, 1976), 221ff.

leading Hebraists of his day he was happier on the Old
Testament than on the New, where he leaned heavily on
previous writers – how heavily in Romans we shall see. It
would be misleading to think of these commentaries as works
of close scholarship. On the contrary, they are intended to be
clear and simple works for the literate but perhaps unscholar-
ly country parson. How they came to be written, and to what
end, we may let him tell mainly in his own words:

'Through nearly the whole of my life, in fact until my
fifty-fourth year, it never entered my mind to write anything
on the Canonical Scriptures . . . From a boy I was, I confess,
devoted to the Sacred Readings [*sacris lectionibus* – does he
mean readings of Scripture in public worship?] and always
desired that some godly scholar might, in place of the *Glossa
ordinaria* (which is really too allegorical), produce from the
best interpreters and expositors, old and new, a more certain
and richer exposition for preachers of the divine Word'
(Sig.aaa2ᵛ). He waited for someone to publish such a work,
but nothing came. At last 'several good men, learnèd and
friendly', urged him to undertake the task himself by putting
in order and publishing what he had assembled for his private
use. 'The Lord supplied me with leisure', and so far as his age
and energies permitted, he obeyed his friends' promptings.
He had a good library of 'holy theologians as well as
commentaries by the Hebrews [= Rabbis]' (Sig.aaa2ᵛ) which
he had read from his youth up. He was therefore well
prepared for the work.

So he chose out and wrote down and transferred to his
commentaries whatever he thought useful for simple people
and for those who did not possess a lot of books or were
ignorant of the languages. He did not always make a
verbatim transcript, but adapted the passages in such a way
that the godly reader might receive more abundant and holy
fruit. 'What the holy men spent much time on, I contracted
into a compendium; what seemed more obscure, I tried to
clarify; what was brief (a rare occurrence), I have explained
more fully in a more free sense' (Sig.aaa2ᵛ).

He had one class of reader especially in mind, for he had
been greatly worried by 'the perilous state of the plain

country parson' (*periculosa conditio simpliciorum in rure praes-byterorum*) (Sig.aaa2ᵛ). They had been forbidden by their overlords, the Christian magistrates, to preach the sermons of mendicant friars and ordered to proclaim the Word of the Lord, *solum ac purum*. But they had received little or no help for performing a task to which they were unfitted by training. What was lacking to them, and how could they be helped? What was lacking was a knowledge and understanding of Holy Scripture. The best help was to supply them with easy commentaries.

Two commentaries there were of particular value, by Bullinger and Bibliander, both followers of Zwingli here in Zürich. And we should thank God that in our church in Zürich 'there has been for these fifteen years the greatest agreement of teachers, the most Christian teaching, and the most exact explanation of the holy Canon according to the words and phrases, and with so much learning. . . so that I believe I have lived in Paradise itself all these years, after my wretched Babylonian captivity, and have been with comrades of an apostolic school – whatever some may think of our preceptors' (Sig.aaa2ᵛ).

He gets back to the point and says that Bibliander's lectures (*ordinariae praelectiones*) on the Old Testament had been taken down and copied for the use of the country clergy. (Zürcher draws our attention to the interesting fact that we have here a continuation in this of the archaic mode of dissemination by manuscripts.[36] After a while Bibliander's commentaries were published).

'Many of us paid a great price for the multiple commentaries on Lombard and we hoped to have copious fruit from them. Much more surely may we hope for the divine and holiest fruit from the most divine and holy seed of the divine Word, cultivated sincerely, faithfully, and in the spirit of godliness, unto the reforming of faith and morals and of sound doctrine among the elect' (Sig.aaa2ᵛ).

The title of Volume VII accords with the above account: *Commentaries of Conrad Pellican, minister of the Church in Zürich, on all the apostolic Epistles, of Paul, Peter, James, John,*

[36] Zürcher: *Op. cit.*, 88.

and Jude, composed and edited to bring together the best interpreters, for the use of those with a zeal for apostolic theology.[37] It is a large book, with a type-face of 22 × 13.5 cm., and is printed in roman throughout. There are two prefaces, the first, which we have used above, is addressed 'To all Readers of Holy Scripture, but especially to the bishops [= pastors] of the Churches of God, brethren honoured and dear, Conrad Pellican prays that they may know, love, live, and teach Christ'. Romans occupies pages 1-176 in this volume. In keeping with his aim of simplicity he gives no Greek and avoids textual criticism. There is also little explanation of individual words. His text (is he unique among the Reformers in this?) is the Vulgate, corrected where he judges it necessary.

The principal question to be asked concerns the source or sources of his *Romans*. We have already seen that his avowed purpose was to present selections from other writers, either copied verbatim or worked over by himself in order to simplify and clarify them. One does not read him for long before it becomes plain that in *Romans*, or to be more precise, for I have not made a comparison over the whole volume, in the passages with which we shall be concerned, his quarry is Martin Bucer.[38] Whole passages are lifted, sometimes abridged, from the *Metaphrases et Enarrationes* of three years before. There are no acknowledgments of these borrowings, apart from a critical remark on the usual lines of Bucer's prolixity and difficulty (18). But he has to be placed as a satellite of Bucer.

Also in this year appeared a second impression of Gagney's *Scholia*, and a third of Bullinger's Pauline Epistles, as well as the third of Melanchthon's *Dispositio*, and Gagney's French translation of Primasius.

---

[37] The copy I have used in Cambridge University Library bears on the title page the signature "H. latymere".

[38] This is confirmed by a letter to Myconius, in which Pellicanus explained that he used Bucer for Romans, Chrysostom for Corinthians. (Zürcher, 139).

8: 1540

The March of 1540 saw the appearance of the first of the splendid series of Biblical commentaries by Calvin, which was, according to Beza,[39] prevented from including the whole of Scripture only by Calvin's death fifteen years short of what might have been expected to be his allotted span. Although it was his first Biblical commentary, he was not new to the commentary form, for he had, eight years previously, written his humanist virtuoso piece on Seneca's *De clementia*. The new work, composed from a different motive, breathes a different spirit. But at this point we must remind the reader, who, if he has read "Calvin's Romans" will probably have read the final edition, that only the first edition falls within the period of our present study. The second is eleven years in the future, after Trent; the third another five beyond that.

Although I have already twice written at some length on the origins of Calvin's commentating, an account must also be given here, or we should leave an ugly gap. As with Bullinger and Bucer, however, I will try to avoid repetition by allowing Calvin to speak for himself at greater length.

The source for our information is to be found in the dedicatory letter addressed to Simon Grynée of Basel and dated from Strasbourg, October 18, 1539. It begins by reminding Grynée of conversations they had had 'three years ago', that is to say, in 1536. But the three years must surely be interpreted somewhat loosely. Calvin lived in Basel, where these talks must have taken place, from February 1535 until February or March 1536. His interest in the method of Biblical commentating should therefore be dated at the latest in the first two or three months of 1536. The letter also seems to suggest that Calvin talked with Grynée on this subject because he himself was contemplating writing a commentary. Grynée, according to Pollet, also began to expound Romans in lectures at Basel on March 21, 1536.[40] His

[39] Dedication of Praelectiones in Ezechielis Prophetae Viginti Capita Priora, OC XL, 11-12.

[40] J.V. Pollet: *Op. cit.*, II, 390. Grynée's lectures remained unpublished and are now lost (390 n.4).

conversations with Calvin were therefore no doubt as much for his own sake as for Calvin's.

They could hardly have had Bucer's *Romans* in mind when they talked, for they would not have been able to see a work which was published only in March 1536. On the other hand, it is not impossible that the later reading of Bucer's commentary may have both fired Calvin's enthusiasm to write a commentary and aroused his critical faculties to find a better method than Bucer's.

We may now turn to the letter itself.

'You will remember that three years ago we were talking together about the best way of commentating on Scripture, and the method which you liked best I also put first. For we both thought that the chief virtue of an interpreter lay in clear brevity, and that almost his only duty was to disclose the intention and meaning of the writer whom he had undertaken to explain. To the extent that he leads his readers away from the intention and meaning, he deviates from what he should be aiming at and unquestionably strays outside his true field. And so we were wishing that among those on whom is today laid the task of helping theology in this way there might be someone who would both cultivate easiness, and also take care not to detain the friendly reader unreasonably with long-winded comments. I know that this is not the opinion of everyone and that those who disagree can also bring forth arguments for their case; but I cannot be parted from my love of the concise [or, the *compendium*?]. But the variety of men's minds means that they have their preferences. Let each be allowed his own judgment, so long as he does not want to subjugate all others under his own rules. In this way we who prefer brevity will not reject or despise the labours of those who are more copious and diffuse in expounding the sacred books. And they on their side must bear with us, even if they do think us too compressed and concise' (1[5-24]).

He felt impelled to attempt a commentary himself. He was not confident that he had achieved their ideal, but he had never expected to, though he had so adapted his style that people might see that he was aiming at that mark.

But was there room for yet another commentary on

Romans? 'For when so many men of the greatest learning have already laboured at interpreting it, it is unlikely that there is anything better left for others to say' (1^{32-34}). At the outset he was deterred, he says, by the thought of how many commentaries there were, from time past and at the present. But the number is not surprising, for Romans occupies a special position in Scripture: 'if anyone understands this, he has an entrance opened to him into the understanding of the whole of Scripture' (2^{39-41}). More briefly than Bullinger, and without names, he praises the commentaries of the church fathers; 'their godliness, learning, holiness, and age gives them such authority that we should despise nothing that comes from them' (2^{41-43}). Of the moderns, however, he writes at length, and, in so doing, reveals further his views on method. It is noteworthy, by the way, that he refers by name only to reformed commentators, not to Romanists.

'There would be no point in mentioning by name all the living commentators; but I will say what I think of those who have done the most important work. Philip Melanchthon has shed much light on the Epistle by his unique gift of teaching and industry and skilfulness in every sort of discipline, and in these qualities he surpasses all his predecessors. But because it was his intention to deal only with the main subjects, he dwells on them to the exclusion of many things which could worry ordinary minds' (2^{45-50}). (We note, therefore, that Calvin considered Melanchthon's commentary unbalanced and insufficient; it concentrated on the discovery of *loci* and neglected exegesis). 'Bullinger came next, who received the praise he deserved. His great virtue was that he combined easiness with the gift of teaching' (2^{50-52}). (A rather brief comment, this; and no reference to Bullinger's advice on method, to which, if I am not mistaken, he was greatly indebted). 'And last of all, Bucer, whose lucubrations said the last word with the colophon to the volume.[41] As you know, he is a man of the most profound learning with a full knowledge of many subjects; he has a most perspicacious mind, has read widely, and has many other and various

[41] Presumably meant for a joke on the size of Bucer's commentary, a colophon usually consisting of only two or three lines.

qualities, almost unrivalled today. Equalled by few, he surpasses nearly all. To him belongs the praise that he has engaged in the interpretation of Scripture with more careful diligence than anyone else' (2^{52-59}). (At this point, nothing but the strongest praise for Bucer.)

'It never entered my mind to compete with such men or to steal the least part of their laurels – rivalry like that would have been too shameless . . . On the other hand, I trust it will be allowed that nothing was ever so well performed by men that there was no place for the industry of successors in the way of polishing, adorning, or clarifying. It is not for me to advertise myself, except to say that I judged this work would not be useless. I undertook it for no other motive than the common good of the Church. And I hoped that by a different kind of writing I should escape the charge of rivalry, which I was chiefly afraid of' (2^{59-69}). He is, by this last sentence, making it clear that, with all his admiration for the three predecessors, he was following his own way, not theirs. And so he goes on to criticise Melanchthon and Bucer. Whether his silence on Bullinger implies approval we cannot tell.

'For Philip attained his main goal of casting light on the necessary subjects (*capita*). And he was so occupied with these that he omitted many things which ought not to be overlooked; but he did not want to stop anyone else from expounding them. Bucer is too prolix to be read in a hurry by busy people. He is also too profound to be easily understood by superficial and careless readers. For whatever argument he treats of, the incredible fertility of his mind suggests so many things to his hand that he cannot stop writing. Thus, since the one expounds less than the whole, and the other expounds more fully than can be read in a short time, it seems to me that what I intend has no appearance of rivalry at all' (2^{69}-3^{79}).

No doubt Calvin is protesting so much because he does not wish his very close friendships with Melanchthon and Bucer to be jeopardized by his criticisms. But this does not alter the sincerity of the criticisms or the genuineness of the statements of his methods and principles. As he continues, we can see that his consciousness of his predecessors (expressed no doubt with the over-modesty of convention) was restricting his freedom in choosing the right form of commentary. 'I was undecided for a long time whether it might not be better to glean, so to say, some things after them and others which I considered might be helpful to those of average understanding, or to write a continuous commentary, in which it would be necessary to repeat many things which had been said already by them all, or at least by some one of them. They not infrequently, however, differ among themselves, and this presents a lot of difficulties to less sharp readers, so that they are unsure whom they should agree with. I therefore thought it would also be useful if I indicated the best interpretation and relieved of the burden of judging those who are not able of themselves to make such decisions, especially since I had determined to deal with everything easily and concisely, so that readers would not spend very much time reading in me what others had said' (3^{79-91}).

He again shows his sensitivity to the charge of singularity and at the same time tries to remove the offence which the unlearnèd might take at the variety of interpretations of the same text. 'It is only fair that I should be forgiven because I sometimes dissent from others, or at any rate am somewhat different from them. The Lord's Word ought to have too much veneration among us than that we should perplex it at all with various interpretations. For somehow or other this detracts from its majesty, especially if it is done with little judgment or sense' (3^{94-99}). It is criminal and sacrilegious to handle Scripture, as any other holy thing, with impure hands; to twist it in any direction we like, and to play tricks with it, as many have done. But this is not the point here: 'even those who cultivated godliness and were reverent and sober in treating the mystery of God by no means always agreed with one another. For God never bestowed on his servants such a blessing that any one man was endowed with full and perfect understanding in every respect . . . Therefore since we may not in this present life foster that most desirable hope of always agreeing among ourselves as to the meaning of passages of Scripture, we must, when we depart from the opinions of past writers, take care not to be motivated by a lust for originality, by an itch to be critical, or by antagonism or ambition. We should do it only when it is necessary and we should seek only to be useful' (3^{15}-4^{15}). If Scripture were expounded in this way and in this spirit 'less liberty would be taken in the dogmas of religion; and it is in these that the Lord wishes our minds especially to be in agreement. Readers will easily grasp the fact that all this is what I am trying to do' (4^{16-19}).

Anyone who wishes to understand Calvin's commentaries ought to read and ponder this *apologia* cast in the form of a dedication. He should note not only what is said, but also what is not said. Nothing about the actual mechanics of commentating, of which we have so much in Bullinger. Calvin prefers to leave himself a fair degree of liberty, using now this, now that method. He will not, like Caietan, tie himself down by announcing on the title page that he will keep to the *sensus literalis*, for sometimes (although probably not in *Romans*) it will be necessary for him to interpret according to any other sense that the text itself demands. This is not to say that he had no principles of interpretation or that he did not make consistent use of the tools which Renaissance philosophy and scholarship offered him. In particular, M. Bernard Girardin has gone very fully into the use of rhetoric in this commentary.[42]

The literary history is soon told.[43] It is probable that the commentary was based on lectures given in Geneva between autumn 1536 and Easter 1538. An abridgement was translated into French, not by Calvin, in 1543. Both books were condemned by the Paris Faculty of Theology before March 1543. A revision of the first edition was included in the collected edition of the commentaries on all the Epistles in 1551 and a further and more thorough revision, in which it was greatly enlarged, in 1556. The deletions were very few, and we can say that, with many alterations, 1540 was carried

[42] B. Girardin: Rhétorique et Théologique. Calvin. Le Commentaire de l'Épitre aux Romains. (Théologie Historique 54) Éditions Beauchesne, Paris, 1979.

[43] For a fuller account of the genesis of the Commentary, see my edition, Iohannis Calvini Commentarius in Epistolam Pauli ad Romanos (Leiden, 1981), IXff.

over almost entire into the definitive edition. This last is the form from which all the English translations have been made. A French translation of the complete first edition was published in 1550. The edition of 1540, the only one which concerns us in this book, cannot be said to have enjoyed the outstanding popularity of some of our other commentaries; yet it still ranks at their head, as an example of the highest virtues of a commentator – deep penetration into the author's thought, a self-less faithfulness to his views, and clarity and force in expression. It is for these qualities that Calvin is the only one of our commentators who is read today by those who are not professional theologians.

Calvin's first *Romans* was a small (type-face 11 × 6.5 cm) but quite thick book of four hundred and thirty pages. The *Praefatio* and Biblical text are in large roman, with twenty lines to a page; the *Argumentum* in smaller roman, with twenty-four lines, and the commentary itself in italics, with twenty-six lines. At least one copy (that in the Speer Library, Princeton) gives on the second title-page the author under an anagram pseudonym he sometimes used: *Commentaria Alcuini*.

This year were published four other works, the fourth edition of Melanchthon's *Commentaria* (twice), the second of Titelmann's *Elucidationes*, and new impressions of Ambrose and Primasius.

The only work to appear in **1541** was the third edition of Aquinas.

9: 1542

On Marino Grimani we have little enough information. The Grimani were a family that made a fair amount of hay while the sun of the Renaissance Papacy shone. Domenico, to whom Erasmus dedicated his Paraphrase of Romans, was a son of a future Doge of Venice. He became Cardinal, and Patriarch of Aquileia. It was he who judged the famous case of Pfefferkorn versus Reuchlin. Of his nephews one, Giovanni, succeeded to the Patriarchate of Aquileia when the other, Marino (c.1489-c.1545), our present author, relinquished it. Marino, also a cardinal, is mentioned briefly in Oldoinus' *Vitae et Gestae* (III,485) and *Athenaeum Romanum* (484) and in the *Dictionnaire des Cardinaux* (1057), but none gives us more than a factual outline. He comes for a moment to life in a letter from Erasmus to Augustine Steuchus, librarian in St Antony's monastery in Venice. The splendid library afforded Steuchus the opportunity of writing a book on the Old Testament, which he dedicated to Marino as the nephew of Domenico, from whom a large part of the library had come. Erasmus is reminded of his own contact with the two Grimani when he had been staying in Rome. Domenico had received him not as an inferior but as a colleague and had talked with him for more than a couple of hours. He had called in his nephew 'already at that time an archbishop, a youth endowed with a divine talent. As I was trying to get up, he stopped me with "The disciple must stand in the presence of his master"'(PSA IX, 206).

The talent appears as less than divine in his commentaries on Romans and Galatians, published in Venice in 1542 and dedicated to Pope Paul III. *The Commentaries on the Epistles of Paul to the Romans and to the Galatians* consists of one hundred and seventy three folios, of which *Romans* forms fol. 3^r – 130^r. It has a type-face of 15 × 9.5 cm., with the Dedicatory Epistle in roman, the Preface and Commentary in italic and the running heads in roman capitals.

All that Grimani has new to contribute to the exposition of Romans is an easy and clear humanist style. Originality of thought or creativity of interpretation should not be looked for from him. He follows the text of the Vulgate, but records some variant readings. His exegesis is sensible and unadventurous, but on the whole he expresses his exposition in a humanist fashion and in humanist categories. Nevertheless so insistent is he on "grace alone" that he often appears more evangelical than the evangelicals. When he has completed his exposition of justification his real position becomes clear.

Although his name is spelt Guillaud on the title page and in the prefatory matter of our edition of the book, the later editions all supply a second *i*; we will therefore call him Claude Guilliaud. He was by no means the least interesting of our authors and he is certainly one of the pleasantest. He was of that unusual species, a Sorbonnist who was, as we shall see, sufficiently well-disposed to the Reformers to be accused of heresy.

He was born in 1493[44] near Lyons and went to the University of Paris, apparently taking his arts' degrees at the Collège de Bourgogne; at any rate he was teaching arts subjects there in the mid fifteen-twenties. He was, however, also a member of the Collège de Sorbonne, holding various official posts there and often representing the college in business matters. He took his doctorate in theology in March, 1532. But this university period of his life ended in 1534 when, having apparently failed to be rewarded with a college living, he was taken up by Jacques Hurault, the Bishop of Autun in the Duchy of Burgundy. He was made canon theologian of Autun, penitentiary of the diocese and provost of the benefice of Sussez-en-Auxois. The first post entailed lecturing on Scripture to clergy of the diocese; in the second he was responsible for the spiritual care of those condemned to death for heresy, visiting them in prison and accompanying them to execution – no very pleasant office, one would think. It is said that he saved the lives of two booksellers from Geneva. The story accords with what we know of his tolerance.

According to Farge, he collaborated in editing and annotating a Bible in six volumes published by Hughes de la Porte at Lyons in 1540. Further, his collaborator was none other than Villeneuve, that is, Michael Servetus working as physician to the Archbishop of Vienne under the name of Villeneuve. Darwell and Moule, however, date the Bible in 1542

---

[44] On biographical facts I am largely indebted to the *Dictionnaire de Biographie Chrétienne*, ed. F.X. de Feller and F. Pérènnes (Paris, 1851) art. Guilliaud, and to Farge: *Op. cit.*, 213–216.

(No.6120), mention only the one editor, Villeneuve, and say nothing of more than one volume.[45]

However that may be, Guilliaud had certainly been occupied in the study of the Bible for many years before he brought out his *Collatio*. He tells his patron in the dedicatory letter, 'when I was at the Sorbonne [i.e. up to 1534] I devoted three years to expounding Paul's epistles, which little notes I brought together. And I was especially trained by almost daily study with the most learnèd teachers of that most distinguished College of the Sorbonne. Again, I have kept on with constant public lecturing in your church at your behest and by your authority for the past seven years since you took me from that distinguished College of the Sorbonne to your most celebrated church and house' (Sig. ⋆ 2ᵛ). Later he says that he had lectured at Paris, then at Autun and Lyons, and finally at Eleutheropolis Belliocensis (Villefranche-Beaujeu), 'which is my beloved home-town' (Sig. ⋆ 3ʳ) Hurault it was who persuaded him (practically all our commentators were, if we are to believe their prefaces, modest and retiring characters who needed a good deal of prodding before they dared to venture into print) Hurault persuaded him to make selections from his wide reading of commentaries on Romans

---

[45] The permission to print (quoted in Baudrier) shows us the part played by Guilliaud. After saying that M. Michel de Villeneuve, doctor in medicine, had undertaken to correct for a Bible in six volumes the *Glossa ordinaria* (or, at least, I suppose that is what is meant by 'de prélire la glose ordinaire'. Littré explains prélire as proof-reading, which is not what Servetus was asked to do), it continues: 'Also, to regularise the spelling, to put in accents, to punctuate, and to put in diphthongs; also to restore the Greek or Hebrew words which are in Latin letters and write them in Greek or Hebrew. Also, to mark the places where are to be inserted the annotations of Haugubinus (= Pagninus?) on the Old Testament and the annotations of Erasmus on the New, according to the advice of M. Michel de Villeneuve and M. Claude Guilliaud, doctor in theology of Paris, canon of Autun. Also to write in the margin the marginal additions contained in the Bible of Robert Estienne, following the decision of the said Guilliaud, and also paying regard to the interlineary glosses, which are not to be duplicated if they are the same as the marginal [glosses]' J. Baudrier: Bibliographie Lyonnaise (Lyons and Paris, 1908), Tom. 7, 265-266. This Bible was placed on the Index of prohibited books for its Annotations.

and compose a commentary of his own out of the *congesta farrago* (Sig. ★ 2ᵛ – ★ 3ʳ). The resulting work was the *Collatio – A Collection on all the Epistles of St Paul, made according to the Judgment of the Learned, by Claude Guillaud of Beaujeu, Doctor of Sacred Theology, Praepositus and Canon Theologian in the famous Church of Autun.*

This is a medium sized book, the type-face 18 × 11cm. The Scripture text and the running headlines are in roman, the exposition in italics. The Epistle to the Romans occupies pages 1 – 107. On the reverse of the title page are two verses. The first is a 'tetrastich', or stanza of four lines, addressed 'To Claude Guillaud, Canon Theologian and Curio of Ville-franche, by Philip Crozet, quaestor of tributes in Beaujeu'. It runs:

> Whatever the old poet-augurs once did sing,
> What echoes from the great Apostles' choir,
> In fourteen Pauline letters he doth bring,
> To help your feet ascend that mountain's spire.

The second is a Distich to the reader:

> Hark to the true Apollo's words divine,
> Not him of Cumae but of Palestine.

Although it falls outside the scope of our study, the future career of the book ought to be mentioned. The second edition, greatly enlarged, according to a preface by the printer (Sig. ★ᵛ), appeared in 1544. The following year Guilliaud was accused of heresy by the Faculty of Theology at Paris and forced to revise his book.[46] This he did and it was published, no longer at Lyons but at Paris. In the meanwhile Hurault had died and the new edition was dedicated to the Dean and Chapter of Autun.

As we have seen, the work was a deliberate collection of other men's expositions. Guilliaud's own account is that 'a good part is taken from the holy doctors', meaning the fathers and, pre-

---

[46] See also J.M. De Bujanda, F.M. Higman, and J.K. Farge: Index de l'Université de Paris, 1544, 1545, 1547, 1549, 1551, 1556 (University of Sherbrooke & Geneva, 1985) 186–188.

sumably, schoolmen, while other works are used as subsidiary, 'yet without giving authors' names' (Sig. ★3ᵛ). The work is therefore eclectic. In the first of our passages we shall find him principally borrowing from Bucer, in the second he is more selective, using among others Caietan and Bucer.

We should not leave this survey without speaking of Erasmus of Rotterdam. A mere mention of the fifth edition of his *Novum Testamentum* and *Annotationes* was made under 1535 because they were largely written long before our period begins. But such was his standing among his contemporaries and such was his influence on New Testament studies that we cannot omit him now.

We can see three lines of influence from Erasmus reaching to our authors. The first comes from his edition of the Greek New Testament. Not only is it inconceivable that any of them should not possess a copy of one or other of the editions, but it would be safe to conjecture that most of them used it regularly as their text. Calvin, I think, used Colinaeus at this time, but he certainly also used Erasmus. It is not improbable that the cardinals, being wealthy men, could own the expensive *Complutensis* and it is possible that Caietan might make that his text for Romans; but it is more likely that the humanists Grimani and Sadoleto would use Erasmus' text. Only a careful textual study would show the truth; until that study is undertaken, the probability may be allowed to stand.

Apart from the use of one text rather than another, however, the fact stands out that now, within twenty years of Erasmus' first edition, every one of the authors will either treat the Greek as authoritative or at least grant it a certain subsidiary authority. Some will do this by using the Greek as their text and supplying a fresh Latin translation, others by correcting (usually in their notes) the Vulgate which they take for their text. During the fifteen-thirties it would appear that the strangle-hold of the Vulgate on the Roman Church was to a certain extent loosened. But only to a certain extent, for these Romanists (before the Council of Trent, be it noted, with its notorious but possibly misinterpreted *Decretum de vulgata editione Bibliorum*) made the Vulgate their actual text; but it is impressive that the most of them were ready to bring it into accord with the Greek.

Alongside an indebtedness to Erasmus' Greek Testament must also be set a liberal use of the linguistic and textual notes in his *Annotationes*. Our sections of Exegesis will show examples of these notes being taken over by other writers and reproduced, sometimes with acknowledgment of the true author, sometimes as their own. Most of them, of course, laid no claim to careful scholarship; and indeed, only Erasmus' *Annotationes* and Bucer's *Interpretationes* concentrate on this sort of study. The rest are, in a higher or lower degree, theological commentaries which use textual and linguistic studies only in the service of their main object. Nevertheless, the point is that they did so use them and to that extent were "modern" commentators.

The third line of influence was his insistence on observing the context. Plainly, there was nothing new in this; but, if Erasmus could hardly be said to have invented it, he certainly re-instated it as the *conditio sine qua non* of commentating. After him, its place in expounding a document was accepted. Again, all our authors agree that this is necessary in their task, even if they do not all have a keen enough perception to ferret out what a passage is saying, and even if sometimes the attraction towards an irrelevance proves too strong for their self-control.

PART TWO

ROMANS 1.18-23

18. 'Αποκαλύπτεται γὰρ ὀργὴ θεοῦ ἀπ' οὐρανοῦ, ἐπὶ πᾶσαν ἀσέβειαν, καὶ ἀδικίαν ἀνθρώπων, τῶν τὴν ἀλήθειαν ἐν ἀδικίᾳ κατεχόντων. (*Erasmi editio 1527*)

ουρανου επι Compl   ασεβειαν και   Compl
ανθρωπων των Compl   κατεχοντων,   Col

Revelatur enim ira dei de caelo super omnem impietatem et iniustitiam hominum eorum qui veritatem dei in iniustitia detinent. (*Stephanus Vulgata 1528*)
hominum, Er[4]Vg   detinent: St[32] Compl Er[4]Vg

Palam fit enim ira dei de coelo, adversus omnem impietatem, et iniustitiam hominum, qui veritatem in iniustitia detinent: (*Erasmi versio 1527*)
Palam fit] Manifestatum Er vers[1]   coelo adversus Er vers[5]   impietatem et Er vers[5]   detinent, Er vers[1]

EXEGESIS

'Αποκαλύπτεται – **Revelatur**] Erasmus: 'That is, uncovered and opened. When what was previously covered becomes plain' (A[1]420; A[3]289; A[5]346). And Bullinger: 'For the wrath of God is uncovered' (9).

ὀργὴ θεοῦ – **ira dei**] There is general agreement that it should be understood as the vengeance of god, *vindicta Dei* (Caietan: *iusticia vindictiva* (III F) or *ultio Dei* (Bucer, 82[a]); Calvin: 'condemnation and vengeance' (28[7-8]), Caietan: 'the vengeance of eternal condemnation' (III F)). Caietan and, more fully, Calvin, take *ira* metaphorically: 'Wrath is used, as commonly in Scripture, ἀνθρωποπαθῶς, for the condemnation or vengeance of God, inasmuch as, when he punishes, God bears, in our

84

opinion, the appearance of one who is angry. This therefore refers to the feeling of the sinner who is punished' (28[7]-29[10]).

ἀπ' οὐρανοῦ – **de coelo**] Calvin, *e coelo*. Variously understood. Caietan refers it either to vengeance – vengeance from heaven, to distinguish it from vengeance effected through men – or to "revealed" – that is, revealed in that particular way. The former will mean that 'the wrath of God from heaven is the vengeance of eternal condemnation' (III F); the latter refers to the Gospel: 'revealed in that way (that is, in the Gospel) it explains that the Gospel revelation is from God' (III F). Similarly Bullinger: 'in the same heavenly proclaimed Gospel is opened or revealed both the righteousness and vengeance of God' (9); and Melanchthon: 'that is, declared in the Gospel [*1540 adds*: divinely delivered]' (34[r];LXXXI[v]). But Grimani: [from heaven] 'because we read that many punishments are sent from heaven on the wicked angels and on ungodly men' (13[r]), e.g. the Flood, the fire on Sodom, fire in the time of Elias, etc. 'From heaven also, that is, from God who is in the heavens' (13[r]). He contrasts "heaven" with "the Gospel"; the wrath of God is not revealed in the Gospel, which, according to its name, is good news, but from heaven (13[r]). Bucer also says that the wrath of God is not revealed in the Gospel, which is *proprie* the revelation of nothing but the righteousness and goodness of God; but he adds that the Gospel does declare negatively that God's wrath remains on those who will not believe (83[a]). *De coelo* is intended to express the awfulness of God's wrath (82[b]). Calvin takes it to mean "universally": 'the wrath of God is poured out on the whole world, as far and wide as heaven stretches' (29[13-15]).

ἐπὶ πᾶσαν ἀσέβειαν καὶ ἀδικίαν ἀνθρώπων – **in omnem impietatem et iniustitiam hominum**] According to Bucer (83[b]) and Melanchthon (34[r];LXXXI[v]), a Hebraism for 'all men are ungodly and unrighteous' (Bucer). Calvin agrees (28[2-3]). The distinction between *impietas* and *iniustitia* is interpreted variously. Bucer (83[b]) and Bullinger (9) apply *impietas* to God, since it means to be without religion or the true worship of God, and *iniustitia* to duty towards men. Thus Bullinger: 'By . . . ungodliness Paul understands all superstition and false religion, and . . . by unrighteousness all iniquity, all the crimes and sins which result from false religion' (9). Melanchthon, however, restricts *impietas* to the first table of the Law but takes *iniustitia* as embracing all sins, whether against God or against men (34ʳ;LXXXIᵛ-LXXXIIʳ). Grimani refers both words to God: 'He calls idolatry *impietas* and infidelity *iniustitia*. For what greater impiety is there than to give to the creature the honour due to God alone? and since righteousness is of faith . . . infidelity is deservedly called unrighteousness' (13ᵛ). For Caietan *impietas* is a species of *iniustitia* (III F). Calvin accepts the earlier distinction, but connects the two words as representing different aspects of ingratitude towards God: 'for sin is committed in two ways; ἀσέβεια is a certain dishonouring [*inhonoratio* – failing to honour] of God, while ἀδικία means that man unjustly snatches God's honour by transferring to himself what belongs to God' (28³⁻⁷).

τῶν τὴν ἀλήθειαν – **eorum qui veritatem Dei**] Erasmus: 'The word "God" does not appear in the Greek or in the old Latin copies [*add:* nor does Chrysostom mention it (A⁵)]. He means the truth known to the philosophers, which is theirs rather than God's' (A³ 289; A⁵ 346). Nearly all our writers understand "truth" as the knowledge of God, although there are differing shades of opinion on the meaning of "knowledge". For Bucer it is the knowledge of what man owes to God (83ᵇ); for Melanchthon 'the knowledge of God [*1540 adds:* or the natural law]' (34ʳ;LXXXIIʳ). But Bullinger takes "truth" to be 'God himself and true religion, just as unrighteousness is superstition' (10). Similarly Haresche: 'Here "the truth of God" is taken for God himself and for those things which truly belong to God' (xxiʳ).

ἐν ἀδικίᾳ κατεχόντων – **in iniustitia detinent**] Again a variety of opinion. Bucer interprets the phrase to mean that they do violence to the truth (83ᵇ). Caietan makes a metaphor of it: 'to imprison within the will the intellectually known truth by, as it were, the bolts of unrighteousness . . . They imprison it, I say, so that it shall not escape into affections and works which conform to the truth they know' (III G). Similarly, but without the metaphor, Melanchthon: 'that is, man's will or heart does not assent or conform (*obtemperare*) to these knowledges' (LXXXIIIʳ). But Pellicanus: The truth is held down 'when we maliciously follow wrong paths and sacrilegiously despise

known truth and oppose the Spirit urging better things' (15).
Grimani continues with the theme of idolatry: 'To hold down
the truth in unrighteousness is not to worship and venerate the
known truth by consequent works. Although they knew that
God alone was to be worshipped, they bestowed the worship of
the Creator on creatures' (13ᵛ). Gagney says that they hold
down the truth *in iniustitia* who hide what they know (*Schol*. 2ʳ).
Similarly Calvin: 'To hold (*continere*) the truth is to suppress or
obscure it'; and he reverts to his earlier point: 'whence they are
accused as if they were robbers' (29¹⁵⁻¹⁶).

19. Διότι τὸ γνωστον τοῦ θεοῦ, φανερόν ἐστιν ἐν αὐτοῖς ὁ γὰρ
θεὸς αὐτοῖς ἐφανέρωσε.   (*Eras ed. 1527*)
θεου φανερον Compl   αυτοις. Er²,³,⁵ Compl Col
αυτοις, Er¹   εφανερωσεν, Er¹,²   εφανερωσεν.   Col

Quia quod notum est dei: manifestum est in illis. deus enim illis
manifestavit. (*Steph Vulg* 1528)
dei,   St³² Er⁴Vg

propterea quod id quod de deo cognosci potest, manifestum est
in illis. Deus enim illis patefecit. (*Eras vers* 1527)
id quod] omit Er vers¹   cognosci potest] cognobile Er vers¹
est, Er vers¹   manifestum] id manifestum Er vers¹
patefecit.] manifestavit, Er vers¹

EXEGESIS

Διότι τὸ γνωστὸν τοῦ θεοῦ – **Quia quod notum est dei]**
Some understand the phrase as denoting possibility, perhaps
following Erasmus: 'that is, what is knowable of God, that is,
what can be understood and known (*sciri cognoscique*) about
God' (A¹420; A³289: A⁵346). Thus Melanchthon (35ʳ-
36ʳ;LXXXIIIᵛ), Bullinger (10), and Pellicanus: 'Because they
do not take care as they ought to worship the God whom
they can understand by grace and the benefit of the intellect
(*ingenii*)' (15). The stressing of the possibility is not intended
to deny that the possibility has been attained; but the actuality
is brought out by Caietan and Calvin. 'As his intention is to
prove that they "hold down" the truth, his starting-point is
that the truth of divine things is known to them' (III G);

Calvin translates τὸ γνωστὸν first as *quod cognoscitur* and then, in the running head, following the Vulgate, as *quod notum est*, and explains it as 'that which it is lawful or expedient to know about God' (29[19-20]).

φανερόν ἐστιν – **manifestum est**] Melanchthon renders it *notus est*: 'in so far as God can be known, he is known to them' (34[v];LXXXIII[v]).

ἐν αὐτοῖς – **in illis**] Stressed by Caietan: 'that is, in their inmost being' (III H). Calvin takes *in* as used for emphasis, but in a different sense: 'He seems to want to indicate a manifestation which presses them so closely that they cannot escape it' (29[31-32]). There is general but tacit agreement with Erasmus that the phrase refers to those who are addressed and not to created things in general (A[3]289;A[5]346).

ὁ γὰρ θεὸς αὐτοῖς ἐφανέρωσε – **Deus enim illis manifestavit**] Caietan distinguishes between *manifestavit* here and *revelavit* in v.18. The latter should be used in speaking of the light of grace, *manifestavit* of the light of nature (III H).

20. τὰ γὰρ ἀόρατα αὐτοῦ, ἀπὸ κτίσεως κόσμου τοῖς ποιήμασι νοούμενα καθορᾶται, ἥ τε ἀΐδιος αὐτοῦ, δύναμις καὶ θειότης, εἰς τὸ εἶναι αὐτοὺς ἀναπολογήτους,   (*Eras ed* 1527)
αὐτου απο   Compl   κοσμου,   Er[1,2,3] Col
αυτου δυναμις   Er[1,2] Compl Col   αναπολογητους.
Compl

Invisibilia enim ipsius: a creatura mundi, per ea quae facta sunt intellecta, conspiciuntur: sempiterna quoque eius virtus et divinitas: ita ut sint inexcusabiles. (*Steph Vulg 1528*)
ipsius a Compl Er[4]Vg   mundi per Compl Er[4]Vg   sunt, Er[4]Vg   intellecta conspiciuntur Compl Er[4]Vg   divinitas, Er[4]Vg

Siquidem quae sunt invisibilia illius, ex creatione mundi, dum per opera intelliguntur, pervidentur ipsaque aeterna eius potentia ac divinitas, in hoc, ut sint inexcusabiles, (*Eras vers 1527*)
pervidentur, Er vers[1,2,3]   potentia ac] omit Er vers[1]   hoc ut Er vers[5]   inexcusabiles: Er vers[5]

EXEGESIS

τὰ ἀόρατα αὐτοῦ – **Invisibilia ipsius**] There is agreement that
the term refers to the attributes of God, which Caietan and
Grimani call *conditiones*. In this context *conditiones* may be taken
as the ways or modes in which God is God. Caietan: '*Invisibilia*,
that is, the invisible *conditiones* of God' (III H). The reason, he
goes on, for the singular verb *notum* with the plural noun lies in
the simplicity of God: 'that most simple entity which is God is
not known by us under his own unique and most simple mode
but by multiple *conditiones* (that he is *actus purus*, immutable,
eternal, and the like)' (III H-I). Similarly Grimani: 'By *invisibilia*
are meant the invisible *conditiones* of God, those indeed which the
philosophers knew (that he is *actus* or *potentia*, first, infinite,
immutable)' (14ʳ). Gagney's 'such are goodness, wisdom, and
the like' (2ʳ) is repeated by Guilliaud (7). Bucer keeps closer to
the text, reading the first and last parts together, with *a creatura
. . . conspiciuntur* as parenthesis. Therefore, 'God's eternal power
and divinity – that is, that he holds in his hand and governs all
things (these are included in the term "eternal power"), and that
in the best way, showing himself to be the *summum bonum* and
Father to those who seek him (this is contained in the term
"divinity") – these, I say, are the *invisibilia Dei*' (84ᵇ). Repeated
by Pellicanus (16).

ἀπὸ κτίσεως κόσμου – **a creatura mundi**] This phrase posed
difficulties for some of our commentators. Their first problem
was caused by the Vulgate translation of κτίσις as *creatura*. If
this referred to created entity it became necessary to decide on
the identity of created entity, whether it was individual or a
collective group of entities. Then, as a further and consequent
problem, because this sense of *creatura* threw a strain on the Latin
word *a*, "by" or "from", in itself not clear, the place of *creatura
mundi* in the sentence is made ambiguous. Erasmus reflects the
ambiguity. He says that κτίσις can be rendered either as the act
of creating or as the thing created. By using *creatura* the Vulgate
seems to refer κτίσις to man and τὰ ποιήματα to created
entities, with the meaning that those things which cannot be
perceived by the corporeal eye are seen by the creature, that is,
man who was created a soul. Others may take a different view;

for himself, Erasmus thinks that both can be referred to the
creating of the world, 'so that you will understand that the
invisibilia dei are perceived from the very creation of the world
when they are understood through the works, which declare the
power, wisdom, and goodness of God the Creator' (A¹420;
A³289; A⁵346-7). Caietan: 'The sentence can be punctuated so
that *a creatura mundi* may be taken either with *invisibilia dei* or
with *conspiciuntur* (perceived). If the former, it means that the
conditiones of God, which, of course, are visible to God, are
invisible to the creature. If the latter, it means that the invisible
things are perceived by the creature of the world, and this
creature is defined by the word *intellecta* (being understood) – in
other words, perceived by the intellectual creature of the world.
The Greek word can mean either "creature" or "creation". The
former fits the context better' (III I-K). Similarly Gagney: 'In
Greek ἀπὸ τῆς κτήσεως (sic!), that is, "From the foundation of
the world"; in other words, from when the world was founded;
or, "By the creature of the world", that is, man, who is
understood chiefly of all creatures. For how the invisible things
of God are known from the consideration of visible things, see
the excellent Book VII of Hugh of St. Victor in his *Didascalicum*'
(*Schol.* 2ʳ). Bullinger and Calvin follow Erasmus' translation *ex
creatione mundi*.

τοῖς ποιήμασι– **per ea quae facta sunt**] All are agreed that the
phrase means 'by the works, as by an instrument' (Er A¹420;
A³289; A⁵347). Caietan makes the point that it is to be taken
strictly as *per* and not as *in* (III A).

νοούμενα – **intellecta**] Erasmus: A present participle and not a
perfect (A¹420; A³289; A⁵347); echoed by Caietan (III A).

ἥ τε ἀΐδιος – **sempiterna quoque**] In Greek not *quoque* (also)
but *que* (and), says Erasmus; but the Vulgate translated it
correctly 'if Origen's interpretation is true, that *invisibilia* refers to
invisible creatures, [that is to say, separate entities], and not to God
[whom he later brings in separately]' (A¹420; A³290; A⁵347.
Passages in square brackets do not occur in A¹).

εἰς τὸ εἶναι αὐτοὺς ἀναπολογήτους – **ita ut sint inexcusabiles**] Caietan: '*Ita* (So), for *in hoc*(unto this)'[1] (IIII D). Similarly
Calvin, whose own translation *ut sint* is strengthened in the

---

[1] *hoc* accusative, not ablative. Cf. Beza: *ad hoc ut*

running head by *in hoc* (30[45]). They are both following Erasmus'
version; he says: 'Ita is not only redundant but ruins the sense.
The Greek is. . .that is, "in order that they may be inexcusable",
or "to this end, that they may be inexcusable", or, that they may
be brought by their knowledge of God to the point of being
unable to plead ignorance as a pretext when they sin, or, that
God granted them knowledge of himself so that afterwards they
should have no pretext for their unbelief if they rejected Christ'
(A[1]420; A[3]290; A[5]347). Caietan refers *in hoc* to what follows, i.e.
that they may be inexcusable in this, that when they knew God
they did not glorify him as God (IIII D). But Haresche: 'Not that
God made them become inexcusable, but this happened
consequentially. Their ungodliness and unrighteousness and
malice and fault made them inexcusable, because they had not
the ignorance which makes men excusable' (xxii[v]). Calvin,
apparently alone, has had this verse in mind throughout, and
treats it as a climax, taking ἀναπολογήτους in its strict forensic
sense: 'At God's judgment men can offer no defence against the
just charge of guiltiness' (30[46-48]). Bucer comes close to the same
theme: 'that is, destitute of all defence, having nothing to plead
in excuse' (86[a]); but it is not central in his exposition and he does
not pursue the point.

21. διότι γνόντες τὸν θεὸν, οὐχ' ὡς θεὸν ἐδόξασαν ἢ
εὐχαρίστησαν, ἀλλ' ἐματαιώθησαν ἐν τοῖς διαλογισμοῖς αὐτῶν,
καὶ ἐσκοτίσθη ἡ ἀσύνετος αὐτῶν καρδία,   (Eras ed. 1527)
καρδια.   Er[1,2,3] Compl

Quia cum cognovissent deum, non sicut deum glorificaverunt,
aut gratias egerunt, sed evanuerunt in cogitationibus suis, et
obscuratum est insipiens cor eorum, (Steph Vulg 1528)
deum non   Compl   glorificaverunt aut   Compl
egerunt: Compl   suis: Compl Er[4]Vg   eorum.
Compl   Er[4]Vg

propterea quod cum deum cognoverint, non ut deum glorificaverunt, neque grati fuerunt, sed frustrati sunt per cogitationes
suas, et obtenebratum est insciens cor eorum. (Eras vers 1527)
cum] quum Er vers[5]   frustrati] vani facti Er vers[1]
per cogitationes suas] in cogitationibus suis   Er vers[1]

EXEGESIS

ἀλλ᾽ ἐματαιώθησαν – **sed evanuerunt**] Erasmus: 'i.e. are
vain or useless (*vani sive supervacanei*).' Commonly, he says,
vanus means boastful or proud, and this is how Lyra takes it.
'Latin scholars use *vanus* either for what is not true or what is
trifling [and empty], without any solidity. . .But Paul means
that they were deceived and unsuccessful (*frustratos*)' (A[1]420;
A[3]290; A[5]347). Caietan follows Erasmus' original rendering:
'for, *sed vani facti sunt*' (IIII D) and explains it thus: 'For to
become vain is to become devoted to those things which are
vain, to those which are trifling, like fame' (IIII D–E). Calvin
uses the (according to Lewis and Short) rare word *exinaniti
sunt*, to empty or to make empty and desolate. His gloss
reads: 'That is, derelict of the truth of God, they were turned
to the vanity of their own minds (*sensus*)' (31[84-85]).

ἐν τοῖς διαλογισμοῖς αὐτῶν – **in cogitationibus suis**] Erasmus: 'not simply "thinking" (*cogitatio*), but the thinking
which is reasoning and weighing and judging' (A[1]421; A[3]290;
A[5]347). Caietan: 'the sharpness of their natural abilities
(IIII E). Bullinger: 'not so much *cogitatio* as rather what
accords with one's powers (*nervis*), like the reasonings of the
wise and the disputations of philosophers, which from
probability prove as well-nigh inevitable' (10–11).

---

22. φάσκοντες εἶναι σοφοὶ, ἐμωράνθησαν,   (*Eras ed. 1527*)
εμωρανθησαν.   Compl

dicentes enim se esse sapientes, stulti facti sunt. (*Steph Vulg
1528*)
[no variant readings in relevant edd]

Cum se crederent esse sapientes, stulti facti sunt, (*Eras vers 1527*)
Cum] Quum   Er vers[5]   sunt: Er vers[5]

EXEGESIS

φάσκοντες εἶναι σοφοὶ – **dicentes enim se esse sapientes**]
Erasmus: 'φάσκοντες εἶναι signifies rather "who, when they
thought, or professed, themselves to be wise"' (A[1]421; A[3]290;
A[5]347). Similarly Calvin: 'when they thought themselves wise'

(28[79]). Caietan: 'The two particles *enim* and *se* are superfluous. The interpreter added the pronoun *se*, which is somewhat forced, to bring out the meaning' (IIII F).

ἐμωράνθησαν – **stulti facti sunt**] Erasmus: 'that is, "became mad" (*infatuati sunt*)' (A[1]421; A[3]290; A[5]347). Calvin follows him: 'Therefore they became *infatuati* by the just judgment of God' (31[8]).

23. καὶ ἤλλαξαν τὴν δόξαν τοῦ ἀφθάρτου θεοῦ, ἐν ὁμοιώματι εἰκόνος φθαρτοῦ ἀνθρώπου καὶ πετεινῶν καὶ τετραπόδων καὶ ἑρπετῶν.   (*Eras ed. 1527*)

θεου εν   Compl

Et mutaverunt gloriam incorruptibilis dei, in similitudinem imaginis corruptibilis hominis, et volucrum, et quadrupedum, et serpentium. (*Steph Vulg* 1528)

hominis: Er[4]Vg   om. succeeding commas   Er[4]Vg

mutaveruntque gloriam immortalis dei, per imaginem, non solum ad mortalis hominis similitudinem effictam, verum etiam volatilium et quadrupedum et reptilium. (*Eras vers* 1527)
[no variant readings in relevant edd]

EXEGESIS

τὴν δόξαν – **gloriam**] *Gloria* is taken in two senses. The former, the glorifying or praise of God, is adopted by Caietan: 'the glory due to the incorruptible God' (IIII G). Calvin prefers the latter sense, understanding *gloria* as the *maiestas Dei*, which is contrasted to the mortality and wretched condition of man (32[25]).

ἐν ὁμοιώματι – **in similitudinem**] How God's glory can be changed creates a problem for some of our authors. *In similitudinem* should not, says Caietan, be taken as indicating the *terminus ad quem* of the change, as if God's glory were changed into the similitude. Rather, the similitude is the occasion of the change, that in which the exchange of the glory due to God gets its opportunity (IIII G). He therefore corrects the accusative of the Vulgate to the ablative of the Greek. Erasmus had already done this: '*In similitudine*, or rather, in the formation (*affictione*) or counterfeiting (*assimilatione*) of an image. For he does not think that they changed God's glory into the image of a man, but that they thought otherwise of God than they should have done when they gave him the image of a man' (A¹421; A³290; A⁵348).

ἀφθάρτου θεοῦ – **incorruptibilis dei**] Erasmus: 'Some translate this *immortalis* [*add*: as in I Tim. 1 [v. 17], *immortali deo*, ἀφθάρτῳ θεῷ – A⁵], and this certainly fits the context better; for he opposes the immortal God to the image of mortal man, [*add*: φθαρτοῦ – except that ἄφθαρτον means more than ἀθάνατον. Men's minds are ἀθάνατοι but certainly not ἄφθαρτοι– A⁵] (A¹421; A³290; A⁵347-8). But Calvin disagrees. His own rendering is *incorruptibilis Dei. . .corruptibilis hominis*, with the comment: 'For this is how I prefer to translate it rather than with Erasmus, "mortal"; for Paul opposes not only God's immortality to man's mortality, but God's glory, liable to no faults, to man's most wretched state' (32²⁶⁻²⁸).

EXPOSITION

Within a general agreement on the meaning of the passage in its context there is not inconsiderable difference among our authors, not only in details, but even in approach, in emphasis, and in important elements of the argument. The general agreement is easily expressed: Paul wishes to establish that Gentiles are sinners; he achieves this by arguing that they had a certain knowledge of God which they stifled, so that it did not lead to the worship and service of God; by stifling knowledge, they were impaired intellectually and morally.

The first, and rather surprising, difference of opinion, concerns the identity of those addressed. Almost all the authors take them to be 'the philosophers'. This will, of course, mean philosophers contemporary with or previous to Paul himself, and therefore the philosophers of ancient Greece and Rome. But these are usually seen as representative of the Gentiles in general, either in that it was they who first attained the knowledge of God and then passed it on to others in their teaching, or with the argument that if this was the best the wise men could do, what chance was there for the rest? But Calvin firmly rejects the identification: 'It is commonly assumed from this verse [v.22] that Paul was dealing with philosophers, who particularly claim that they are wise. And so they think the argument runs that when the excellence of the great has been abased there will be nothing praiseworthy left in the common herd. But it seems to me that this is very weak. It is not only philosophers who think they are wise in the knowledge of God' (31[91-97]). The identification is sometimes connected with the idea that *Graeci* is to be taken literally as referring to the Greek nation and not to the Gentiles represented by the Greeks in particular. It is therefore a natural progression to associate the wise of this world with the Greek philosophers.

On another particular point we shall see that, in spite again of a general agreement on the sense of v.20, the word *invisibilia* is given different meanings. On the one hand it will be understood of the Godhead within Itself and on the other of the Godhead in Its relation to man. The former will appear in the use of the term *conditiones* and of their identity – *actus purus*, immutability, unity, incorporeality, etc. The latter is best expressed by *virtutes*, indicating God's use of his power; which *virtutes* are, for example, his goodness, mercy and faithfulness.

And thirdly, we shall see differences on the place of the passage in its wider context. In this respect many of the Romanists are in a happier position than the Reformers in that they are able without difficulty to integrate it into their doctrine of justification as an element in the "first grace". The Reformers, having dropped that scheme of justification, are left with 1.18–23 on their hands. In the event, it too often seems to be at best attached to their doctrine of justification rather than a part of it. The outstanding exception here, as so often, is Calvin who, by interpreting the earlier chapters of Romans forensically, finds the passage, with an emphasis on inexcusability, necessary to the argument, and therefore to the doctrine.

Melanchthon

We first notice that Melanchthon's view of the place of this passage in the Epistle will be shared by Bucer but rejected by Calvin. Melanchthon sees justification as the *principalis propositio* of the Epistle. But before this main theme the passage 1.18-2.29 forms a *prima propositio* or first theme (33ʳ;LXXXᵛ). He is using *propositio* in its technical rhetorical sense, as we find it defined in Quintilian and in Melanchthon's own *Rhetorica*.[2] Indeed, Melanchthon's 1529 *Dispositio* on Romans describes Paul as deliberately dividing the *propositio* into clauses according to a proper *rhetorica distributio* or rhetorical arrangement. So here he is saying that justification is the principal theme of Romans and that this is preceded by the theme stated in 1.18-2.29. 'The first proposition is this: The Gospel accuses all men and pronounces them all under sin; that is, answerable for sin and [*1540 adds*:bound to] eternal death, they cannot be freed from sin and eternal wrath by their own righteousness' (33ʳ; LXXXᵛ). And certainly this must precede the principal proposition, since no consolation can be given until sins have been accused and repented of (33ʳ;LXXXIᵛ). In Melanchthon's exposition, therefore, we have the straightforward movement of accusation – repentance – justification.

After accusation and repentance comes the comfort of justification. Therefore Paul says that the wrath of God is revealed in the divinely delivered Gospel against the breaking of God's Law, against *impietas* (and Melanchthon (1540) gives many instances of *impietas*; e.g. a lack of fear, love, and trust towards God, being resentful and fretting against God in afflictions, fleeing from dangers involved in confessing Christ, loving the errors of the Epicureans or the Academy and not truly consenting to the Word of God (LXXXIᵛ-LXXXIIʳ) and against *iniusticia*, that universal disobedience (34ʳ; LXXXIIʳ).[3]

---

[2] C.R. XIII, 429: 'in every matter or controversy we must first and foremost consider what the *status* is, that is, what is the principal *quaestio* or *propositio*, which contains the sum of the matter, to which all arguments are to be referred'.

[3] 1532: *Impietas* 'that is, contempt and hatred of God. It signifies not only outward faults but natural uncleanness in the heart, which by nature is empty of any fear of God, trust in God, love for God, etc.'(34ʳ).

These men hold down the truth in unrighteousness. Here "truth" means 'the knowledge of God [*1540 adds*: or the law of nature]' (34ʳ;LXXXIIʳ). By introducing the law of nature Paul is saying that all men have some knowledge of God, and on this basis he can accuse and condemn all. For some knowledge of the law is inborn in man and, although in the depraved state of human nature it is more obscure, it is not obliterated completely. The knowledges (in the plural) about God are these: That God is one, infinitely powerful, wise, righteous, good, the Creator and Preserver of nature, punishing the unrighteous and wicked, hearing and saving the righteous and pure; that he is to be obeyed, that he commands virtuous things and forbids crimes, that he implants in our minds the distinction between virtuous and wicked things. 'These are natural knowledges, which we hear continually preaching to us in our consciences' (35ʳ;LXXXIIᵛ). 'This is the natural voice of conscience' (LXXXIIᵛ). It has no knowledge of free forgiveness of sins; it is simply knowledge of the Law, demanding the condition of our obedience (35ʳ;LXXXIIᵛ).[4]

But these men hold down the truth in unrighteousness. Man's will or heart does not assent or submit to these knowledges (LXXXIIIʳ). For it is just at this point that the philosophers go astray. They know that God exists; but when they are confronted with the injustices and cruelties in the world, they conclude that God is either himself cruel or has no care for human affairs (LXXXIIIʳ⁻ᵛ). And this conclusion begets the frame of mind that lacks the fear, trust, and love of God. Without this bridle it accommodates itself to concupiscences (*cupiditatibus*) in opposition to the natural knowledges (LXXXIIIᵛ).

This, then, is the *prima pro-positio*. We now enter upon its *ex-positio*.

Melanchthon explains the *divinitas* and *aeterna potentia* of God as meaning 'that God exists, eternal, powerful, wise,

---

[4] 1532: 'But the knowledge of God should not be understood of speculations, in which is sought an understanding of God's essence, but the knowledge of God is the knowledge of God's will towards us and the knowledge of God's Law' (36ʳ).

righteous' and so on (LXXXIIII^r),[5] repeating, in fact, what we have already quoted. All these the mind knows as it views the workmanship of the world (*opificium mundi*). They are the many *vestigia*, footprints or traces, from which we can reason about God. But it is necessary to bear in mind that this reasoning cannot take place unless the knowledge or πρόληψις (preconception) about God is implanted in the mind (LXXXIIII^r).

It was the will of God to reveal himself to the human race and so to be known and praised. Therefore a wonderful and brilliant light shone in man's mind and a clear knowledge of God was implanted in his nature (*conditione*). If sin had not shed its darkness, 'the human mind would have been like a mirror showing, so to say, an image, that is, many clear knowledges about God' (LXXXIIII^{r-v}). Therefore, if man's nature had remained sound, philosophy's chief occupation would have lain in reflecting upon the *vestigia divinitatis* in nature, which would have proclaimed the wisdom and goodness of the Architect (LXXXIIII^v). But darkness came, the image ceased to shine, the natural knowledges became obscure, and the heart or will did not assent sufficiently to those knowledges or strive after them, and so it lost the true knowledges of God and became directed to other objects. This can be illustrated from providence, and Melanchthon supplies several examples from classical authors.

In face of sin, the divine Law was given to renew the recognition of God. But it does not completely supersede or make unnecessary the natural knowledge, which had not been utterly blotted out of our minds, and by which we survey 'the *vestigia Dei* in the nature of things' (LXXXV^r). We should therefore continue to do this, remembering, however, to hold fast to the *regula*, the Word of God (LXXXV^r). As an example of such a survey, Melanchthon points to the physical sciences: 'Philosophers who treat

[5] 1532: '*Potentia* does not signify idle power, as Epicurus imagines an idle god. But it signifies the power which creates, preserves, and governs things. *Divinitas* does not signify secret essence, for this is not seen. But it signifies those things which are proper to God, wisdom, goodness, righteousness, or God governing things, caring for humanity, hearing and saving the righteous and punishing the unrighteous' (36^v).

physics skilfully, like Galen, think more honourably about
God. On the other hand, the Epicureans throw physics into
disorder and will not survey the *vestigia Dei* in nature'
(LXXXV^v). And he goes on to recite at some length nine
arguments from nature 'which bear witness that God is the
Creator and Preserver of all things' (LXXXV^v-LXXXVIII^v).

But although the possibility of arriving at these knowledges of God lay open before men, they did not take the next
step of glorifying God as God, that is, of giving him the glory
that he is God, i.e. eternal, of infinite power, Creator and
Preserver of things, wise, righteous, punishing the unrighteous, hearing and helping the righteous, that we should obey
him, fear his judgment, believe in him, and seek and expect
blessings from him, and so on. In other words, of fulfilling
the works of the first and second commandments. But
because the world thinks nothing of them, the Gospel in
every age accuses the world of sin. For some men are
ἄθεοι, and others are idolators. Melanchthon now continues with the themes of atheism and idolatry, giving
examples from the classics (38^v-39^v;LXXXVIII^v-LXXXIX^r).

After this, however, instead of taking up the clause *ut ita
sint inexcusabiles*, he deals with repentance, in accordance with
his view that this passage is part of the *prima propositio* on sin
and repentance: 'Since, then, ungodliness remains. . .let us
repent, let us seek the Word of God, and let us learn to
worship God aright and to call upon him with a true faith; let
our faith and works be ruled by the Word of God' (XC^v).

Caietan

Formally Caietan's exposition is not scholastic. But the
mental approach and the thought-forms show that it is rooted
and grounded in the scholasticism of which he was the foremost
contemporary exponent. We are therefore presented with a
scholastic Paul. It is not simply that Caietan interprets Paul
scholastically but that he is bringing out the scholastic meanings
he believes Paul intended.

The purpose of the passage is 'to treat of the grace, or
power, of the Gospel (*euangelica gratia seu potentia*)' (III E) and
to abase (*deprimere*) both Gentiles and Jews by relating them
to the Gospel (*relatos ad rem euangelicam*), which is the power

of God unto salvation. He does not, however, allow this understanding to govern his exposition of the passage; the very next sentence shows that the unity he has perceived is soon broken: 'Intending to set forward this for his theme, and afterwards to unravel individually the points he has proposed' (III E). Thus in practice, if not in theory, Caietan divides the passage into two parts which are only loosely related in his exposition. The first, vv. 18–20a, he treats as a statement of a natural knowledge of God. The second, beginning at v.20b, *ita ut sint inexcusabiles*, certainly makes use of and carries on the first but in a detached sort of way. *Ita ut sint inexcusabiles* has had no place in the first part and it does not govern the second. It is, at best, a bridge between the two parts.

God's wrath is revealed from heaven on all ungodliness and unrighteousness of men who hold down the truth in unrighteousness. There is nothing peculiar to himself in Caietan's understanding of the situation depicted here. The common view of the soul was that it was composed of fundamentally two faculties, the intellect and the will; the one grasped what was perceived, the other assented and assimilated it or dissented and rejected it. All our authors are operating with this theory of cognition. Caietan therefore explains the verse as meaning that these men imprison by their wills the knowledge they have about God. Hence it is unable to influence their affections and actions, to make them conform with the truth they know.

This by itself, however, is a mere assertion. Paul must prove his case. To prove that they held down the truth in unrighteousness, he must first establish that they knew the truth about divine things. But it is not enough that only some should have this knowledge by the light of divine revelation; it must be a knowledge common to all, whether believers or unbelievers, for Paul is here dealing with the heathen or Gentiles (III G). This knowledge is expressed in the phrase *quod notum est Dei*, 'that which is known of God'. Now, there is a negative implication in these words. They suggest that some "attributes" of God (the word he consistently uses is *conditiones*) are not known to them. They do not know, and cannot of themselves learn, that God is threefold and one. So we may understand by *quod notum est Dei* that which by the light of nature the human intellect knows about God. And this comprises a nexus of knowledge: that God is one, that he is the sovereign (*princeps*), that he is *actus purus*, that he is eternal, 'and other things of this sort' (III G–H).

It must be emphasized that this is a knowledge attained by natural means. St Paul makes this clear in his next words 'For God manifested it to them'. He does not say 'revealed' but 'manifested'. 'Revealed' implies the light of grace; 'manifested' signifies 'the divine assistance (*concursum*) by the mediation of the light of nature, which itself is God's gift' (III H).

We next learn the *modus quo*, the way in which, man attains to *quod notum est Dei*: 'it is the way of natural understanding from the effect' (III H). Or perhaps *ex effectu* would be better translated as 'what has been effected'. Certainly Caietan is thinking of a movement or inference from effect to cause, but he is very conscious that the effect is that which God himself has brought into being. The reason why the beginning must be made at the effect is that the *conditiones Dei* are themselves invisible; they are the *invisibilia* of v.20a.

But before the argument can be developed, the text demands, according to Caietan, an assertion of the *simplicitas Dei*, the inner unity of God. *Invisibilia* is plural, in contrast to the singular *quod notum est Dei*. We are, of course, in a traditional and well-worked area, for orthodox Christian theologians have always, when they have come to deal with the Divine attributes, taken pains to emphasize that the various attributes in no way imply a breaking of the Divine unity, or simplicity. For Caietan the interpretation becomes a qualification. It means that we do not know God as he is in himself but in his *conditiones*: 'that most simple entity which is God is not known to us under its unique and most simple wise (*ratione*) but by manifold *conditiones* (for example, that he is *actus purus*, that he is immutable, that he is eternal, and so on)' (III H-I). It will follow from this inferred knowledge which we have about God that we do not know God, that is, that most simple entity which he is in himself (III I). Of course, the invisibility does not apply to God, for necessarily he knows himself. This is brought out by the phrase *a creatura mundi*: the *conditiones* cannot be seen 'by the creature of the world' – i.e. man (III I). (Unless, he says, we take *a creatura mundi* with 'perceived' and therefore with *intellecta*, being understood; then we shall have to understand it, not only of man but of all intellectual beings – in which he includes the angels.)

We return to the interrupted argument, the way in which man attains to this knowledge about God. Those who are not God perceive the *invisibilia Dei* 'through the things which are made, which are effected by God: the cause is perceived by its own effects' (III K–IIII A). And again, the manner in which the things which God has effected are perceived appears in the next word, *intellecta*, 'being understood'. It is therefore an intellectual and present mode, not sensory and not merely imagined (*intellecta in praesenti, non sensata, non imaginata*). It is not a superficial knowledge but an intellectual penetration; that is, presumably, it is not a knowledge of some surface appearance of God which is not consistent with the inward nature of God, but it is a knowledge of the *conditiones* which are genuine perfections of the Divine nature. Caietan sums it up by introducing the very common metaphor of a mirror. The things God has effected are mirrors in which God shines (IIII A). Obviously, to see someone in a mirror, you need the sight of a mirror. Similarly, to see God through the things which have been made we need an understanding of those things. An understanding and not a sight or view; for this is not a matter of a simple and straightforward sight and identification. The word Paul uses is 'through', not 'in': 'Through those things which have been made'. The *invisibilia*, the *conditiones Dei*, are not seen *in* these creatures. When *through* the creatures we reach an understanding we rise up to perceive the *conditiones* themselves.

He clarifies this when he comes to *conspiciuntur*, 'are perceived', which conveys the manner of seeing. There are two modes of seeing. The one is direct, by way of sight or intuitively (*visionis seu intuitus*) of the thing itself. But, as we have already seen, the *conditiones* are invisible in this sense. The other is also clear, but it is indirect (*in alio*), as we see something in a mirror (IIII B). Thus the creatures become a mirror in which the *conditiones Dei* are perceived when a certain assumption has been made and inferences drawn. The assumption is that the creatures are the *effecta* made by God; the inferences are, that he who brought these things to pass must be of such and such a nature.

Invisibilia is a generic term, comprehending that God is incorporeal, immaterial, one, living, intelligent, and blessed in himself. The two words that follow are specific; God's eternal power (*potentia. . .quatenus potestas*), which is never exhausted by action and which is able to achieve an eternal effect, and his divinity or essence (IIII B-C).

So far Caietan's touch has been sure, his exposition clear and commanding; but as soon as we reach 'that they may be without excuse', the whole tone of the exposition changes. It is as if his interest in what is being said flags. The statement is to be referred to what follows: 'And the sense is, that they are inexcusable in this, as it is added below' (IIII D). They are made inexcusable because they hold down the truth in unrighteousness, that is, 'by having knowledge in their intellect and not glorifying him as God', whether by words of praise or by deeds of sacrifice and worship (IIII D). But they did not merely sin by omission; they went astray in their inward intention and desire; they fell into the besetting sin of philosophers and, in their desire for human glory, became empty and frivolous. Their very thinking became a subject of vainglorious delight to them (IIII E-F).

In the final verse he becomes involved in a fruitless struggle with the words, which could mean, taken literally, that God's glory or man's glorifying of God was itself changed into the similitude of men, birds, quadrupeds, and reptiles. But 'he is not indicating the *terminus ad quem* of the change; it does not mean that they have changed the glory due to God *into* the similitude etc. But in the text is signified without *terminus ad quem* the change of the glory due to God. The similitude is described concurrently as the occasion of the change, as the thing in which the change of the glory due to God obtains its occasion. For the plain and literal sense is that by worshipping the images of men or animals they change the glory due to God' (IIII G). This is true, even if somewhat surprising, of philosophers; they too change the glory due to God.

On this disappointing, involved, and tautologous note Caietan ends his comments on the passage.

Bullinger

For Bullinger the passage puts forward a contrast between true and false religion. The latter, along with its cognate, superstition, is, under the name of unrighteousness, the object of God's wrath in v.18. The former appears in the same verse as the truth which is suppressed in unrighteousness: 'For the Apostle, truth is God himself and true religion' (10). This contrast largely governs his exposition and certainly sets its tone, so that he interprets the passage less in terms of an intellectual knowledge than of *pietas* and *religio* and consequently sees the object of knowledge, the *invisibilia Dei*, not so much as the essential attributes of God, although this is true, but of those attributes in respect of mankind (10).

The heart of his exposition comes under v.20: 'For the invisible things of him, even his eternal power and divinity are understood from the creation of the world' – to which he adds his own gloss: 'namely, if we ponder his works' (10). God, he says, revealed himself to the Gentiles, not as to the Jews, by means of writings and oracles, but by the universal structure of the world (*mundi mole*), by benefits, and by marvels, and by things created and visible. By these he willed to place before men's eyes the invisible things, that is, he himself who is invisible, and to declare his eternal power and ineffable divinity. 'In himself God is the subsistence of all things, omnipotent, supreme (*summus*), true, eternal, good, and wise' (10). If the work of God, the *moles mundi*, which is 'the most certain evidence of these things' (10), is pondered with a nice and careful judgment, the knowledge will be attained. For the *moles mundi* subsists in God, was founded by his power and wisdom, is ruled by his righteousness and truth, and is most beautiful and useful by his goodness. But God's attributes towards men are one with his attributes in themselves; none of what has been said could be true except because God himself is eternal, omnipotent, and truly supreme (10).

At this point Bullinger seems to want to grant the Gentiles an actual and positive knowledge of God. He takes St. Paul's argument as a declaration that the Gentiles did not lack God or truth and true religion, even if they made no use of their knowledge. In support of this he appeals to the usual New Testament passages in Acts chapters 14 and 17. 'Again, we see that there was no small knowledge of God and of divine things in some honourable Gentiles. But these things are explained fully in histories and books of philosophy. Certainly, to take one example out of many, Seneca alone left to posterity more true theology than almost all the books of all the schoolmen' (10).

In spite of these bold words Bullinger submits to the text and allows that the Gentiles' knowledge proved in vain; they refused to accord God his rightful position as God or give him the glory due to him. Thus they suppressed the truth in unrighteousness (10).

The attitude of Bullinger's exposition is, in common with many other of our authors, firmly historical. No doubt he believed that Romans was addressed no less to sixteenth century readers than to its original recipients, but his purpose was to convey the teaching of Romans and in the mirror which he holds up to this passage his contemporaries saw, not themselves, but the Gentiles of the ancient world. Again, he lays the main emphasis on the possibility of a knowledge of God for the Gentiles, especially for the so-called "virtuous" heathen, with Seneca selected as the shining example. Such men, apparently, possessed for themselves and were able to impart to others a genuine if limited knowledge of the Creator. Are we to take Bullinger's statements at their face value? Did he really believe that this "natural" knowledge had any positive value, perhaps as a preparation for faith? Certainly he is not careful, like Calvin, to introduce qualifications; nor does he stress here the general theme of judgment, defense, and inexcusability.

A further point to be noted is that, like Melanchthon and Caietan, he keeps his elucidation of man's perception of "natural" revelation vague. All we have is a generalized statement of a doctrine common to all orthodox Christians of the age – God is the Creator; the world, the universe, is his workmanship; study the workmanship and you will gain knowledge about the Workman. Even if the most of Gentile humanity were ignorant, a few choicer souls took the trouble to observe more carefully and were able to draw the correct conclusions, that God exists, that he is the Creator, and that he is 'omnipotent, supreme, true, eternal, good, wise, and righteous' (10).

Sadoleto

Sadoleto's exposition exhibits the spectacle of Renaissance Platonism super-imposed on a traditional medieval foundation. In spite of the mystical flavour of other parts of his work, he looks at the present passage historically, almost with detachment. Even his right view of the human predicament is at the last vitiated by a qualification.

In his first comments we can see that the relationship between the Old and the New Testaments constitutes an unresolved problem for him. "Revealed" in v.18 is used in a different sense from "revealed" in v.17. There the revelation was of the Gospel, which had previously, in the Old Testament, been hidden and unseen. But the wrath of God was active in Old Testament times. Hence "revealed" in v.18 means that it 'is now for the first time perceived' (27;36). Only when the truth had begun to be perceived did falsehood also appear; only the clear sight of dawning day gave knowledge of the shades of night. For truth and falsehood, dawn and night, cannot be known separately, especially to men accustomed to live in perpetual twilight 'unless their darkness and blindness are suddenly surprised by the rising rays of the sun' (27;36).

The Creator set before the eyes of men many and plain works for them to behold and consider, for 'he wished the power of his divinity to appear in the contemplation of them' (27;37). It was the task of philosophy to understand the universe and in this understanding to arrive at the knowledge of God. Not that this implied a special quality peculiar to the minds of philosophers, for the human mind generally has an innate aptitude for the investigation of things created and formed by the divine counsel and so for understanding the invisible things by means of the visible (28;37). Does not the Psalm say, 'The heavens declare the glory of God and the firmament sheweth his handy-work . . . Their sound is gone out into all lands and their words into the end of the world' (Ps.19.1,4)?

Had men, and especially the philosophers, embarked on this journey of discovery and been led by these guides, they would have come to know God's greatness and majesty and would have learned that he alone is Lord of nature. Then they would have adored, venerated, and glorified him with a complete worship. But suddenly they were blinded by a certain vanity of spirit and error of mind and broke the unity and infinity of the omnipotent God into a thousand fragments. And so they became vain and made images and fell into terrible sins (28;37).

At this point Sadoleto introduces his qualification in the form of the word "almost". This error and fault, common to almost all the human race, (*commune pene humani genus*) was brought into the world by the wise of the age and by the philosophical writers (28;37). Who escaped the error and fault? Sadoleto does not tell us.

Bucer

It would be going too far to say that in Bucer's exposition of March 1536 the passage becomes hardly recognizable as that in the commentaries of the preceding years. The general argument is the same, much of the exegesis is the same or similar; but in one important respect Bucer is original. At first, however, he treads in Melanchthon's footsteps.

'The divine indignation and vengeance is plainly seen today to rage furiously against all mortals, however much the Greeks with their philosophy and the Jews with their Law may please themselves and seek righteousness from them' (82[a]). This sums up the section, which is the *prima propositio* of the Epistle. It is followed by the cause, why the wrath of

God is revealed; that is, because they hold down the truth in unrighteousness. The wrath of God in all its terrors is revealed (not, strictly speaking, in the Gospel, which declares God's righteousness and goodness and only proclaims his wrath against those who remain in unbelief) on the ungodliness and unrighteousness of men who do violence to the truth – and by the truth here is meant the knowledge of what they owe to God and men (83ᵇ).

Paul wishes to establish and emphasize that they are ungodly and unrighteous who hold down the truth in unrighteousness. This can be done only by first proving that they have the truth. The term τὸ γνωστὸν τοῦ θεοῦ, *quod cognosci de Deo potest*, is explained as 'his eternal power and divinity', and this it is that 'God gives to all men everywhere to know about himself' (84ᵃ). Men can infer God's power and providence and divinity from an observation of the *machina mundi* and from there can be led on to the worship of God. 'But all this truth they hold down in unrighteousness, in that perversity which is a withdrawal from and resisting (*revocante et reluctante*) of the knowledge about God, and so they take care to look to their own interests, to govern themselves without any trust in God's providence and good pleasure, and to love, not their neighbours, but themselves, and to seek all things for themselves' (84ᵃ).

And now we come to what makes Bucer's commentary individual. He has already said that the knowledge about God is the gift of God. He now expresses this, or explains it, by means of the Stoic epistemology as it comes in Cicero's *de natura deorum*. He does this, not by allusion but deliberately and openly, referring twice to the characters in the conversation whom he is quoting.

The first thing that happens is that the concept of knowledge has to be temporarily replaced by the Stoic concept of *notio*; it is a notion that 'he has power over all things and is the *summum bonum*' (84ᵇ). This *notio* is impressed and infixed by God in the minds of all men, so that the awareness that God exists is innate and is, as it were, engraved on the mind, and that not simply once for all, but it is continually renewed and is inexpungeable. Bucer tells us that his source is the character Lucilius Balbus, in *de natura deorum* 2 (84[b]).

But *notio* is not the *cognitio* of God's eternal power and divinity. Between the two lies a gap. All men possess the *notio*. No man is able to apprehend the power and divinity of God; they are the *invisibilia* – by which Bucer understands here those things which are imperceptible, to any sense. For God to reveal himself, for the *invisibilia* to become perceptible, it is necessary that the knowledge of him should be infused into man. But how does this take place and by what means? By means of the *machina mundi*, by the workmanship so much to be admired, by those things which are created and made by him, the ποιούμενα (84[b]).

Bucer now returns to *de natura deorum* 2 and expounds the four *notiones* put forward by Balbus as the Stoic creed – that man's foreknowledge of the future, his awareness of temporal benefits, his awe before the forces of nature, and his perception of astronomical order, are all "notions" of the existence and nature of deity implanted at birth. This done, he supports Cicero with evidences from Holy Scripture (85[a]), clearly believing that they are saying the same thing, save that Scripture advances an argument for the *divinitas* which is not found in Cicero, and that is God's judgment on sin (85[a]).

He now considers that *quod de Deo cognosci potest* has been satisfactorily explained. But it has to be added (if I understand this passage aright) that such knowledge demands a mind in harmony with God. It is for those 'on whom God at the same time breathes his *numen* and to whom he imparts light about himself. Our mind is a particle of the divine breath *(aurae)*, ἐντελέχεια,[6] a certain perennial *actus*, as dependent on God as the day on the sun, the river on its spring' (85[b]). This would seem to be a translation of the Stoic's engraving of the *notio* on man's mind into Aristotelian categories, with the additional idea that therefore there is a relation between the

---

[6] ἐντελέχεια: '*the absoluteness, actuality, actual being* of a thing, Lat. *actus*, opp to δύναμις (simple *capability* or *potentiality*...) a philosophic word coined by Arist., who calls the soul the ἐντελέχεια of the body' (Liddell and Scott: A Greek-English Lexicon).

mind and the *notio* and even between the mind and the *cognitio Dei*.

But Bucer is recalled to the Pauline argument. This whole revelation seems to have been fruitless, for it does not issue in the worship of God. The fault is man's, not God's. God reveals what is good, and we know it clearly enough; but we incline to evil from our own perversity. Yet, says Bucer, there seems to be an inconsistency here: our wrong-doing is deservedly to be imputed to our own fault, and yet we have no strength to do what is right, in fact it is completely impossible for us to will and to do the right unless the Lord effects it in us (85ᵃ). They are therefore ἀναπολόγητοι, 'destitute of any defence, having nothing to plead in excuse' (86ᵃ). They are *inexcusabiles* because, when they knew God, they did not glorify him as God. But at this point Bucer is led away from this concept into a discussion of what it is to sin in ignorance and of the relation between sinning willingly and sinning knowingly. We need not follow him. He claims the support of all the church fathers except Origen for his interpretation of the passage. Section VI ends with an essay at reconciling passages of Scripture, some of which ascribe and some of which deny the knowledge of God to the ungodly (86ᵇ-88ᵃ). The heart of the matter is that 'there is a twofold knowledge of God, the one general which, because God irradiates it to all mortals who are sound in body and mind, is usually called "natural"'. This avails to take away excuse and to convict of ungodliness. 'But the other is so full and solid that immediately of itself it brings forth love and a worthy reverence of God, and is therefore called eternal life. This is what the Lord promises to his elect through Christ, and he makes them participators of the new Covenant' (86ᵇ).

With Section VII of the *Enarratio* he returns to the subject. The verses 21ff. are an explanation of what has been said. 'For he explains more fully why they who suppress the truth in iniquity are inexcusable' (89ᵃ). They knew the eternal power and divinity of God, that is, his supreme goodness (*summum bonitatem*), from the *machina mundi*, by God manifesting himself to them. But they did not worship him or give him thanks. He again takes up the point of excuse of ignorance,

this time with a metaphor. If a man meets the king and does
not pay him honour, he is doing wrong. But if he is not
aware that the one he meets is the king, his fault is
pardonable. Similarly with God. None can worship what he
does not know. But this was not "their" situation. They
knew, but they did not worship or give thanks. Even worse,
instead of worshipping the one they knew, they transferred
their worship to others; they made images of God in the form
of men, animals etc. and gave them glory. God therefore
gave them up (89[b]). Once again, therefore, Bucer has slipped
away from an exposition of inexcusability.

Haresche

Haresche's main interest lies in analysis. It is his chief
strength and his chief limitation. He is never happy until he
has separated out all the parts of a sentence, taken it to pieces,
and examined each piece in its every aspect. Only when he
has done this in the *Notulae* (and it is his conception of
exegesis) does he feel at liberty to put it all together again and
expound the passage literally. Even then analysis will take
charge at slight provocation and he will lead us into minute
explanations of words or phrases. In the *Notulae* on 1.18-23,
for example, the word *ira* has to be distinguished as either *ira
Dei* or *ira hominis*. The latter has then to be defined: 'an
inherent quality of soul by which the blood is kindled and
inflamed, and thus, the blood being kindled, it excites the
man to wrath' (XX[v]). The former is defined: 'a power which
rules the ministers of punishment and by which execution is
done upon sinners' (XX[v]). It is called *ira Dei* from similitude
(i.e. analogy) to *ira hominis* (XX[v]). The same way is followed
with *pietas – impietas, iustitia – iniustitia*.

God's wrath, so runs his exposition, this power by which
execution is done upon sinners, is brought out of obscurity
and secrecy into the light of knowledge. Men know the truth,
but they do not put it into practice. What is more, far from
leading others to put it into practice, they hide from them
their own knowledge of God (xxi[v]). That which may be
known about God has been manifested to the Gentiles 'by an
inward light, by which in their hearts (although it may not

appear outwardly in practice) they possess a means of knowing, that is, a natural reason, in which light the face of the Lord is imprinted upon us' (xxi^v) – or so I take the obscure final clause to mean. Putting it another way, it is revealed 'by the influence of the natural light by which the rational soul of the creature is able to perceive (*intelligere*) the Creator, so that the Gentiles not only have the advantage of natural reason, but are also daily helped by God, lest nature alone should seem insufficient' (xxi^v).

We may look at it in terms of communication between God and man. Man speaks to man either by the spoken or the written word or else by some outward sign. But God, for his manifestations to man, 'infuses in him an inward light . . . And in another way, by setting before him outward signs of his wisdom, that is, the sensible creatures' (xxi^v). By "sensible creatures" is meant creatures perceptible to the senses.

By means of the inner light, man is able to know God and to distinguish between Creator and creature and in the outward, visible things he could, so to say, read off the knowledge of God as from a book (xxi^v – xxii^r). These visible entities are left, uncharacteristically, somewhat vague and are defined simply as 'man and the *machina mundi*' (xxii^r). The perception of them is intellectual and, indeed, can only be intellectual, in that the object of perception is a unity: 'viewed intellectually and which can be seen by the intellect alone, just as God and those things which are in God and with God are one' (xxii^r). The wonderful works of the visible creation are the *vestigia Creatoris*, the foot-prints of the Creator. If with 'the intellectual and pure eye of the mind' (xxii^r) we contemplate vigilantly these outward things, we are recalled by them to inward things and thus arrive at the knowledge of God (xxii^r). There is, then, according to Haresche, a certain ascending order of being which can be followed from step to step in logical procession until the correct conclusion is drawn. Only those men who are wiser than their fellows, that is to say, the philosophers, are capable of such success: 'Philosophers perceive an order in things and see that one thing proceeds from another and is caused and governed by it. Thus they arrive at the knowledge of one first and supreme

Being, who must be eternal, perfect, and, consequently, omnipotent, supremely wise and supremely good (xxii^r).

He has proved his case, at least to his own mind. The Gentiles can, even without the aid of the written Law, gain from the creation a knowledge of the Creator. Haresche is now checked by his scholasticism. He has to analyse the word "knowledge" and he must give proper place to the distinction between explicit and implicit faith. What sort of knowledge are we considering? It is an *obscura* and *obumbrata cognitio* (xxii^r). Not, certainly, a knowledge of the Trinity and of the Persons (the province of explicit faith), yet nevertheless of the attributes of the Trinity, that is, of the omnipotence which is ascribed to the Father, of the power (*virtus*) which belongs to the Son, and of the goodness which is the quality of the Holy Spirit (xxii^r – xxii^v). On the argument that the attributes must not be divorced from the being, Haresche can even grant the Gentiles, if with qualification, a knowledge of the Trinity: 'from these creatures the Gentiles knew, or could know, God and the Trinity' (xxii^v).

'Knew, or could know' – they did not make use of the knowledge which lay within their grasp, and therefore they were inexcusable. Haresche accepts the fact, but he does not emphasize it or draw out its meaning. His interest lies rather in causation: it was not God who made them inexcusable; they themselves were to blame: 'Not that God brought it to pass that they were inexcusable, but this happened as a consequence of their ungodliness and unrighteousness, and their malice and defect rendered them inexcusable because they did not have the ignorance which makes men excusable' (xxii^v).

Pellicanus

As we saw in the opening *Survey* Pellicanus is extensively indebted to Bucer on this passage. Although he refers to Bucer and Bullinger as two of the best expositors of 1.18-23, it is to Bucer that he refers most frequently; indeed, many passages are verbatim copying.

The Apostle's intention here, says Pellicanus, is to demonstrate that, just as we receive righteousness by faith, so, if we have no faith, we are all the servants of unrighteousness. The Gentiles were devoted to the world; and the Gentile Christians in Rome, with whom Paul was concerned in this part of Chapter 1, had formerly been without true faith and had been laden with superstitious idolatry and abominable crimes. Indeed, all mortals stand under the vengeance of God for their wicked lives (15).

All of us human beings sin against the light that we have: 'We men were so created that we might know what is true, right, and good, and we are incited to pursue the same truth impressed on our mind' (15). But we suppress the truth by following after other desires: 'We maliciously chase after all sorts of things and sacrilegiously despise the truth that we know' (15). Nevertheless, the fact that we despise and neglect the truth and do not devote ourselves to worshipping God as we should, does not mean that we do not know the truth. In particular, 'the wise of the age' (he means, but does not say, the philosophers) 'understand well enough that there is a certain power by which all things are caused and ruled, and that there is a certain fountain of all good things, and therefore a divinity. Hence they ought to revere and worship it and commit themselves to its providence. By the dictates of natural reason they understand that whatever pleases it should be followed and that they must approve themselves before it and obey it' (15).

The content of the knowledge is not absolute but is limited by man's creatureliness. It is 'whatever it is lawful for man to know about God – that he has power over all things, that he is the *summum bonum*' (16). This is made more precise when he explains the *invisibilia*, copying Bucer's words, as 'partly his sempiternal strength and power (*virtus et potentia*); that is, he holds all things in his hand, and governs all things; and partly also his divinity when he shows himself to our minds as the *summum bonum* and a father to those who seek him' (16).

In explaining how man arrives at this knowledge, Pellicanus somewhat cautiously follows Bucer's use of Cicero. He adopts some of the terms but falls short of taking over the theology of *de natura deorum* as the key to interpret the passage. The knowledge of the existence of a god is universal, 'so innate and implanted in all men that this *notio* cannot be blotted out of their minds by anything earthly. For the judgment is from nature and therefore from the maker of nature who, by the perennial influx of his light into men's minds irradiates them and leads them to the knowledge of himself by the things he has created' (16). He is here stringing together and adapting sentences and phrases from Bucer. He follows him also in being faithful to Scripture in a way that many of our commentators fail to be at this point. They will all speak of the light of nature as being God-given and some of them will use the phrase 'God irradiates them' or its equivalent. But Pellicanus (after Bucer) makes it clear that he intends a special revelation of God: 'And hence also we learn that the truth is known only by God's revelation' (16 = Bucer 84[b]); more precisely, known by the illumination of the Holy Spirit: 'Those things which are known about God are invisible and are gathered from the visible creatures of this world – but not without the peculiar teaching and movement of the divine Spirit' (16 = Bucer 84[b]). Indeed, the *invisibilia* transcend the perception of man's sense and cannot be known by man's unaided mind, but as God's revelation 'they are gathered together and perceived by the reasoning (*cogitatio*) of the mind, that is, they are known clearly and surely' (16 = Bucer 84[b]).

The means by which the *invisibilia* are known are *ea quae facta sunt*, created entities, and it is in expatiating upon them that Pellicanus gives his one reference to *de natura deorum*: 'Through those things which were created and made by himself, with their greatness of movement, their actions and positions, and also for the presence of future things, from the greatness of the harmonious agreements which are perceived in the heavens, from the various terrors of the elements and of many other wonderful powers that impress themselves upon us, and from the perpetual movement of all the heavenly bodies. Concerning which, see Cicero *de natura deorum,* and, far more clearly and simply, Holy Scripture' (16 = Bucer 85[a]).

To explain inexcusability, he takes a passage from Bucer's second *Enarratio*: 'If the Gentiles, of whom he speaks, had not known that there was a God by whom all things were created and ruled . . . they would be excused. But when he manifests himself to them so that they truly know him . . . to be omnipotent and omniscient, the highest good and the benefit of all, this excludes all pretext of ignorance and impotence, so that they are completely inexcusable' (17 = Bucer 89[a]).

Pellicanus has at least succeeded in presenting Bucer in a readable form, even if, by ironing out his difficulties, he has removed his peculiar force and profundity.

Calvin

Here we have an example of an exposition which was deliberately based on two or three predecessors and yet managed to be original and creative. Like Melanchthon and Bucer, Calvin interpreted the passage in terms of classical rhetoric; but he came to his own conclusions. 'It seems to some', he wrote, 'that this is the *prima propositio*. According to this view, Paul is taking repentance as his starting point. But I consider that it is the beginning of the *conflictatio*, the *status* of the case put in the previous proposition' (28[89-92]). To understand him fully we must go back to the close of his comments on vv. 16–17: 'Now we have the *status* or chief hinge on which everything turns (*cardo principalis*) of this first part of the Epistle: "We are justified by the mercy of God alone through faith" ' (27[64-66]). We have already seen that *status* means the substance of the *causa*, or case, being pleaded. Here Calvin also calls it the *conflictatio*, or debate. What he is saying, therefore, is that l.18ff. is the arguing through of the essential, vital case stated in l.16–17, 'We are justified by the mercy of God alone through faith'. And his opening comments on l.18 are: 'He argues from a comparison of contraries, by which he proves that righteousness is communicated only through the Gospel. For he shows that, apart from the Gospel, all men are damned . . . And first he takes up an argument of accusation (*damnationis argumentum assumit*)' (28[82-85]). In contrast to Melanchthon's accusation – repentance – justification, the movement in Calvin's exposition of the passage is: Gospel – condemnation without the Gospel – salvation in the Gospel alone. This is borne out by the *Argumentum*, where he traces the successive steps in Paul's thinking: First Paul commends to the Romans his apostolate; but his apostolate is bound to the Gospel, and so he 'falls into' (*incidit*) commending the Gospel (i.e. 1.16-17); but because there is a correlation between the Gospel and faith, he 'slips into' (*delabitur*) a *disputatio* on faith (1.17); and thus he comes to the principal *quaestio* of the Epistle, that we are justified by faith (5¹⁵⁻¹⁹). Our passage is therefore concerned to show that, apart from faith in the Gospel, man stands under the condemnation of God.

A further central point in understanding Calvin's interpretation here lies in the significance of the rhetorical terms which he uses in common with Melanchthon and Bucer. I would suggest that whereas they were using the terms in the general sense which they had come to bear in the humanist climate of the day, where pleading in court had been translated into lecturing in the schools, preaching in the Church, or just writing, Calvin has his mind, in these earlier chapters of Romans, filled with the image of the court-room, so that the *termina rhetorica*, born of the lawcourt, are the right language to use in this context. The general image centred on *ut sint inexcusabiles*, crystallizes into the image of the author Paul, or rather his Gospel, which is the Word of God, as *advocatus*.

The first part of the argument *ex comparatione contrariorum* deals with the condemnation of man. Although the contemplation of the *structura mundi* and this most beautiful composition of the elements ought to lead men to glorify God, there is none who does what he should. All are therefore guilty of sacrilege and ingratitude (28).

The wrath of God is revealed everywhere under heaven against man's ingratitude, ingratitude that is both a failure to honour God and a stealing from God of his glory and appropriating it to ourselves. This act of robbery is expressed in the clause 'who hold down the truth in unrighteousness', that is, who unjustly suppress or obscure the true knowledge of God (29).

This knowledge, the *quod notum est Dei*, is 'what it is lawful or expedient to know about God' (29[19-20]). But the definition is at once explained and strengthened by relating the clause to v.21 'did not glorify God'. Thus *quod notum est Dei* is what pertains to making illustrious (*illustrandam*) the glory of God, or, what comes to the same thing, whatever should move and excite us to glorify God. By saying that this knowledge is manifest *in ipsis*, there is suggested a manifestation which presses them so closely that they cannot escape from it (29).

In himself God is invisible. But his majesty shines forth in all his works and in all creatures. Men should therefore recognize him there. The Epistle to the Hebrews (11.3) calls the worlds the mirror or stage-play of invisible things. The passage (Rom. 1.18ff.) does not set out to be a complete guide to the understanding of the attributes of the Creator through his creation. It teaches only how we can arrive at his eternal power and divinity, 'for he who is the author of all things must be without beginning and from himself' (29-30). His divinity can only exist with his individual *virtutes*, which are all comprehended under his divinity (30).

This is all that Calvin has to say on vv.19-20a. It is remarkable that nowhere, either on these verses or on the rest of the passage, is there any mention of the *de natura deorum*. Even in the *Institutio*, whose early chapters reflect the pattern of Romans 1. 18ff., there are only two references to it and one is in disagreement.

The exposition of the clause *in hoc ut sint inexcusabiles* makes clear the direction of Calvin's thought. He sees man as accused before his divine Judge. The whole passage is concerned, as we saw, to show that, apart from the Gospel, all men are condemned. And here, in the *inexcusabiles* clause, man's defence in his case before God breaks down: 'Men can advance no defence at the judgment of God that they are not justly to be condemned' (30[46-48]).

Why can man advance no defence? The manifestation or demonstration by which God makes his glory plainly appear in the creatures is sufficiently clear in its own light. It is only because of our blindness that it is insufficient. Yet we are not so blind that we can excuse our ignorance without at the same time accusing our perversity. We conceive a Divinity. We reason that it, whatever it is, ought to be worshipped. But at this point our mind *(sensus)* fails us, and we have still not arrived at who God is or what he is like *(aut quis, aut qualis sit Deus)* (30[52-55]). This is a knowledge that God himself put, imperceptibly, into their minds. That is to say, he demonstrated himself through his works, so that they necessarily perceived him. But there are varying degrees of knowledge, and we must note the degree which they reached (30[68]), for they did not take the next step of glorifying God as God (v.21).

To explain what it is to glorify God as God Calvin returns to the *divinitas* and *virtutes* or attributes of God and rejects the nominalist separation of God in himself from God in his *virtutes* as known to us. 'God cannot be conceived without his eternity, power, wisdom, goodness, truth, righteousness, mercy . . . Therefore, he who has a conception of God already owes him praise for his eternity, wisdom, goodness, righteousness. When men do not recognize such *virtutes* in God but dream of an empty phantom, they are rightly said to rob him of his glory' (30[69]-31[81]). (Note also that to fail to glorify God is an act of robbery). When they had deserted the true knowledge of God, they turned to the emptiness of their own minds and were thrown into errors and lies (31).

It is at this point, in expounding v.22, that Calvin dissociates himself from the general view that the "they" in this passage referred to the philosophers. Philosophers are not alone in thinking that they are wise in the knowledge of God. It is an arrogance common to all races and orders of men. Therefore Paul accuses all men of making themselves glorious and pulling down God to their own level (31).

They left the true knowledge of God and fabricated a new god in his stead (v.23). The excuse that they were aware that God himself was in heaven and not in their idol is invalid, for beneath the action lay a wrong conception of God. Instead of respecting his majesty, they lowered him to the level of the image which they had made to correspond to him. This fault was universal. The common people, priests, rulers, philosophers (even Plato!) tried to search out some form in God, to

give him a figure. Calvin here registered disagreement with
Erasmus. By rendering ἀφθάρτου and φθαρτοῦ as "immortal" and "mortal" (see *Exegesis*, p. 94), Erasmus brought
in the idea of man's transitoriness in opposition to God's
eternity. Calvin, however, sees this latter part of the passage
dominated by the concept of glory. Paul's meaning therefore
is that 'they defiled God's majesty [by comparing it] with the
similitude of a corruptible man' (32^{25-26}), opposing his glory
to man's most wretched condition (32).

Grimani

This exposition, coming from a friend of Erasmus, might
be expected to show all the signs of humanism. Many of the
signs, in form and style, it does show; but this does not
prevent it from betraying also a certain scholastic temper.
Humanism and scholasticism were by no means necessarily
mutually exclusive. In Grimani's work the humanist method
and approach dominate, and the scholasticism is less apparent; but it is present all the time in the background. This is a
straightforward, sensible exposition taking an historical, and
not a theological view-point, and seeing the passage as
concerned with first century Jews and Gentiles, the Jews
subject to their Mosaic Law, the Gentiles, and especially the
Greeks, to their philosophers.

We begin with the common difficulty of the Gospel and
wrath. If God's righteousness is revealed in the Gospel (v.17),
how can his wrath and indignation also be said to be revealed
there? The answer is that they are not revealed there. From its
very name the Gospel is good news, not bad. Wrath and
indignation, on the contrary, are revealed from heaven, a fact
which has a twofold significance. On the one hand 'we read
that many punishments are sent from heaven on the wicked
angels and on ungodly men' (13^r); examples are given, the
Flood, the fire that destroyed Sodom, and so on. And on the
other hand, "from heaven" means 'from God who is in the
heavens' (13^r).

The wrath and indignation are revealed against idolatry
and unbelief, for so Grimani interprets 'ungodliness and

unrighteousness'. His not very convincing reasoning is that there is no greater ungodliness than giving to the creature the honour due to God, and this is idolatry. Similarly righteousness comes of faith; where there is no faith there is no righteousness; therefore unrighteousness is unbelief (13ᵛ). The change of concepts determines, or perhaps accords with, Grimani's understanding of the passage. There is nothing to suggest that the unrighteousness and ungodliness are universal; rather, the scene is set in ancient times when idolatry and unbelief flourished in the known world. In his own world of sixteenth century Europe idolatry was non-existent and unbelief only to be found among the many heretics and few atheists. He therefore keeps to the past tenses and, usually, the third person plural; thus, 'although they knew that God alone was to be worshipped, they bestowed the worship of God on creatures' (13ᵛ).

The Gentiles might at this point object in their own defence that they had not suppressed the truth of God, for the simple reason that they had never known God. The Apostle deprives them of this excuse by asserting that they had known God, for that which can be known naturally about God or about divine matters by man (that is, what is necessary to afford an adequate worship of God) has indeed been revealed to them. And so we have the familiar argument that 'no-one has ever existed so ignorant as not to know from the very fabric of the world that God exists, granted that none has arrived at a perfect and absolute knowledge of him' (13ᵛ–14ʳ).

Grimani refrains from proceeding into the details of Stoic theology and keeps to the relative generalities of "light" and "seed". The knowledge of God was communicated to the Gentiles by God himself, 'for he not only shed upon us from the beginning a certain light by which we [= mankind] knew the good and arrived at the truth of God, but he also naturally sowed in us the first principles of all arts and doctrines, by which we receive the more easily the knowledge of himself' (14ʳ). More than this, however, the Gentiles had the advantage of being instructed by wise men among them: 'the Gentiles, and especially the Greeks, enjoyed the benefit of philosophers, not only in the knowledge of natural things, but also of God and of other entities separate from the body' (14ʳ). Therefore, summing it up, 'he either shed in them a certain divine light, or gave them philosophers or Prophets, or published the Law; by which things they might be able to know, not only earthly matters, but also divine' (14ʳ). It would seem that the knowledge of God was a real possibility for the Gentiles of the Roman world and the failure to achieve it only accidental.

The knowledge of God that Grimani understands St Paul to mean is comprehended in the three terms *invisibilia*, *sempiterna virtus*, and *divinitas*. By *invisibilia* are meant the *conditiones Dei*, the attributes of God – we have already met the word in Caietan. And these (which the philosophers also knew) are that God is *actus* or *potentia*, act or power, *primus, infinitus, immutabilis*. The *sempiterna virtus* shows that God's power does not come and go but is everlasting. The philosophers reached the knowledge that the *virtus* is *sempiterna* from their observation of the everlasting movement of the heavens (14ᵛ). With *divinitas* Grimani goes much further. It is the essence and nature of God. It is true that men cannot know God's divinity perfectly, yet they can know that he is essence (*substantia*) and not merely *accidens* and that he is *simplex* without any *concretio* (admixture) (14ᵛ).

He explains the way in which this knowledge was attained. It was 'understood by those things which were made' (v.20). We are therefore at the concept of making and workman and workmanship: 'Even as the skill of the workman (*artifex*) is shown by his works, so all these things [i.e. the *conditiones Dei*] were manifested by the works of God' (14ᵛ). But the conclusion – more tame and inconclusive in Grimani than in St Paul! – was that the Gentiles made no use of the knowledge of God which they possessed. Instead of worshipping the God whom they knew, they transferred their worship to creatures and so became idolators.

Guilliaud

Since the greater part of Guilliaud's comments on 1. 18–23 are verbatim or near verbatim quotations from Bucer, he need not keep us long.

He begins, however, rather apart from Bucer. Instead of classing the opening sentence as the *prima propositio*, he takes it as the *probatio*, or demonstration of the faith spoken of in 1. 17, 'the righteousness of God is revealed from faith to faith . . . The just shall live by faith': 'faith in Christ, that is, that by which we are justified and numbered among the just' (6).

From this point he turns to Bucer and hardly departs from him until near the end. The only difference lies in length. Guilliaud compresses into four small pages what occupied Bucer for above twenty large pages in double column.

"To reveal" is here used for "to exhibit openly" (6 = Bucer 82^b). "The wrath of God" is put for "vengeance" (6 = Bucer 82^b). "From heaven" suggests 'a more severe vengeance, which appears to be heavenly and divine. For the power and majesty of God come before our eyes nowhere more plainly than in the heavens' (6–7 = Bucer 82^b). That the wrath of God comes upon all ungodliness means that it comes 'upon all ungodly and unrighteous men. It is a Hebraism' (7 = Bucer 83^b). They suppress the truth in unrighteousness, that is, 'Who hide the known truth of God. The emphasis is on the word "suppress", for it signifies that they did violence to the truth' (7 = Bucer 83^b).

There is no need to continue further with this series of abridged quotations from Bucer, for we have seen them already. Guilliaud also follows his guide into and through the pages of *de natura deorum*, curtailing the quotations but inserting some references. But we note that he ends this section with a reference (following Gagney) to Hugh of St Victor's *Didascalicum*, Book VII.

Not until we are near the close do we find that Guilliaud has by no means surrendered to Reformation theology. His *Conciliatio in Primum Caput* aims at deciding various doubtful points. The second is on the verse 'What may be known of God has been revealed to them' (1. 19). At first he sticks fast to Bucer: 'the knowledge of God is two-fold, the one general, which, because God irradiates it to all mortals who are sound in body and mind, we are accustomed to call natural. This is such as to take from us all excuse' (10 = Bucer 86^b). But the next sentence shows what is really in his mind and very far from Bucer's: 'For to him who does what lies in his power (*Facienti enim quod in se est*), say the theologians, God does not deny grace' (10). This phrase is, of course, a very common formula in the medieval scheme of justification. Guilliaud therefore takes the gift of the *lumen naturale* as the first step. The reward, or merit, for making the best use one can of this gift is the infusion of grace.

PART THREE

ROMANS 2.13-16

13.'Ου γὰρ οἱ ἀκροαταὶ τοῦ νόμου δίκαιοι παρὰ τῷ θεῷ, 'αλλ' οἱ ποιηταὶ τοῦ νόμου δικαιωθήσονται. (*Eras ed.* 1527)
[no variant readings in relevant edd]

Non enim auditores legis iusti sunt apud deum: sed factores legis iustificabuntur. (*Steph Vulg* 1528)
deum, Er⁴Vg

Non enim qui audiunt legem, iusti sunt apud deum: sed qui legem factis exprimunt, iusti habebuntur (*Eras vers 1527*)
[no variant readings Er vers¹⁻³,⁵]

EXEGESIS

οἱ ποιηταὶ τοῦ νόμου – **Factores legis**] The intention of this verse is understood variously. For Bucer it is 'the *probatio* of the last part of the premised *propositio* (123ᵃ); for Melanchthon 'a general statement [1540 adds: on the righteousness of the Law]' (45ʳ;XCVIIIᵛ); and for Calvin 'a *prolepsis* by which he forestalls an objection which the Jews could raise' (44⁵¹⁻⁵²). Erasmus brings out the ambiguity in the word ποιέω /*facio*, "doing" or "making": 'that is, Those who work and do the precepts of the Law; or else, They make the Law who frame the Law' (A³ 295;A⁵354). Caietan: 'They are called doers of the law, not as makers (*conditores*) of the Law but as practising in their actions those things which are of the Law' (VII A).
δικαιωθήσονται – **iustificabuntur**] Grimani fastens on the future tense, to which the others pay little or no attention. He therefore interprets the verse of the Jews who lived before the Incarnation and who kept the Law; 'He did not say that they who did the works of the Law have been justified (*iustificatos*), but that they are to be justified (*iustificandos*)' (22ᵛ). This idea,

which has for background the Harrowing of Hell, appears
also in Haresche under 3.25 (which see).

14. ὅταν γὰρ ἔθνη τὰ μὴ νόμον ἔχοντα, φύσει τὰ τοῦ νόμου ποιῇ,
οὗτοι νόμον μὴ ἔχοντες, ἑαυτοῖς εἰσι νόμος,   (*Eras ed. 1527*)
εχοντες εαυτοις Compl

Cum enim gentes quae legem non habent, naturaliter ea quae
legis sunt faciunt: eiusmodi legem non habentes, ipsi sibi sunt
lex: (*Steph Vulg* 1528)
habent naturaliter Compl   habentes ipsis Compl

Nam cum gentes quae legem non habent, natura quae legis
sunt, fecerint, eae legem non habentes, sibiipsis sunt lex,
(*Eras vers 1527*)
fecerint: Er vers[5]

EXEGESIS

τὰ τοῦ νόμου – **ea quae legis**] Calvin relates vv.14–16 to
1.18ff.: 'He now repeats the *probatio* of the first member'
(45[77]) – for I take "first member" to mean the first part of
Paul's whole argument in the Epistle and not to some first
clause in chapter 2. Caietan makes the point, which he builds
into his exposition, that the language is left vague: 'He does
not say that they do all of the Law, but indefinitely "the
things which are of the law"' (VII B). (Cf. Calvin on the
following verse: 'We must not gather from this that they have
a full knowledge of the Law, but only that some seeds of
righteousness were sown in their minds' (46[7-9])).
φύσει – **naturaliter**] Caietan: 'that is, without the help of
the Law, by the natural light of reason' (VII B). Melanchthon: 'that is, by natural knowledge, teaching honourable
things and reproving wickedness' (XCIX[r]). And Calvin: 'He
sets nature over against the written Law, meaning that a
natural beam (*fulgor*) of righteousness shines in the Gentiles'
(45[91-93]). And Melanchthon: 'By this word Paul witnesses
that the knowledge is the work of God effected within the
mind, as light is in the eyes' (45[v];XCIX[r]).

15. οἵ τινες ἐνδείκνυνται τὸ ἔργον τοῦ νόμου γραπτὸν ἐν ταῖς καρδίαις αὐτῶν, συμμαρτυρούσης αὐτῶν τῆς συνειδήσεως, καὶ μεταξὺ ἀλλήλων τῶν λογισμῶν κατηγορούντων, ἢ καὶ ἀπολογουμένων, (Eras ed. 1527)

γραπτον, Er[1]   κατηγορουντων η   Compl

qui ostendunt opus legis scriptum in cordibus suis, testimonium reddente illis conscientia ipsorum, et inter se invicem cogitationibus accusantibus aut etiam defendentibus, (Steph Vulg 1528)

cogitationum accusantium: aut etiam defendentium Er[4]Vg Compl (omitting colon)   suis: Compl   ipsorum: Compl

qui ostendunt opus legis scriptum in cordibus suis simul attestante illorum conscientia, et cogitationibus inter se accusantibus, aut etiam excusantibus, (Eras vers 1527)

suis, Er vers[2,3,5]   excusantibus in Er[5]

EXEGESIS

συνειδήσεως/λογισμῶν – **conscientia/cogitationum**] Caietan distinguishes between the two: 'Conscientia signifies the application of knowledge to something done or to be done, examining it, whether done or not done, a good or bad deed, and likewise whether to be done or not to be done, good or bad. But cogitationes either accusing or defending are as it were parts assembling to the examination of conscientia or alleging out of natural reason arguments for or against' (VII E).

συμμαρτυρούσης – **testimonium reddente**] Erasmus: 'Translators remarkably nod here, when they turn one of the Greek genitives into a Latin ablative . . . and leave the other. It ought to be translated, "Their thoughts accusing or even defending one another".' Er A[5] continues with a fairly long note against the bad translation (354–355).

16. ἐν ἡμέρᾳ ὅτε κρινεῖ ὁ θεὸς τὰ κρυπτὰ τῶν ἀνθρώπων, κατὰ τὸ εὐαγγέλιόν μου διὰ Ἰησοῦ Χριστοῦ. (Eras ed. 1527)
[no variant readings in relevant edd]

in die cum iudicabit deus occulta hominum secundum
euangelium meum per IESUM CHRISTUM, (*Steph Vulg
1528*).
Christum. Er⁴Vg Compl

in eo die, cum iudicabit dominus occulta hominum, iuxta
euangelium meum per Iesum Christum. (*Eras vers 1527*)
[no variant readings Er vers[1-3,5]]

EXPOSITION

The general agreement among our authors on the exegesis
of these verses diminishes when they come to interpret
the meaning. In this respect their differences are not merely
formal but fundamental, both in regard to method of
interpretation and also to theological presuppositions. The
difference in theological presuppositions lies in the view
taken of the relation between God and man and may be traced
back by stages from the empirical means of the revelation to
its ultimate, the view of God himself. At every stage either a
difference will appear or, if agreement at any stage, then an
inconsistency between that and the previous stage will have
been brought to light. The difference of method of interpretation is, at any rate immediately, to be ascribed to
whether they observe the context strictly or less strictly or
not at all. If v. 13 is taken by itself and therefore given an
independent validity and authority (the authority of the
infallible Holy Scripture) it will at once create the problem of
contradiction by 3.20, also taken by itself and possessing the
same individual validity and authority. The first task of some
of the writers is therefore to still their readers' anxiety, if not
their own, by reconciling the two verses. But something
more occurs than the stilling of anxiety. The most common
outcome of attempting a reconciliation between contradictions is compromise. And so it is here. Such is the joy of
some of the authors to have the clear authority of Holy
Scripture on their side that they forget the dreaded word

"Pelagianism" until it is almost too late. Almost, but not quite, even if it has to be a final assurance that the Pelagianism he has just been proclaiming is not really Pelagianism because he says it is not. The need to reconcile the two passages is seen not only in Caietan, Grimani, Guilliaud, and Haresche, but also in Bucer, who also supplies a *Conciliatio* (129^b-130^b). A few writers (e.g. Bullinger, Melanchthon, Pellicanus) virtually or entirely ignore the argument. Calvin shows his perfect respect for the context by damning both sides roundly: 'Those who misuse this verse [2.13] to set up justification by works deserve to be laughed at by schoolboys. It is also inept and irrelevant to pour out long *quaestiones* for the solution of such a futile quibble' (44^{58-61}).

In this section we will take the writers in the two groups into which they most clearly fall, Romanists and Evangelicals. And first we come to *Caietan*. His point of departure is the apparent contradiction between 2.13 and 3.20. This is, he says, a *magna quaestio*. But the *quaestio* will vanish 'if we realise that the subject here is the divine judgment rendering to each man according to his works' (VI K). Clearly Caietan intends to deal with the verse in its context, which he sees as 2.6-11. Moreover, he had already, at the beginning of Chapter 2 (V G), reminded us of 1.16-17, as if he wished those verses to govern his exposition of Chapter 2. It is therefore the meaning of the verse in its context that he first puts forward to resolve the *quaestio*. But instead of dismissing the problem as irrelevant, in Calvin's way, he drops the argument of the context and attempts a solution by means of the scholastic distinction between the merits of works and absolute merits: 'he is not treating of merits *absolutè* but of the merits of works. And indeed by speaking of the merits of works it is very truly said that the doers of the law are justified before God. It implies how much the merit of works is worth. But this does not exclude the merit of faith, which exceeds the merit of works' (VII A). Merely by introducing the concept of merits into the discussion Caietan betrays his view of the standing of man over against God. For the rest of the exposition on this passage he is having to offer disclaimers and to make corrections to his course as he sees where his thinking is taking him.

The next verse ('For when the Gentiles which have not the law do by nature the things contained in the law') Caietan regards as confirmation that some Gentiles actually do observe the Law and will consequently be justified before God: 'And so he proves that doers of the Law will be justified before God from the fact that Gentiles doing the works of the Law will be justified before God' (VII A). It is the Mosaic Law of which the verse speaks. Although the Gentiles lack that Law and the seal of circumcision, they can nevertheless "do" the Law 'by the natural light of reason' (VII B). A strict exegesis of the words at this point narrows down the Mosaic Law from the whole system with its ceremonies to the moral Law alone: 'He does not say that they do all the things of the Law, but indefinitely the things of the Law' (VII B). And as we already know from 1.18ff. that Gentiles have a knowledge of genuine morality, we can say that this verse 'speaks of morals which they know by natural light and not of ceremonial or judicial matters' (VII B). The *moralia* are such precepts as honouring parents, not stealing, not murdering, worshipping one God, revering his name and so on. These things some Gentiles do by natural light (VII B).

But if so, if Gentiles actually keep the *moralia* of the Law, are they not thereby justified? For 'the doers of the law shall be justified'. No, says Caietan, for 'note well that it is one thing to do the things which are of the Law and another to do meritoriously the things which are of the Law' (VII B). The Apostle is here speaking of the former, which is simply a matter of keeping the moral precepts *quantum ad substantiam operis*. But Paul will go on to speak of a keeping of the Law *quantum ad modum operandi*, 'a manner exceeding the power of natural light and the faculties of man' (VII C). Caietan is here making the distinction between merely observing the Law without regard to motive or spirit and observing it from a willing and selfless heart. He does not, however, work out this point but returns to his previous distinction between the things of the Law indefinitely and all the things of the Law. All men can do some of the things of the Law; only 'sound' man [i.e. Adam] can do all the things: 'Naturally to do all the moral precepts of the Law is for the healthy man; and man as he is constituted *in naturalibus* after the fall of nature in our first parent is not healthy. But naturally to do some of the moral precepts of the Law belongs also to weak man, such as is man after the fall of our first parent' (VII B–C).

What is to be concluded from all this? That there is no discrepancy between 2.13 and 3.20. The doers of the Law will indeed be justified; but that means, those who do it meritoriously – and no doubt Caietan intends those who have received the first grace and so are enabled to merit justification by doing their utmost to keep the Law. And on the other hand, by the works of the Law there shall no flesh be justified; and these are works done by those whose hearts are not so renewed. He concludes Chapter 2 with a summary which shows both the drift of his general interpretation and also his intention to keep to the context: 'God does not praise the carnal professor of the Law or circumcision, but him who is a Jew and circumcised in deed and in inmost spirit. The praise which responds to true merits is divine and not human. And in this Paul abases the Gentiles in two respects, in regard to their wisdom and to their judging. He abases the Jews also in two respects, in regard to their Law and to their circumcision without deeds, by showing that the Gentiles are their equals according to the merits of deeds. And he said all this in declaring that the wrath of God was revealed in the Gospel on all who suppress the truth in unrighteousness' (VIII G).

Guilliaud solves the problem posed in his *Conciliatio* of *Factores legis* and *Ex operibus legis* . . . by recourse to the penitential system of the late medieval church, the tacit presupposition of Caietan's interpretation. Of the two stages in justification, the first is by the sheer and unaided grace of God, the second by the person's coöperation with grace. The first grace is gratuitous, unmerited; the second is merited on the basis of coöperation. Guilliaud's argument therefore is that 2.13 refers to the second part of justification, 3.20 to the first part. 'By the deeds of the law shall no flesh living be justified' because man is unable to merit the first grace. But 'the doers of the law shall be justified' because they coöperate with grace and therefore merit justification. 'Doers of the law are justified because, having already received justification freely, they advance in the works of the Law and in merit. Which merits come from the first justification (by which from ungodly a man becomes godly) as from a root . . . But they are not justified by the works of the Law, or they do not merit the first grace, by which sin is remitted to them. For this is of Christ and not of ourselves' (15).

Cardinal Grimani goes another way to work. He starts with the same problem of contradiction: 'But how shall doers of the Law be justified, when he says later that none can receive justification by the works of the Law?' (22^v). But he is able to settle it "easily", as he says, by making the sentence in 2.13 be dominated by the word *iustificandos*, into which he concentrates the future tense: 'he did not say that those who did the works of the Law were justified (*iustificatos*) but are to be justified (*iustificandos*) in order to show that those who did the works of the Law were not justified by virtue of the Law, but in the time to come, so that those who did the Law, that is, who fulfilled the works of the Law, might attain justification at last – which is after Christ's passion' (22^v). His somewhat involved argument runs thus: Among those who lived before the Incarnation were some who "did" the Law. But the doing of the Law is not meritorious in its own right or by virtue of the Law itself. It becomes meritorious by virtue of the death and passion of Christ. But Christ had not yet died when such people "did" the Law and therefore their works were not yet meritorious and they themselves could not yet be justified. When, however, Christ had suffered and died, there was conferred on these same works the saving merit of his death, so that they became meritorious and their doers were justified.

By attempting to resolve the question in terms of Christ's crucifixion Grimani's exposition can be preferred to Caietan's. It is in the inferences that he goes on to draw that his ambivalence is revealed. On the basis of his argument he can say that we are justified partly by the death of Christ and partly by our works: 'If we weigh these things carefully it becomes clear that, if the doers of the Law will be justified, our works are necessary for our justification' (22ᵛ). Of course, he reminds us very quickly that this is not on our own account or from an inherent power in the Law, but for the sake of the death and passion of Christ: 'for by dying for us he justified us and made satisfaction for us and caused our work, which before his death was invalid for the obtaining of eternal life, to become valid and meritorious on account of his death and passion. Therefore both are necessary for our salvation – our work and the passion and death of Christ. And by grace and his kindness salvation is brought about without any precedent human merits and activities' (22ᵛ-23ʳ).

Haresche deals with the problem of the apparent contradiction very fully, even granted that his usual prolixity spins out his exposition to perhaps half as long again as it needed to be. His *forte* lies, as we have seen, in definition. To resolve the problem he begins by analysing Law. He first divides Law into human and divine Law, and then subdivides the latter into *lex naturalis* and *lex divina purè positiva*. Human law is law given by a human legislator, whether ecclesiastical or lay. The purpose of ecclesiastical law is the embracing of virtues and the repressing of vices. The purpose of "lay" law is the conservation of common peace and union. The *lex divina naturalis* is the law that dwells in all who are capable of reason, so that by reason they are able to judge of the things which the *lex naturalis* says should be done or omitted. The *lex divina purè positiva* is the Law given by God and declared in Holy Scripture, or through the mystical body of Christ which is the Church, or through its prelates, mediating what is prohibited or commanded – which cannot be known by natural instinct. Sin is the transgression (*praevaricatio*) of the Law, whether the *divina naturalis* or the *divina purè positiva* or the *humana* (xxxixʳ⁻ᵛ).

There are also two kinds of hearers of the Law. There are 'those who hear the Law declared to them and think and judge that it should be fulfilled in the literal and carnal sense and not in the spiritual sense and also those who hear the Law declared to them and, although they judge that it should be fulfilled in the spiritual sense, yet do not fulfil it'(xl^r). He then couples the verse with Jas. 1.22ff. ('Be ye doers of the word and not hearers only').

The next word to be defined is *iustificabuntur*, which Haresche first looks at in terms of Baptism and regeneration: 'Some are called just before God either because they are already blessèd' – that is, in Paradise – 'seeing God clearly, or if they are *viatores*' – on earth – 'and also infants, because they are regenerated by water and the Holy Spirit. If they are adults and born again of water and the Holy Spirit, because they are justified by faith which works by love' (fo. xl^r-v). In other words, *viatores* are just because they have received the first grace in Baptism.

But Haresche has not said his last word on *iustificabuntur* yet. He now makes a fourfold distinction in justification: *effectivè, meritoriè, exequutivè* and *dispositivè*, and *reputativè*. Three of these are straightforward enough. To be justified *effectivè* is to be justified by God alone, for he alone *effects* our justification. *Exequutivè* or *dispositivè* refers to the justification of the man who *executes* the works of righteousness pleasing to God and necessary for salvation. For proof of this Haresche points to Jas. 2.24, 'by works a man is justified, and not by faith only'. For works *dispose* a man for grace, as we see both in the example of the Ninevites in Jonah 3.10, according to the Vulgate: 'And God saw their works, that they were converted from their evil way, and God repented of what he had said he would do to them and did it not', and also in the example of Cornelius, to whom the angel said, 'Thy prayers and thy alms are come up as a memorial before God' (Acts 10.4). And thirdly, 'he is said to be justified *reputativè* who is reckoned righteous in the *repute* of men, even if sometimes he is a sinner (*iniquus*)' (xl^v).

The term *meritoriè* may be explained by a literal translation of Haresche's own definition. 'He is said to be justified *meritoriè* by merit not depending on the merit of another who is justified in the merit of the passion of Christ exhibited and of his blood shed; for the merit of Christ does not depend on the merit of another, and Christ by his passion exhibited and his blood shed for believers in Christ (*Christifidelibus*) merited justification' (xl^v). Like Grimani, Haresche clearly saw the theological compulsion of linking the merits of believers with the merits of Christ won on the Cross and imparted in the Sacraments. But he is also convinced that merit must be personal, it cannot 'depend on the merit of another'; he therefore has no place for imputed merit. This dictates the form of his conclusion: 'To be justified *meritoriè* means to be justified partly by the merit of another and partly by one's own meritorious act, and this because, when he is justified, he is justified not only by his own meritorious act, but also in the merit of the passion of Christ exhibited and his blood shed' (xl^v).

The way is now clear for Haresche to apply his distinctions and definitions to the verse he has undertaken to elucidate. The reader will probably be glad to be reminded that the verse under discussion is 'doers of the law will be justified'. Doers of the law (they are so called 'because they fulfil the commandments of the Law in heart and word and deed as God wishes' (xli^r)) are justified *effectivè*, *meritoriè*, and *dispositivè*. The passage in question, unclear enough in itself, is further confused by erratic punctuation; but we can make out that what he is saying is that (1) doers of the law are justified *effectivè* by the act of God; (2) they are justified *meritoriè* in the merit of the passion of Christ exhibited and his blood shed, by a merit not depending on the merit of another, and by mediating faith which works through love; moreover, *meritoriè* partly by the merit of another and partly by the merit of having such faith as is necessary for justifying an adult, the primary factor being the grace which makes a man acceptable to God, so that he receives an eternal reward; (3) they are justified *dispositivè* in that their works proceeding from faith and love dispose them to justification (xli^r).

It will have been noticed that Haresche has been careful to give the initiative in justification to God and his grace, a fact which comes out even more strongly as he goes on. There can be no question of man's forestalling grace by works done before he believes. 'Those who do the works of the Law are not justified by works preceding faith; and properly speaking it is not such who are called doers of the Law but those who do the works from out of faith (*mediante fide*)' (xlii^r). The point at which faith intervenes and therefore works become meritorious is Baptism.

These eight pages may be fairly summarized by saying that justification is the work of God, that it depends on the merits of Christ, that it also depends on man's coöperation with grace, and that good works flowing from faith working by love are meritorious.

Sadoleto deals with 2.13–16 as a section, but at no great length, giving it no more than twenty-seven lines. The argument of the passage he summarizes as: 'either to have the Law or to observe the Law justifies before God' (33;45). If the former is true, then good works are irrelevant; only the fact of belonging to the Jewish nation is sufficient, and all the Jews are completely safe – even those who sin against God and the Law. Moreover, the Gentiles will be entirely lost; although some of them were honourable and righteous and even led a pious life, ruled by reason and with a desire for God's honour, yet all this will be in vain and the faith they had set on the most high God will prove a deceit and they will be lost. 'But if it is rather the observance of the Law which effects righteousness, even those who do not observe that Law on tables, but observe the works and precepts of the Law by the gift of nature and the intention of the will, these are made righteous (*iusti sunt effecti*) before God' (33;45). But for the work to be truly good, it must come from 'a mind which is aware of what is right' (33;45) and after weighing the various possibilities comes to the definite decision. Sadoleto now turns at once to v.16 and devotes the last ten lines to it.

It would appear that this was not one of the passages censured by Paris and the Vatican, for it stood unchanged in the revised edition of 1536. We therefore place it with the other Roman Catholic expositions, although it seems hardly to chime with them. But it is not difficult to see that only the form is humanist. The substance could have been written scholastically as the *conciliatio* of the difficulty: 'Whether to have the Law or to observe the Law justifies before God'. And if his words are taken in a generous spirit as expressing more theologically than they say, he can be cleared of

Pelagianism and seen as a loyal acceptor of the medieval system of penance.

With our next author, *Martin Bucer*, we move on to a completely different level of scholarship and understanding altogether, but even he cannot resist an attempt at reconciliation of contradictories. His view of 2.13 is that it is 'a tacit irony' (123[a]) directed against the Jews, who had such great advantages and yet went astray at this elementary point of thinking it enough to hear without practising what they heard. The statement that the doers of the Law will be justified he takes at its face value and brings round to his own beliefs by supplying a gloss on the word "doer". His interpretation becomes the same as the others we have looked at; in different language he also is saying that genuine doing of the Law comes only from a regenerate heart. 'So to do the Law, or to be a performer (*patrator*) of the Law, is nothing other than to be devoted to the Law, to practise (*meditare*) the Law, so that one's whole life may be conformed to the Law. . . Hence it is that God recompenses (*rependat*) eternal life to those who do the Law, that is, seriously devote themselves to it' (123[b]). Hence his *Conciliatio* is concentrated on "doer": 'The Apostle here writes that οἵ ποιηταὶ, those who do the Law, are justified. . . How is "those who do the Law are justified" any different from "they are justified by the works of the law"?' (129[b]). Bucer's answer runs thus: Those who do the Law are those who do the works of the Law; and we know from Holy Scripture that it is according to our works that God will judge us. But to do the Law means to devote oneself seriously to what the Law commands and not merely to perform some of the actions demanded by the Law. This can be done only by those who truly believe in the Lord (129[b]).

Bucer has taken us back, in fact, to justification by faith. But he then moves in a fresh direction. If we look at the actual deeds performed, those which are done by the doers of the Law, we see that these acts of obedience are not our own but the works of Christ in us. It would be incorrect to interpret Bucer here as meaning that we are justified by our own activities inasmuch as they are inspired or activated by the indwelling Christ ('Remember, O Lord, what thou hast wrought in us, and not what we deserve'!). The sense of his following passage is that we are justified by the merits of Christ (that is, by the works of Christ, his life and death of obedience to the Father's will), which become our own through union with Christ by faith: 'God saves us of his pure mercy and by contemplating the merit of Christ, which is given to us and becomes our own when we believe in Christ. For the deeds [of the Law] according to which God justifies us . . . are Christ's works in us, given with him, out of a sheer and gratuitous benevolence of God. So the goodness of God is always, *per se*, the first and complete cause of our salvation' (129[b]).

We must defer our judgment on Bucer until we have seen whether his eirenical spirit influences his exposition of 3.20 seq in the direction of compromise. For the present we note that, with most of the authors we have examined, the attempt at reconciliation leaves a balance between the two verses. We are justified by grace but also by works. Both Caietan and Bucer, however, reconcile 2.13 with 3.20 rather than the other way round; that is to say, they take 3.20 as the dominant and undoubted truth and explain 2.13 to agree with it. And, although we have said that the others also left a balance between the verses, that balance is uneasy and consists largely of a non–Pelagian statement of faith at the end of the passage. The general drift of their exposition is, in fact, a reconciling of 3.20 with 2.13 as the dominant truth.

Our next three authors do not, at least openly, engage in reconciliations but confine themselves to expounding the passage.

Bullinger takes a straightforward view of 2.13, understanding it as an impossible possibility: 'But none of the Jews, in fact no man at all, keeps the Law. Therefore, none is righteous before God, but all are sinners. This is Paul's meaning and not, as some contend, that salvation is owed to our righteousness' (24). In other words, if a man does the Law, he will be justified; but no man does the Law; therefore no man is righteous before God. Similarly with v.14, although Bullinger does not here refer directly to 'doing the law' but confines himself to the natural law, he assumes that none has in fact observed that law: 'But with their eyes shut they fell away and inclined more to the affections of the flesh, so that they could have no excuse for sin. And so the Gentiles are sinners' (24).

On vv.15-16 Bullinger seems inconsistent with what he has already said and what he will say later. He takes the two verses in one context and eschatologically. At the day of Christ the consciences of the Gentiles will either accuse or excuse them; and Bullinger seems to envisage that some will have a clear conscience: 'again, the conscience of some upright man, conscious of no evil, will excuse him' (24); and, 'if you find anything honest, true, and just among the Gentiles, you ascribe it all to the divine wisdom' (25). It is arguable that he is referring to believing, regenerate Gentiles. At any rate, his main argument is clear, that all men, Jews and Gentiles, are sinners and need the redemption of Christ.

Melanchthon's exposition in the 1532/1540 *Commentarius* is also straightforward. Verse 13 is 'a general statement' about the righteousness of the Law. The righteousness of the Law does not consist only in hearing it or professing its ceremonies but in doing it, in fulfilling the complete obedience of the Law. 'So Paul speaks of a possibility (*de Idea*) and accuses the Jews that they are not righteous by the Law, because no one satisfies the Law' (XCVIII[v]).[1]

As in his exposition of 1.18 seq, Melanchthon is not explicit about the natural law. It is a *noticia naturalis de moribus* which distinguishes between good and evil (*honesta et turpia*) and which teaches *honesta* and reprehends *turpia* (45[v];XCIX[r]). It is a knowledge that is the *opus Dei conditum in mente*, analogous to light for the eyes. Augustine, he says, imports difficulties into Paul here, whereas the text itself is not obscure. Paul is discussing knowledge and judgment. It is plain that even the unregenerate can do the external works of

[1] 1532: Paul 'accuses the Jews of guilt, because, although they heard the Law, they did not do it' (45[r]).

the law by their natural abilities (*viribus naturalibus*) and practice discipline and civil works. Paul is therefore speaking of doing external works; but he does not say that the Gentiles are righteous before God by the Law but means that both Jews and Gentiles did external civil works. Melanchthon then goes on to speak of the so-called "virtuous heathen", of Fabius, Scipio, and Atticus (XCIX[r-v]).[2] Later, however, he insists on the universality of guilt and condemns those who, though they accept that 'most at Rome are guilty, yet, make out that from that number just a few are to be excepted, Scipio, Atticus' (CVI[v]).

Pellicanus restricts himself to exposition, without reference to controversy. It is not enough to have heard and to know the Law; one must also obey. The Jews had heard the Law and the Gentiles knew the natural law, but both had transgressed the Law and therefore both were guilty.

Calvin, as we saw, will have nothing to do with attempts at reconciling 2.13 with 3.20 or with defending 2.13 from attack, but gets on with the task of elucidating the meaning of the passage in its immediate and wider context. Verse 13 is intended as, so to say, part of the debate between Paul and the Jews. In it Paul anticipates that the Jews will make an objection against the condemnation of themselves as well as the Gentiles as sinners. They argue that they have the Law, the perfect rule of righteousness, and that they alone know the Law. Therefore they cannot be classed with the Gentiles as sinners. Against this "hallucination" Paul asserts that the Law must actually be done; hearing it or even understanding it will not convey righteousness. It is true that the doer of the Law will be justified. But – and this is where Calvin always puts the emphasis – he must fulfil the Law perfectly and in every respect. This by itself refutes the interpretation of the verse as somehow teaching justification by works: 'For if only those who fulfil the Law are justified by the Law, it follows that none is justified, because none can be met with

---

[2] 1532: 'But it is certain that among the Gentiles there were many honourable and excellent men, whose morals were no lower than those of honest men among the Jews' (46[r]).

who can claim to have kept the Law' (44⁶⁷⁻⁶⁹).

He interprets vv.14 and 15 in relation to 1.20 and inexcusability. The Gentiles cannot plead ignorance as an excuse, for their very actions show that they have a *regula iustitiae*, a rule or standard of righteousness. All peoples have some laws, and laws would not have been thought of unless 'some conceptions of righteousness and uprightness (which conceptions the Greeks call προλήψεις) were naturally innate in men's minds. Therefore they have law without the Law' (45⁸⁵⁻⁸⁷). Their law is rudimentary, however; they do not possess a full knowledge of the Law. It is only that certain seeds of righteousness are put into their minds. These are, for example, that they should have a religion, that adultery, theft, and murder are forbidden, that good faith in business contracts is commended (46⁹⁻¹¹).

But Calvin should not be taken as meaning that the non-Christian Gentiles are better than the Jews in that they obey the *lex naturalis* inscribed on their hearts whereas the Jews are disobedient to the Law of Moses. On the contrary, the purpose of the *lex naturalis* is to make them guilty and inexcusable. He is careful to distinguish between the understanding and the will and so between knowing and doing. They have the power of differentiating and adjudging between the good and the evil and even of approving the good: but Paul 'did not mean that it was engraven on their will so that they desired it (*insculptum eorum voluntati ut appetant*) and strove earnestly after it, but that they were so overcome by the force of the truth that they were unable not to assent to it' (45⁹⁷⁻⁹⁹). And again: 'Therefore it is unsuitable to infer from this passage the power of our will, as if Paul were saying that the keeping of the Law lies within our ability (*facultati nostrae subiectam*). For he was not speaking about the power to fulfil the Law but about knowledge' (45¹⁻⁴).

Thus, the passage is taken in conformity with 1.18-23 and the complete universality of sin among the Gentiles is asserted and pressed. There are no exceptions; there are no Gentiles who entirely and whole-heartedly obey the Law written in their hearts. The difference between Calvin and Bullinger and Melanchthon on this point is striking.

PART FOUR

ROMANS 3. 20-28

20. Διότι ἐξ ἔργων νόμου δικαιωθήσεται πᾶσα σὰρξ ἐνώπιον
αὐτοῦ. Διὰ γὰρ νόμου ἐπίγνωσις ἁμαρτίας. (*Eras ed. 1527*)
[no variant readings in relevant edd]

quia ex operibus legis non iustificabitur omnis caro coram
illo. Per legem enim, cognitio peccati. (*Steph Vulg 1528*)
enim cognitio St[32] Compl Er[4]Vg   peccati: Compl

propterea quod ex operibus legis non iustificabitur omnis
caro in conspectu eius. Per legem enim agnitio peccati. (*Eras
vers 1527*)
legis, Er vers[5]

EXEGESIS

ἐξ ἔργων νόμου – **Ex operibus legis**] A major disagreement
appears at once on the word *lex*. The larger number take it as
a reference to the whole Law in all its parts; but not a few
restrict it to the ceremonial Law alone. For the whole Law are
Bullinger, Caietan, Calvin, Melanchthon, Pellicanus, and
Sadoleto. Thus, for example, Caietan: 'He calls the Law of
Moses "the law of works", embracing the moral, ceremonial,
and judicial laws . . . And in this is also included the natural
law, which is likewise a law of works' (XI G); and Calvin:
'The phrase "the works of the law" is taken in two ways by
the learnèd. Some extend it to the observance of the whole
Law, others restrict it to ceremonies. The addition of the
word "law" moved Chrysostom, Origen, and Jerome to
agree with the former view.[1] They thought that the addition

---

[1] Not as Calvin Translation Society, 'with the latter view'. The word
priorem was allowed to stand in all the editions revised by Calvin himself
and has survived in all the subsequent editions, including Corpus
Reformatorum.

contained a particular connotation that the word should not
be understood only of works in general. . . And what some
scholars adduce is too weak to support their opinion. By the
mention of circumcision [in 3.1] they think an example is
advanced referring only to ceremonies . . . And they argue
from the Epistle to the Galatians, where, when Paul treats of
the same subject, he writes only of ceremonies . . . But with
good reason we contend that Paul is here treating of the
whole Law' (66[81]-67[17]); and Pellicanus, who does not follow
Bucer here: 'Paul does not distinguish the works of the Law,
but only speaks of them in general. I also prefer not to
distinguish, with Augustine. . . who insisted that by the
works of the Law should be understood all the works of the
Law' (42); and again: 'all glorying of merit is excluded; also
excluded is any glorying of works – of works, I say, of the
whole Law, the Decalogue as well as the ceremonies' (45).
But Bucer: 'He concludes from his premises that none can be
justified by the ceremonies of the Law' (176[a]); and again:
'ceremonies, about which alone is the argument, are called in
this place "the works of the law"'(177[a]); and: 'He calls those
things which the Law commands "the works of the law".
And in this place the Apostle thus calls the ceremonies of the
Law (which are a part of the things commanded in the Law)
by autonomasia or synecdoche' (179[a]). The following passage
suggests that Calvin's reference to Galatians was perhaps
directed against Bucer: 'By "the works of the law" Paul
meant the ceremonies of Moses. So that this was the whole
question that he was disputing, both here and in the Epistle to
the Galatians. . .The holy fathers think the same thing about
the works of the law. Only Augustine contends that by the
works of the law all the precepts of the Law, even the
Decalogue, are to be understood. . .But we agree with the
holy fathers that the Apostle meant here by "the works of the
law" particularly to express ceremonies. . .*De caeremoniis
enim erat omnis quaestio*' (179[a-b]). Similarly Grimani: 'And "the
works of the law" is what he calls circumcision and those
sacrifices which were performed in the law of nature or the
written Law, which were performed as ceremonies' (30[v]);
and Haresche: '*Because from the works of the law* preceding faith

or observed in a carnal sense, as ceremonies and sacrifices
were observed carnally by the Jews' (lxiiii^r).

πᾶσα σὰρξ – **omnis caro**] Bucer: 'He said this for "every
man"' (179^b); and Pellicanus: 'that is, all men of whatever
nation, race, condition, or law' (42). Calvin extends the
meaning a little: '"Flesh" without a qualification means
"men" – except that it seems to suggest something more
general. Rather more is expressed when one says "all
mortals" instead of "all men", as you have it in Gellius'
(67^{24-28}). But for Sadoleto it means 'every man devoted to the
flesh and trusting in the works of the flesh' (41;59 – this is the
opinion of Julius, not necessarily of James). Grimani again
looks at it a little differently: 'He says "all flesh" so that we
may understand by "all flesh" all men living in the flesh' (30^v);
and Haresche: 'or every man living in this pilgrimage (*via*)
with a carnal body' (lxiiii^v).

21. Νυνὶ δὲ χωρὶς νόμου δικαιοσύνη θεοῦ πεφανέρωται,
μαρτυρουμένη ὑπὸ τοῦ νόμου καὶ τῶν προφητῶν. (*Eras ed.*
1527)
[no variant readings in relevant edd]

Nunc autem sine lege iustitia dei manifestata est: testificata a
lege et prophetis. (*Steph Vulg 1528*)
est, Er^4Vg

Nunc vero absque lege iustitia dei manifestata est, dum
comprobatur testimonio legis ac prophetarum. (*Eras vers*
1527)
[no variant readings in Er vers^{1-3,5}]

EXEGESIS

Νυνὶ **-Nunc**] Taken in two ways. (1)Bullinger: '*Nunc* is
not temporal, but rather connects and carries on [the
argument]' (33). (2) Calvin: 'The particle *nunc* can be taken
simply as adversative, without relation to time. If you prefer
to refer it to time, the meaning will be that the righteousness
of faith was revealed by the preaching of the Gospel after

Christ was revealed in the flesh'[2] (69[5]-70[12]); and Bucer: 'Here is an opposing of Gospel and Law; for when he said, "without the law the righteousness of God is revealed", he meant the revelation of the Gospel' (180[b]). Melanchthon also takes it temporally, but incorporates this into his rhetorical framework: 'He had earlier made a beginning on the principal proposition by saying that all men are guilty of sin and under the wrath of God and cannot be set free from sin by the Law. Now the principal *propositio* itself follows, which is the *status* of this controversy. . .this *propositio* contains the proper and chief statement of the Gospel about the benefit of Christ . . . The arguments must be referred to this *status* as the head' (CVIII[v]).[3]

χωρὶς νόμου – **sine lege**] Haresche: 'Mosaic, by taking the Mosaic Law for the Pentateuch or the five books of Moses' (lxvii[r]). But Bullinger: '"Law" cannot be taken for the written Law here; but by metonymical substitution (*per Metalepsim*) it is put for "work" or "merit" ' (33). Similarly Calvin: 'without the law, that is, without the help of the law; so that "law" is understood as taken for "works" ' (68[50-51]); and Bucer: 'He said "without the law" for "not from the observing of the law" ' (180[b]).

δικαιοσύνη – **iustitia**] Haresche: '"The righteousness of God" is Christ made unto us justification' (lxvii[r]) – perhaps borrowing from Bucer's reference to Origen's interpretation of *iustitia* as Christ (181[a]). Bucer refers also to Ambrose (who takes *iustitia* 'for the mercy of God pardoning and forgiving sins', and says that it is called *iustitia* because it has its origin from the promise: 'For it is the righteousness of God because he bestows what has been promised' (180[b])) and Augustine, that it is not '*manifestata sine lege*', for it is '*testificata per legem*', but it is manifested '*sine legis iustitia*' (181[a]). While agreeing

---

[2] Altered in 1556 to leave the meaning of the word undecided.

[3] 1532: 'The principal *propositio* and *status* of the chief *disputatio* in this epistle is here established. Righteousness is now revealed without the Law – the righteousness of God by the faith of Jesus Christ etc. And the sum of the *propositio* is that assuredly by mercy on account of Christ we are reckoned righteous before God, and not on account of our works or our virtues; but yet this mercy must be apprehended by faith' (56[r-v]).

with Melanchthon that 'The righteousness of God signifies the acceptance by which God accepts us' (56ᵛ), Bucer wishes to include regeneration and sanctification in his definition of righteousness: 'Philip Melanchthon takes the righteousness of God here for the acceptance by which God accepts us; this agrees with our own understanding of it as the incomparable goodness revealed in Christ by which he forgives sins and imputes righteousness and bestows eternal life; and he initiates it by inbreathing a new mind and a devotion to godliness'(180ᵇ). Calvin is undecided whether *iustitia* is man's righteousness or God's: 'It is doubtful why he calls the righteousness which we obtain by faith the righteousness of God. Either because it alone stands firm before God, or because it is that which the Lord in his mercy bestows on us. Either interpretation fits in well and we do not argue for the one side or the other' (68⁴⁵⁻⁴⁹).

πεφανέρωται – **manifestata**] Caietan apparently refers this to the gift of the Spirit: 'In due order the righteousness of God, which justifies a man absolutely, was revealed on the day of Pentecost and without the yoke of the Law' (X G). Bucer, Calvin, and Melanchthon take it of the preaching of the Gospel (see above, under *Nunc*); Grimani seems to agree, although he is by no means clear:'The righteousness of God, which was revealed and preached [foretold?] in the Law and the prophets, we believers now attain through the faith and belief (*per fidem, et credulitatem*) which we have concerning Christ Jesus our Lord, believing not only that he was sent by God, but also that by his death he made satisfaction for our sins' (31ᵛ).

μαρτυρουμένη – **testificata**] Bullinger: 'verified and confirmed' (33).

22. Δικαιοσύνη δὲ θεοῦ διὰ πίστεως Ἰησοῦ Χριστοῦ εἰς πάντας, καὶ ἐπὶ πάντας τοὺς πιστεύοντας. οὐ γάρ ἐστι διαστολή.
(*Eras ed. 1527*)
Χριστου,   Er¹ Compl   παντας και   Compl

iustitia autem dei: per fidem Iesu Christi in omnes et super

omnes qui credunt in eum. non enim est distinctio. (*Steph
Vulg 1528*)

dei per   Er⁴Vg Compl St³²   Christi,   Er⁴Vg

Iustitia vero dei per fidem Iesu Christi in omnes, et super
omnes eos qui credunt. Non enim est distinctio. (*Eras vers
1527*)

omnes et   Eras vers⁵

EXEGESIS

Bucer: 'This is an *occupatio* (forestalling). The Apostle has
said that the righteousness of God is revealed in the age of the
Gospel by faith and revealed to Jews and Gentiles alike. It
might be objected that God manifested himself to the
outstanding saints as their great reward, because it was clearly
revealed. Therefore "There is no distinction" ' (181ᵇ). But
Bullinger: 'This is both a brief explanation and also a succinct
giving of a reason or proving. He has said that none is
excluded from this righteousness. Now he proves it' (33);
similarly Caietan: 'the apostle proves that the righteousness
of God by the faith of Jesus Christ is in all and upon all' (X I).

διὰ πίστεως – **per fidem**] Haresche: 'by the Catholic faith;
and that because whatever a Christian (*christicola*) knows
about the aforesaid righteousness of God he knows by the
mediation of the Faith (*mediante fide*)' (lxviiᵛ).

εἰς πάντας, καὶ ἐπι πάντας τοὺς πιστεύοντας – **in omnes et
super omnes qui credunt**] Bullinger: 'This is a pleonasm.
By this figure he wishes to express that the salvation belongs
to all believers absolutely without exception' (33); and
Calvin: 'He repeats the same thing in different forms of
expression *ad auxesim*, by which he may the better express
that here faith alone is required, and that no distinction is to
be made between Gentiles and Jews' (71⁵³⁻⁵⁶).

23. πάντες γὰρ ἥμαρτον, καὶ ὑστεροῦνται τῆς δόξης τοῦ θεοῦ.
(*Eras ed. 1527*)
[no variant readings in relevant edd]

Omnes enim peccaverunt: et egent gloria dei. (*Steph Vulg
1528*)

peccaverunt,   Er⁴Vg   peccaverunt et   Compl

Omnes enim peccaverunt, ac destituuntur gloria dei. (*Eras vers 1527*)

[no variant readings Eras vers^1-3,5]

EXEGESIS

Melanchthon: 'This is a repetition of the universal statement which teaches that all men are guilty of sin and under the wrath of God' (CXʳ).[4]

τῆς δόξης – **gloria**] This word comes in for considerable comment. We note first the linking of *gloria* and *gratia*, which had been a variant reading in some Vulgate traditions. Erasmus: 'And the Greek is *gloria*, not *gratia* [*add*: just as we read in the more emended Latin codices, δόξης τοῦ θεοῦ. – A³ *add*: For God is glorified in that, in his goodness, he saves the human race – A⁵]' (A¹428; A³299; A⁵358). Grimani refers to *gratia* as a variant reading: 'Some read this verse differently. They say it should read that we lack *gratia*, not *gloria*, *Dei*, because it does not agree with the Greek reading and is not consistent with reason. For those who have sinned seem rather to have lacked the grace than the glory of God, because grace is given to man before glory' (31ᵛ). Calvin does not refer to the variant in his translation or his comments; but it is interesting to note that he has a sentence which reads in 1540: 'It would have been sufficient to set *gloria* against merits' but in which 1551 and 1556 correct *gloria* to *gratia* (71^99&n. – but this may be merely a printer's misreading of a badly written word). The word itself is defined variously. Bucer: *gloria* 'seems here to mean the singular presence and dignity of God shining in a more divine life, that is, a godly and innocent life. This is certainly the highest dignity of man and is, properly speaking, what Scripture calls כָּבוֹד ' (181ᵇ). Bullinger takes *gloria Dei* as the *imago Dei* and therefore as soundness, sanctity and perfection (33). But Calvin: 'He takes *gloria Dei* for that which has a standing before God, as in John 12 [43], "They loved the glory of man more than the glory of God" (72^85-87). So also, apparently, Caietan: 'they lacked glory with God' (X K).

---

[4] 1532: 'He repeats by the way the antithesis of the former *propositio*, why we may not be righteous on account of our virtues' (62ᵛ-63ʳ).

24. Δικαιούμενοι δωρεὰν τῇ αὐτοῦ χάριτι, διὰ τῆς
ἀπολυτρώσεως τῆς ἐν Χριστῷ Ἰησοῦ, (*Eras ed. 1527*)
Ιησου.   Er¹

iustificati gratis per gratiam ipsius, per redemptionem quae
est in Christo Iesu, (*Steph Vulg 1528*)
ipsius per   Compl   Iesu: Er⁴Vg Compl

Iustificantur autem gratis per illius gratiam, per redemptionem quae est in Christo Iesu, (*Eras vers 1527*)
[no variant readings Er vers¹⁻³,⁵]

EXEGESIS

Δικαιούμενοι δωρεὰν – **iustificati gratis**] Erasmus: 'It is a
passive participle, but in the present tense; and so we translate
it "*Iustificantur autem*" (But they are justified, or, But they are
being justified). I have added the conjunction to make the
sense clearer' (A¹428;A³299;A⁵358); followed by Caietan:
'*Iustificati* freely by his grace.   This is a present participle
passive, lacking in Latin. All sinned and are destitute of glory
with God, but are justified, that is, from sinners become
righteous; and freely, not of works but gratuitously' (X K).
Bucer: 'in this *oratio* something seems to be missing. It has
δικαιούμενοι δωρεὰν etc. (being justified freely), when from
the words what ought to follow seems to be δικαιοῦνται δὲ
(but they are justified). Some add of their own accord the
particle   δέ, using it adversatively, and read "*Iustificantur
autem etc.*" (But they are justified). If anyone wishes to join
this with "in all and upon all", so that "there is no distinction
etc." is interposed as a παρένθεσις, it will be an *enallage casus*
(a change of case), for it would have been said εἰς πάντας καὶ
ἐπὶ πάντας πιστεύοντας δικαιουμένους (unto all and upon all
the justified who believe). But it can also be that part of the
oratio is unresolved (*absolutae*); for to admit an *anapodota*
where the *oratio* may particularly serve, is not unusual for the
Apostle. But however we read it, it is at any rate clear that the
Apostle wanted to explain on what condition the righteousness of God is manifested now, that is, in the time of the

Gospel – freely, from his benevolence alone, by the interced-
ing redemption of Christ, God displays it to all who believe
in Christ the Lord' (182ᵇ-183ᵃ). Accordingly the *Metaphrasis*
renders it: 'The righteousness, I say, of God, which exists in
Jesus Christ, is revealed to all Jews and Gentiles who believe.
For there is no distinction; for all have sinned and are destitute
of the dignity of the divine destiny (*sors*). But they are made
righteous freely by his benevolence, by the redemption
effected through Christ Jesus' (44ᵇ).

δωρεάν ' – **gratis**] Bullinger: 'observe the particle *gratis*,
which has its own explanation affixed – *per gratiam*. But grace
takes completely away the merit of our works' (34).

διὰ τῆς ἀπολυτρώσεως – **per redemptionem**] Erasmus:
'which is properly, redemption of a captive, released by a
price paid for him [*add*: which in French is commonly called
rainson (= rançon) A³˒⁵]' (A¹428;A³299;A⁵358). But Melanchthon refers it to sacrifice: 'Because the angry God requires
some sacrifice (*victimam*) for sin'; and 'Here we learn that sin
was so great that God could be placated by no sacrifice but
the death of his Son' (CXIʳ).⁵

25.ὃν προέθετο ὁ θεὸς ἱλαστήριον, διὰ τῆς πίστεως ἐν τῷ αὐτοῦ
αἵματι, εἰς ἔνδειξιν τῆς δικαιοσύνης αὐτοῦ, διὰ τὴν πάρεσιν τῶν
προγεγονότων ἁμαρτημάτων, (*Eras ed.1527*)

| ἱλαστηριον δια | Compl | αιματι εις | Compl |
| αυτου δια | Compl | αμαρτηματων εν | Compl |

quem proposuit Deus propitiatorem per fidem in sanguine
ipsius, ad ostensionem iustitiae suae, propter remissionem
praecedentium delictorum, (*Steph Vulg 1528*)

| ipsius ad | Compl | | suae propter | Er⁴Vg | Compl |
| delictorum in | Er⁴Vg | Compl | | | |

quem proposuit deus reconciliatorem per fidem interveniente
ipsius sanguine, ad ostensionem iusticiae suae, propter

⁵ 1532: 'For there must be a certain price, a certain sacrifice for the
sins of the world, by which sacrifice God is appeased and may be
reconciled to men. And this sacrifice is Christ' (64ᵛ).

remissionem praeteritorum peccatorum, (*Eras vers 1527*)
reconciliatorem, Er vers[2,3]

EXEGESIS

Many parts of this verse occasioned debate. Bullinger
found it difficult: 'The thread of the discourse, or the diction,
and the brevity make the meaning obscure' (35).

προέθετο - **proposuit**] Calvin: 'Here *proponere* does not mean
to produce or display (*proferre*) or to present openly (*in
medium repraesentare*), but to pre-ordain and pre-determine; so
that it refers to God's mercy which spontaneously sought out
a way to help our wretchedness' (73[15-24n]). So also Pellicanus:
'The Apostle here explains on what condition Christ effected
redemption, and says that God determined it from the
beginning; and long before he came in the flesh he had [been?]
destined to this, and that it was no novelty but predestined
before the ages' (44); and Bucer: 'And so, first, he declares
that God so determined in himself from the beginning. For
although the death of Christ is the cause of redemption, yet
that is only because the Father so decreed' (183[a]).

ίλαστήριον – **propitiatorem / propitiatorium / propitiationem**] Our commentators were exercised over the
rendering of this word. Even some who take the Vulgate as
their text change its *propitiationem* tacitly or openly in their
comments or in the text, as does Caietan. Erasmus: 'that is,
Propiciationem, or rather, *propiciatorium*. [*add*:Origen saw this
as referring to the *propiciatorium* of the Jews, a type of our
Christ, as also he mentions the blood. Theophylact expounds
it similarly, and before him, Chrysostom; finally also,
Augustine in the book *de spiritu et litera*, cap. 13. – A[3,5]] Unless
perhaps the translator takes ίλαστήριον as masculine [*add*: as
τὸν σωτήριον – A[5]]' (A[1]429;A[3]299;A[5]358). Bucer has a long
textual and lexicographical note, in the latter part of which he
traces the usage in the rest of Scripture. His earlier comments
are: 'For the most part they render it *propiciatorium*. But the
translator of Origen writes in one and the same sense as the
Apostle that Christ is truly called *propiciatorium*, *propiciatio*,

and *propiciator*; and he says that this is more frequently to be found in the earliest (*novissimum*) Latin codices. All these three words are signified in Greek by ἱλαστήριον ' (183[a-b]). Calvin is not entirely decided: 'The word ἱλαστήριον is best taken as an allusion to the old *propiciatorium*; for he teaches that the reality of what was there figured is displayed in Christ. Yet the opinion of anyone who prefers to take it more simply cannot be rejected, and it may be left undecided' (73[34-37]); his rendering of *propitiationem* in 1540 and 1551 gave way to *propitiatorium* in 1556. Caietan: 'The Greek word for *ad propitiatorium* is ambiguous, for it may be either masculine or neuter, being in the accusative. But the masculine seems to fit the purpose better; so that the sense is "whom God set forth as a *placator*"' (XI B).

ἐν τῷ αὐτοῦ αἵματι – **in sanguine ipsius**] For Bucer *sanguis* is equivalent not so much to death as to violent death, 'for Scripture is accustomed to express violent death (as it is called) by this synecdoche' (183[b]). Calvin, however, refers *sanguis* to the death on the Cross, which comprehended the whole self-giving of Jesus from his birth to his death: 'By naming only the blood, he did not intend to exclude the other parts of redemption, but rather to comprehend the whole under one part' (73[37-40]).

τῆς δικαιοσύνης – **iustitiae**] Grimani takes *iustitia* here as justice in opposition to mercy (33[r]). Melanchthon: 'The sentence will be clearer if we change its form: "To the showing of his righteousness" – that is, that God may declare that he himself is going to justify. [*1540 adds:* And it is an antithesis. Above, he accuses all when he says, "We are none of us righteous, even when we have the works of the law". But now in Christ God reveals his righteousness, that is that he will justify, as he promised in the promises that he would give a new righteousness, new and eternal life, that he would restore the human race, abolishing sin and death']⁶ (CXII[r-v]).

διὰ τὴν πάρεσιν – **propter remissionem**] Erasmus: 'It is

---

⁶ 1532: 'For righteousness here signifies justification, as above; that is, the righteousness by which he reckons us righteous. And the antithesis is also to be held, that at the same time he declares us not to be righteous by our cleanness or works' (65[v]).

surprising that the copy Ambrose followed should read, *Propter propositum praecedentium delictorum* (on account of the purpose. . .). For the Greeks have πάρεσιν, not πρόθεσιν – unless perhaps the Ambrosian codex itself is at fault. And what he adds in interpretation, *Sciens deus propositum benignitatis suae* (God, knowing the purpose of his kindness), suggests that he read *propositum* and not *remissionem*' (A[3]299;A[5]358). Calvin: 'I would prefer, if I might, to take διά as *per* (through); for you will have a frigid sense if you take it causally' (74[44-47n]). But in his translation he retained the Vulgate reading *propter*.

τὴν προγεγονότων ἁμαρτημάτων – **praecedentium delictorum**] Three of our authors take this as meaning sins committed before the Incarnation, linking it with Christ's descent into hell. Thus Bullinger: 'Hence it appears that the death of Christ absolved also the saints of the Old Testament. Peter shows this clearly enough in his first epistle, and so also does the article of faith "he descended into hell"' (35). And, more fully, Haresche: 'The Apostle confines it to preceding offences, so that no-one may think that those are remitted which are done after the receiving of grace. For God remits preceding offences when he bestows his grace on men and justifies them, so that they may then live justly. In the power of the passion of Christ exhibited, sins are remitted which precede the advent of Christ:. . .the sins of men who lived before Christ's Incarnation and were kept in Limbo on account of the guilt of original sin' (lxix[r]). His former point, he goes on to say, applies also to the original sin of infants preceding the grace of God in Baptism and also the *peccata actualia* which in adults precede contrition and grace (lxix[r-v]). Grimani: 'From this it is clear that the merit of the blood of Christ has power to save not only us who are found in this state of grace, but also those before us who lived uprightly, whether in the law of nature or in the written Law' (33[r]). Melanchthon, however, refers it to sins committed after the reception of grace: 'They say that this clause is added to teach us that the Gospel does not give licence for sinning and we know that sins are remitted to those who do penance [*or*: repent], in whom sin is mortified. But it does not follow from this that lapses after remission, if they again repent, cannot be pardoned. . .This is therefore a description of present remission in general, not exclusively of subsequent remissions' (CXII[v]).[7] Similarly Calvin: 'But that he confines remission to those sins only which were in the past gives no support to the error of the Novatians, who deprived Christians of the hope of pardon if after the cleansing of Baptism they were again stained with sin' (74[51-67n]).

26. ἐν τῇ ἀνοχῇ τοῦ θεοῦ, πρὸς ἔνδειξιν τῆς δικαιοσύνης αὐτοῦ, ἐν τῷ νῦν καιρῷ, εἰς τὸ εἶναι αὐτὸν δίκαιον, καὶ δικαιοῦνται τὸν ἐκ πίστεως Ἰησοῦ. (Eras ed. 1527)

αυτου εν Compl

in sustentatione dei, ad ostensionem iusticiae eius in hoc tempore. ut sit ipse iustus, et iustificans eius qui est ex fide Iesu Christi. (Steph Vulg 1528)

dei ad Compl   iustitiae suae, St[32]   tempore: Compl Er[4]Vg   iustus et Compl Er[4]Vg   eius[2]] eum St[32] Compl Er[4]Vg   ex fide est Compl Er[4]Vg

quae deus toleravit, ad ostendendam iustitiam suam, in praesenti tempore: in hoc, ut ipse sit iustus: et iustificans eum qui est ex fide Iesu. (Eras vers 1527)

suam in   Er vers[5]

EXEGESIS

ἐν τῇ ἀνοχῇ– **in sustentatione**] Erasmus: 'that is, in patience and longsuffering' (A[1]429; A[3]299; A[5]358). Calvin: '*tolerantia*; that is gentleness (*mansuetudo*)' (74[70-71n]).

πρὸς ἔνδειξιν – **ad ostensionem**] Calvin: 'Paul's deliberate repetition of this clause is emphatic and very necessary; for nothing is harder than to persuade a man that he should ascribe to God all he has received and not claim anything as his own doing' (75[76-78]). Caietan: 'These words are joined with those preceding, that is, "in his blood", to show the

[7] 1532: 'properly he describes a state before forgiveness. It is not exclusive, as if afterwards none can back-slide, or that sins cannot be forgiven again' (66[v]).

reason why in his blood, why God set Jesus as the placator in his
blood, to show his righteousness' (XI D).
   Ἰησοῦ – **Iesu Christi**] Caietan: '*"Christi"* is superfluous'
(XI E).

27. Ποῦ οὖν ἡ καύχησις; ἐξεκλείσθη. διὰ ποίου νόμου; τῶν
ἔργων; οὐχὶ, ἀλλὰ διὰ νόμου πίστεως. (*Eras ed. 1527*)
εξεκλεισθη · Er³   ουχι.   Compl

Ubi est ergo gloriatio tua? Exclusa est. Per quam legem?
Factorum? Non: sed per legem fidei. (*Steph Vulg 1528*)
Non. Er⁴Vg Compl

Ubi igitur gloriatio? Exclusa est. Per quam legem? Operum?
Non, imo per legem fidei. (*Eras vers 1527*)
Non: Er vers⁵

EXEGESIS

   Grimani seems to refer this verse exclusively to the Jews:
'he now concludes, saying, "O Jews, where is now thy
glorying?"' (33ᵛ). Caietan, less decisively, says that it
excludes all human glorying but is especially directed against
the Jews (XI F). Calvin takes it universally, using the first
person plural throughout (76).
   τῶν ἔργων – **[lex] factorum**] Caietan: 'He calls the Law of
Moses (which comprises *moralia*, *caerimonialia*, and *iudicialia*)
the law of deeds (*factorum*), because it was the law of works
(*operum*), even as also whatever else is written Law. And in
this is also comprehended the natural law, which likewise is
the law of deeds' (XI G). Haresche: 'The law of deeds
(*factorum*) is the old Law viewed in regard to its ceremonial
precepts' (lxxʳ).
   διὰ νόμου πίστεως – **per legem fidei**] Bucer here defines law
as "a certain force, calling us away from some things and
impelling us to others' (201ᵇ – borrowed by Guilliaud (20)),
and accordingly interprets *lex fidei* as 'the power (*vim*) of
faith, which surely governs the whole man' (201ᵇ). But

Haresche: 'The law of faith is that by which we not only believe Christ and in Christ (*christo et christum*) but also into Christ (*in christum*). And this law is inward, disposing the movements of the heart' (lxx^r). Calvin dismissed the phrase tersely: 'The name of law is improperly applied to faith' (76^30–31).

28. Λογιζόμεθα οὖν πίστει δικαιοῦσθαι ἄνθρωπον χωρὶς ἔργων νόμου. (*Eras ed. 1527*)
[no variant readings in relevant edd]

Arbitramur enim iustificari hominem per fidem sine operibus legis. (*Steph Vulg 1528*)
[no variant readings in relevant edd]

Arbitramur igitur fide iustificari hominem absque operibus legis. (*Eras vers 1527*)
[no variant readings Er vers^1–3,5]

EXEGESIS

Λογιζόμεθα – **Arbitramur**] Erasmus: 'We reckon, or We gather, therefore. For [Theophylact – A¹ Vulgarius –] interprets it συλλογιζόμεθα *velut hoc iam argumentando collegerit*' (A¹429;A³299;A⁵358-9). Bucer: 'He has λογιζόμεθα , which he does not take as "to think" or "to reckon" but "to affirm as certain"' (202^a).
οὖν or γὰρ – **enim**] Caietan: '*enim* (for) for *igitur* (therefore)' (XI G).

EXPOSITION

Caietan

To explain the statement 'by the works of the law there shall no flesh be justified before him' (3.20) Caietan differentiates between the righteousness of the work and the righteousness, or justice, of God; or rather, he differentiates between their effects. The *iustitia operis* is limited in its scope and makes only the work to which it relates righteous and, correspondingly, makes the one doing that work righteous.

The *iustitia dei*, on the contrary, is unlimited and justifies absolutely, and this 'because it blots out the sins which it finds in a man' (X E-F). The Law gives only the knowledge and not the remission of sins, for *cognitio* in 3.20 is opposed to *remissio* (X F).

The word "manifested" in v.21 gives rise to the question as to when the *iustitia dei* was revealed. Caietan's answer is that 'the *iustitia dei*, which justifies a man absolutely, was manifested on the day of Pentecost and thereafter without the yoke of the Law' (X G). His reason for this relation is no doubt to be found in Acts 2.38. Those who were 'pricked in heart' by Peter's sermon asked, 'What shall we do?' To which Peter replied: 'Repent and be baptized every one of you in the name of Jesus Christ unto the remission of your sins; and ye shall receive the gift of the Holy Ghost'. Here are all the elements of justification and therefore of righteousness – repentance, Baptism, forgiveness, the gift of the Spirit, the name of Jesus Christ.

Caietan links 'the righteousness of God by the faith of Jesus Christ' (v.22) with 'the righteousness of God has been revealed from faith to faith' (1.17). The earlier verse, however, had not explained what the *materia* of faith is, or the manner in which God's righteousness is connected or joined with us: 'Now we have both. "The righteousness of God by faith" – here is the manner in which the *iustitia dei* is applied to us. "OF JESUS CHRIST" – here is the *materia fidei*' (X H). Both the manner in which and the *materia* are universal, for the verse says, 'in all and upon all'. It is saying clearly that 'through the righteousness of works neither Jews nor Gentiles were justified with the righteousness which remits sins. This is done only by the righteousness of God through the faith of Jesus Christ' (X I).

Verse 24 brings him to the *ratio* or method of justification. It is through 'the redemption which is in Christ Jesus'. Hence in justification the *gratia* and the *iustitia* of God concur. Caietan is certainly at this point (hitherto it has not been clear) thinking of *iustitia* as justice rather than righteousness. Having committed himself in effect to an opposition between grace and justice (for why else would it be necessary to say that in justification they concur?), he is able to assert triumphantly that therefore justification is not by grace alone. This it would be only if God remitted sins without any payment being made, something he never did and does not do. The element of justice consists in redemption, 'that is, in the payment of the price which Jesus made in releasing us from the captivity or slavery of sin' (XI A). But an inconsistency still seems to remain in the use of the word *gratis*, freely. If it is *gratis*, then it is without the payment of a price; if a price is paid, it is not *gratis*. 'The solution is that Holy Scripture does not say that we are justified *sola gratia*, but *per gratiam simul et iustitiam* (by both grace and justice). But these are both of God; that is, by the grace of God and by the justice of God and not by the justice [or righteousness] of men. . . Thus the grace of God excludes, not the justice of God, but the justice [righteousness] of men. And the redemption effected by Christ is the justice of God and not our own justice [righteousness], because Jesus Christ himself is true God' (XI A-B).

In spite of some obscurity, we may take it that Caietan wished to give a more central place to Christ than he had done hitherto, for he not only insists on taking the phrase 'in Christ Jesus' literally (instead of 'by Christ Jesus'), but also uses the ambiguity in the words *propitiator* and *propitiatorium* to make Christ himself, rather than only remission of sins, the gift of grace, and at the same time to extol grace rather more highly than he might seem to have done: 'The redemption of Jesus Christ does not diminish but rather increases God's grace towards us; so that we may understand from divine grace that we are not only given pardon but also the *placator* (the one who makes peace)' (XI B).

Caietan sees the Epistle as a gradually unfolding argument which reaches its first climax here in the phrase 'by faith in his blood': 'Little by little he unfolds the mystery. In the beginning he had said, "from faith to faith". Afterwards he explained that it was "by the faith of Jesus Christ". Now he explains more precisely and clearly the faith of the death of Jesus Christ by saying "through faith in his blood". For faith in the blood of Jesus is faith which depends on the death

which was by the outpouring of the blood of Jesus' (XI C).
Caietan steadfastly accords the primacy to grace in a further
note: 'Notice that three times the Apostle uses *per* (through).
First by saying, "*Through* his grace"; secondly, "*through* the
redemption"; and thirdly, "*through* faith in his blood". Thus
we can understand that for justifying us there coincide, first
from God's side, grace, then on the side of Jesus Christ the
justice of redemption, and finally, on our side, faith in the
blood of Jesus Christ. Grace indeed holds the first place,
inasmuch as it also belongs to the second and third. The
second is of grace in that it constitutes the mode (*rationem*) of
God's righteousness. The third (that is, faith) is the application and conjunction of them both with ourselves' (XI C).[8]

Why did God set forth Jesus as the *placator* in his blood? It
was (v.26) 'to show his *iustitia*'. 'For, to show the divine
iustitia God decreed that Jesus should placate God in his own
blood, paying the price for human redemption' (XI D). In
this we can clearly see the Apostle's reason for differentiating
between *iustitia dei* and *iustitia operum*. Only the *iustitia dei*
remits "preceding sins" (XI D).

Where the verse goes on to say 'that he might be just and the
justifier of him who is of the faith of Jesus Christ' Caietan
comments that two points are to be noted. The first is that God
is not only merciful or gracious but also just *in executione*; 'and
this is precisely the mode (*ratio*) of the divine *iustitia* which he
has shown' (XI E). The second is that God justifies him who is
of the faith of Jesus. 'And this points straight to the circumscrip-
tion of "*iustitia* at this time" – that is, of the death of Jesus. A
man is justified in no other sort of way than by the mode
(*ratione*) of faith in the blood of Jesus' (XI E-F).

Verse 27, with its distinction between the *lex factorum* and the

---

[8] R.C. Jenkins quotes this passage alongside one from Cranmer's
Homily of Salvation to demonstrate that parts of the homily 'were
taken almost *verbatim* from the Commentary of the Cardinal, whose
works were well known to, and often quoted by, our reformers'
(Pre-Tridentine Doctrine, 70). But the supposed quotations are far from
verbatim. That under consideration here agrees both with Caietan and
also with Calvin's three causes of justification. Moreover, the only
English Reformers to mention Caietan were all, according to the Parker
Society index, Elizabethan.

lex fidei, evokes from Caietan an ambiguous statement of faith viewed as works: 'You may ask in what way the law of faith is distinguished by Paul from the law of works, even from moral works, since faith also is included in the class of works – for to believe is our work. The solution is that to believe in him who justifies the ungodly depends on an external *iustitia* (*iustitia aliena*), that is, the *iustitia dei* through Christ. But the other works depend on our own righteousness – that is, a work is good according to itself and makes the one who habitually does it good (*bonum reddit habentem*). And therefore the righteousness of faith is distinguished over against the righteousness of works' (XI G-H). Here on the one hand he classes faith as a work, presumably in the sense of a meritorious work, while on the other hand he places its virtue, not in itself as such, but in its object, in that it apprehends the *iustitia aliena*, the *iustitia Dei*. If we re-phrase this and say that the faith which apprehends the *iustitia aliena* is a meritorious work which is rewarded with righteousness or justification, we see that Caietan is still operating within the sphere of justification by works.

The reconciliation of 2.13 with 3.20, which we saw under the earlier verse, has to be revived here. The Apostle does not mean, in saying that a man is justified without the works of the Law, to go back on the promise that the doers of the Law will be justified. What is intended is the power which justifies a man *absolutè*, the justifying power which remits sins (XI G).

Guilliaud

Of Guilliaud we need again say very little. His exposition is in this section gathered less from Bucer and largely from Thomas Aquinas and Caietan. This is why we have placed him immediately after Caietan. His interpretation is governed by the current Romanist view of salvation. That we are justified by faith does not mean, as the Pelagians say, that faith is itself the meritorious cause of justification, but 'because in the justification by which we are justified by God, the first movement of the mind to God is by faith' (18). The order of salvation is shown by Paul's threefold use of the word *per* – '*per* gratiam ipsius', '*per* redemptionem', '*per*

fidem in sanguine'. These three things concur in justification.
'Grace comes first, which is from God's side, who does
everything by his gratuitous goodness. Then, from Christ's
side, the righteousness of redemption by his own blood shed
and offered as the price of human redemption. Then from our
side faith, by which gift from God we are moved, depending
on the death of Jesus Christ' (18–19).

Haresche

Haresche takes up again, indeed repeats *ad literam*, what he has
laid down on 2.13 on the threefold law, the *lex humana*, the *lex
divina naturalis*, and the *lex divina purè positiva* (see p. 133). But it
is not clear why he thinks he needs to raise this issue again, for
now he is, like so many of our commentators, about to use the
distinction between moral law and ceremonial law and it is to
the fourfold distinction of justification (*effectivè*, *meritoriè*,
exequutivè and *dispositivè*, and *reputativè*) that he will turn to
interpret 3.20 and to square it with 2.13.

'By the works of the law shall no flesh living be justified.'
This refers to works which precede faith, or possibly the
Faith (for it is not always clear whether some of our authors
are referring to works done under the old Covenant and
therefore prior to Christian Faith, or works done by an
individual in Christendom before he believes). Or else it
refers to the carnal and not spiritual keeping of the Law. By
such works a man will not be justified. Haresche at once
points out that there can be no question of any works at all
justifying *effectivè*. What is at issue is whether they justify
dispositivè. In fact they do not, for according to Rom. 14.23
'whatsoever is not of faith is sin', and it has already been said
that these works precede faith. If they are sin, they clearly do
not dispose a man to grace or justification. But then he
remembers 1.20: 'for the invisible things of him are clearly
seen by the creature of the world, understood through the
things that are made, even his eternal power and divinity',
which he has understood to mean that the Gentiles who were
without the written law could have a knowledge of God. He
reconciles the passages by means of the *dispositivè* and so
builds up his picture of justification: 'I do not wish to say that

. . . some were not rewarded temporally, and that, if they did not resist the knocking (*pulsatio*) with which the Holy Spirit knocks at their hearts but acquiesce in it and are illuminated, so that they behold in their minds, through the things which are made, the Lord God also, they will then have a certain faith about God, in the manner already declared in Chapter 1. . . and then the works will be subsequent to this faith and so will not be sins. And therefore these will dispose them to grace'; and, of course, conversely (lxiiij^{r-v}). But, Haresche not only reconciles 3.20 with 2.13 by the argument: 'By the works of the law man is not justified, because such works precede faith'; but he establishes the need for works in justification when he concludes: 'nevertheless, works, done in sin, even mortal sin, avail for a temporal reward and the disposition of grace, so long as they proceed from faith' (lxiij^{v}).

When we turn to his *Expositio textus ad literam* we find only a continuation and repetition of what he has already said under 2.13 and 3.20ff. *Per fidem* in v.21 means the Catholic Faith (lxvij^{v}), that is, apparently, the body of Catholic belief, which is above human faculties and is received from God (lxviij^{r}). In 3.28 *per fidem* is taken as 'the medium necessary for salvation'. Faith is meritorious, 'partly in that it depends on Christ and his passion exhibited and partly for its own act freely brought forth *(elicito)* and accepted for eternal life'. The 'law of faith' is explained in opposition to 'the law of deeds', that is, 'the old Law viewed in respect of its ceremonial precepts'. Unfortunately, the explanation is enigmatic and impossible to translate literally: 'The law of faith is that by which we not only believe *christo et christum*, but also *in christum*' (lxx^{r}). Presumably he intends a distinction between faith as belief, assent, and trust. *Iustificati gratis* is interpreted entirely in terms of the sacramental system of the infusion of grace at Baptism in a first justification, *ex opere operato*, followed by the second justification by which adults are made more just and more acceptable to God: 'because by the gratuitous grace of God exhibited by the passion of Christ infants are justified with the first justification in receiving the grace of Baptism conferred upon them *ex opere operato*, by which they are made righteous without any act of their own. And also because adults are justified with their first justification by the gratuitous grace of God shown by the passion of Christ and the shedding of his blood, and so not by their justifying acts, whether inward or outward. And this because acts preceding the first justification, even if sometimes they are morally good, are yet not meritorious, because they are not produced by the *gratia gratum faciente* of God. And this because such grace does not precede the first justification in time although it may be concomitant with it. And because also in the second justification, by which adults are made more just and more *grati* to God, although a meritorious act of the will may be concurrent with it, partly from the merit of Christ's passion and partly from itself. And this, because it is freely produced by the spiritually mediating help of God and by his *gratia gratum faciente* and therefore is accepted for eternal life, and yet because such an act is produced by the special mediating help of God, which is freely given by God' (lxviii^v).

The *praecedentia delicta* are, as he has already said under 2.13, sins committed before the Incarnation. Those who committed them were kept *'in lymbo*, on account of original sin' (lxix^r). And he expressly denies that it refers to sins of baptized Christians: 'The Apostle determines "preceding sins" so that no one may think that those sins are remitted which he commits after he has received grace' (lxix^r). But, of course, any sin which precedes grace is remitted when grace is received – the original sin of infants is remitted in the grace of Baptism, and the actual sins of adults are remitted in the grace of penance (lxix^{r-v}).

Grimani

Grimani's exposition of this passage is of considerable interest as an example of how far a Romanist could go in the proclamation of *sola gratia* and that without suspicion of heresy. Nevertheless, for all the strong expressions he uses, he cannot be said really to teach *sola gratia*.

His starting point in 3.20 is to identify "the works of the

law" with the ceremonial Law. Indeed, he seems to go even further and to include heathen ceremonies: 'And he calls the works of the law circumcision and those sacrifices which were performed in the law of nature or the written Law, which were performed as ceremonies' (30ᵛ). But, leaving that aside, he has at any rate left himself a loop-hole by differentiating between works. It is on this basis that he returns to the reconciliation of 2.13 and 3.20. Both statements are true if the phrase 'works of the law' is taken in two different ways: 'But how is none justified before God by the works of the law, when he had earlier said, "The doers of the law will be justified"? We have to consider which are the works of the law, indifferently called works of the natural law and moral works and natural works. If anyone did these works before the advent of Christ, then these works would [i.e. in the future] by grace be meritorious. But there are works of the law which we call ceremonial or judicial, like circumcision, immolations, and sacrifices, which are also called works of the flesh, because they are done in the body and in the flesh. Although they satisfy the Law and men, they do not satisfy God; for they are not the works of the spirit or of the soul, but of the body and of the flesh' (30ᵛ).

The purpose of the Law is not to take sin away but to reveal its *qualitas* and *conditio* (30ᵛ). This is chiefly seen moralistically, in that the Law was ordained principally in order that we should know what actions were sins and so avoid them. But it was also given that we should know the gravity of sin. 'This is why he instituted that ceremonies, sacrifices, and sprinklings of blood should be so diligently observed, so that the multiple and grave kinds of sins should be purged by these expiations, so that when the time of grace should come those who had kept the Law should receive justification' (30ᵛ-31ʳ). He calls the Law the *manifestatrix peccatorum* (31ʳ), and clearly means that before the Incarnation men were not justified before God by the works of the Law although those who did keep the Law were *waiting* to be justified. 'He says "the righteousness of God" to distinguish it from the righteousness of men which was contained in the Law and only justified men in their own eyes, because he who did the Law lived in it; but he was not justified *coram Deo*' (31ʳ).

Righteousness, however, is received by faith (*fides* or *credulitas*), faith in Christ as the Son of God, faith in his death as the absolution of our sins: 'The righteousness of God, which was revealed and foretold in the Law and prophets, we believers now receive by the faith and by the simple trust (*credulitas*) which we have about Christ Jesus our Lord, believing not only that he was sent by God but also that by his death he made satisfaction for our sins. This, I say, is the faith which believes that the *iustitia* of God was effected for the absolution of our sins, because those who believe in Christ believe also that God the Father wished his Son, who is Christ, to suffer, so that he might justly make satisfaction for our sins and thence all might attain justification for their sins' (31ᵛ).

It is when we arrive at 3.24, with its unequivocal *gratis per gratiam* that Grimani speaks out remarkably for free grace independently of merit. How many students of the Reformation, faced with the following passage in a set of context questions, would ascribe it to a Roman Cardinal and not to a Reformer? 'It is as if he said, "Do not think that you are righteous either by the good works of nature or by the works of the written Law, so that justification is surrendered to you as a reward and wages of your works and labours, for it will be surrendered to you freely. For what works of ours, what merits could have deserved that God himself should take human nature and suffer a most shameful death for us? Certainly no work, no merit of ours could be such that we could be justified either by ourselves or by the Law. It was therefore by sheer grace that we were redeemed . . . And so it was by the sole grace of God that without any merits of ours, we received justification" ' (31ᵛ-32ʳ).

But in fact, this passage also must be understood in the light of his interpretation of the works of the written Law as ceremonial. And what he is saying is that man is not justified by the ceremonial works of the Old Covenant or by the good works of nature. Moreover, what is given freely is not the actual bestowal of justification, but the divine activity of the

Incarnation, Cross, and Resurrection of Christ, whose justifying efficacy may be acquired by means of moral works which are meritorious on account of the work of Christ. As we have already seen, the only reason why moral works were not meritorious under the Old Covenant was that the Incarnation had not yet taken place. Therefore all the apparently Evangelical statements – 'without any merits or works of ours or any other satisfaction of ours, but by the sole benignity and grace of God are we freed; God alone redeemed us by the death of his Son, Jesus Christ our Lord' (32^r), or 'Wherefore our justification is not from the Law but from the righteousness of God, which is communicated to us by the faith of Jesus Christ in his blood, without which it is impossible for any to be justified' (33^r) – all such statements lead only to the conclusion that, as he says in the earlier section, 'both are necessary for our salvation – our work and the passion and death of Christ' (23^r) and in the present chapter, 'From this it is clear that the merit of the blood of Christ has power to save not only us who are found in this state of grace, but also those who before lived uprightly, whether in the law of nature or in the written Law' (33^r). We may also note a passage which shows that Grimani does not take the word *solus*, which he uses frequently, with the strictness that the Reformers allow it: 'Solus itaque Filius Dei prae caeteris omnibus positus fuit a Deo propitiator ipsius pro nobis' – 'The Son of God alone, above and beyond all others, was set by God as the propitiation for us'. A Reformer would have said 'The Son of God alone, without any other. . .'.

In the last resort Grimani's adherence to "grace alone", "faith alone", even "Christ alone", is seen to be, not absolute, but relative.

Sadoleto

We saw in the First Part that Sadoleto's commentary was censured by Paris, banned by Rome, and seemingly accepted by Bucer; and we postponed the discussion of this curious state of affairs until the present place since both the criticism by Rome and the praise by Bucer concerned the doctrine of justification by faith. Before we turn to this specific topic, however, we must expound Sadoleto's treatment of this passage.

The part of chapter 3 in which this passage occurs he divides into two sections, vv. 19-26 and vv. 27-31. The whole is directed by St Paul against the Jews, those who are "under the Law" (40;56); and Sadoleto emphasizes this point more than once, making it more precise when he says that the passage is to be taken in its historical context, against the Jews who believed in Christ but could not bear to give up the Law (40; 58).

The starting point comes when Julius Sadoleto raises the problem of the apparent inconsistency between 2.13 and 3.20, and asks James for his opinion. James smartly returns the question to him, saying humorously that it is brotherly to communicate. Julius accepts the challenge and takes up the explanation of the difficulty. There is, he says, a twofold comparison here; first, of Jews with Gentiles, and secondly, of the Law with faith. Keeping the Law is not a matter of carnal (i.e. physical) activities and ceremonies; it consists 'in sincerity of heart and in spiritual works; in these alone is the true observance of the Law' (40;58). It is necessary, if we are to understand him aright, to grasp the distinctions he is making here, for he seems to use the contrast to mean different things. 'Carnal activities and ceremonies' are opposed to 'sincerity of heart and spiritual works'. Here it is essentially an opposition of good works done only externally to good works that spring from a genuine inward motivation. Later, when he explains "all flesh" (v. 20) it becomes, – 'that is every man devoted to the flesh and trusting in the works of the flesh' (41;58); but we are still left asking what he means by "flesh", whether he is thinking of the carnal or, a word he also uses, apparently as its synonym, the corporeal. And again, another use of the opposition comes in his view of the relation between the Old and the New Covenants. The Old Testament, he says, is concerned only with the reward of earthly blessings. This is therefore true of the Law; and those who lived under the Law had only earthly blessings held out before them and were therefore 'tending to the earth and with their hope and affection (*amore*) fixed on the earth, and reckoning that help for living and enjoyment and satisfaction of mind will come to them from the good things and fruits of the earth' (45;65). "Carnal activities and ceremonies" thus means the observance, or attempts at observance, of the Law before the coming of Christ and apart from faith in Christ after he had come.

Here, however, the true observance of the Law is placed 'in sincerity of heart and in spiritual works'. As we have already seen under 1.17seq., such spiritual observance was also open to the Gentiles 'if, by the power of the one God and the truth that they knew, they could turn their hearts to worship and imitate him, so far as is lawful for men' (40;58). The 'truth that they knew' is the belief and persuasion that 'God is one and is the rewarder of those who worship him in godly wise' (41;58).

Does this mean, then, that the Gentiles can be justified apart from Christ? Sadoleto's interpretation of 'the doers of the law shall be justified' seems to open Pelagianism like a crevasse across his path. He bridges it by saying that it all depends what you mean by 'justify', a word that has many meanings in St Paul. 'Here it is not taken for full and perfect justification, but for as much as the Law can give and bestow' (41;58). The Publican may be taken as an example. He went down to his house justified, says Luke. But this was not 'with universal and absolute righteousness', for he was, by his own admission, a sinner, void of righteousness. It was, therefore, only with a partial righteousness, and that 'because he showed himself humble and penitent for his sin before God' (41;58).

He turns against the heretics, for they take occasion from such statements as 3.20 'to remove the works of the Law, and to keep faith alone and magnify it alone, so despising works. And they do this that they may be able to sin freely and with impunity' (41;59). He continues at length in this vein of misrepresentation, which we do no more than note as characteristic of his commentary.

After this parenthesis, he tries to explain further how the doer of the Law can be justified but yet how no flesh can be justified in his sight by the works of the Law. Righteousness is not simply one virtue among others but the universal virtue. According to human righteousness, that is, the universal kind of virtue, a man can be justified from the Law and from the works of the Law, but not before God, for divine righteousness transcends human. 'Only he who has been enlightened by the glory of divine righteousness and by the gift from that same God can be justified' (42;61).

Sadoleto's method of working in this passage is by, so to say, circumambulating the topic, drawing closer to the centre at each piece of exposition. Hence, 'by the law is the knowledge of sin' enables him to repeat what he has already said and draw the original contrast into a new form. Now it is no longer between carnal and ceremonial works and sincerity of heart and spiritual works, but between two kinds of righteousness. He has already said that the righteousness of God transcends human righteousness, that it concerns 'sublime things' (43;62). To this he now opposes the righteousness of the Law. Whereas he has just said that there is a certain justification from the Law, he now seems to limit the righteousness of the Law: 'As if he said that the righteousness which is acquired by the Law is only the knowledge of sin, in order that sin may be avoided' (43;62). If this is so, it is hard to see how a righteousness which consists merely in the knowledge of sin can justify, even if only on a human level.

And now, by means of another reconciliation of scriptural passages, he winds round to the centre. How does I Tim.1.9 ('Knowing that the law is not made for a righteous man, but for the lawless and disobedient') agree with what has been said? We must differentiate between the Mosaic Law and the Faith of Christ. The Old Testament is concerned only with earthly blessings given as a reward for the genuine observance of the Law. The New Testament, however, is concerned with heavenly blessings given to faith: 'faith so sets before us the God who should be loved that we completely cast out of ourselves all love of earthly goods' (43;62). The Mosaic Law therefore is unable to justify, but 'that is admirable and solid and sound [faith], and which obtains the strength (*vim*) of complete righteousness before God, which judges that the standards (*exempla*) of its own deeds and manners are to be

sought from the power and deeds of God' (44;64). In other
words, it seems, God is the *exemplar* who is to be imitated.
Man should act as God has acted. For this, however, it is not
enough for him to look at accounts in Scripture of what God
has done; he needs also to be counselled and taught. 'It is clear
that no perfect counsel, such as is given in the Faith, was
given in the Law. For no notable counsel, resulting in
perfection, can be given to those tending to the earth and
with their hope and affection set on the earth, to those
reckoning that help for living and enjoyment and satisfaction
of mind will come to them from the good things and fruits of
the earth' (45;65). Is not the story of the rich young ruler a
perfect example of this? If perfection came from the Law,
would the Lord have said to one who had fulfilled all the
commandments, 'If you would be perfect, go and sell all that
you have and give to the poor'? (45;65). But, as already
shewn, 'this perfection of work and counsel is in Christ alone
and in the Gospel' (45;66). Therefore we must imitate this
and therefore, also, we are not justified by the Law (45;66).

We are now at the very heart of Sadoleto's understanding
of the passage. A man is justified by faith, that is, by the
imitation of God or Christ. Such a view demands that his first
act is to deny the Reformers' teaching that justification
consists of the forgiveness of sins: 'We do not receive this
justification as remission of sins only, as some interpret this
passage. For in this way, too, justification would be by the
Law, in which God put forward remission of sins to those
making offerings for sin and sacrifices for expiation' (45;66).

A little later he sets out the order of salvation: 'Then that
faith in almighty God stirs up righteousness, through which
he, as he is truly good, not only pardons those who come to
him and give themselves to him by faith, but also adorns
them with almost the same righteousness with which he is
endued and with the same kind of goodness. And then he
receives those so adorned and made holy into grace,
friendship, and relationship, and adopts them as sons and
bestows the blessed and immortal life on them' (46-47;68). If
he means us to take the ordering strictly (and a lot of the
trouble with Sadoleto is that we never know how literally we

are to take him) then it will go like this: faith; pardon; gift of righteousness; adoption; life. Should adoption and life really follow the gift of righteousness?

Julius at last asks the question that we have all been wanting to ask for some time: What do you mean by "faith"? James replies, in typical humanist manner, that the *significatio* of this word in common speech and even in Paul is *multiplex*; and he proceeds to give examples from both usages. Heb.11.1 plays a large part, of course. His definitive statement seems to be as follows: 'Thus we understand this sort of definition of faith that it is, either to hope by believing those things which are not subject to the sight of the eyes, that is, spiritual and eternal things, or to believe by hoping. Although the foundation of faith is believing, yet hope contains faith within itself and without hope faith is completely empty. And this is the proper definition of Christian faith. The true faith of Christ, therefore, is to believe God and in God and into God (*Deum, et Deo, et in Deum*), that is, to trust in him, so that you may hope from him eternal blessings' (48;71).

From now on the theme of earthly versus heavenly dominates his exposition, although it has been present, sometimes latent, throughout. 'For this is the faith of Christ . . . to neglect all human and mortal things, not to reckon as our blessings what we hold and possess here, but to aspire to heavenly and incorruptible things and to place and set our hope and trust of receiving them in God alone' (50;75). This, of course, is unexceptionable; no Christian would deny its pious truths. But just how these things can be is left somewhat vague. Verse 24, 'Being justified freely by his grace through the redemption that is in Christ Jesus', is primarily interpreted, not in terms of redemption or atonement, but of the contrast between the earthly and the heavenly. In so far as the work of Christ is treated, it becomes completely exemplarist: 'And so God himself chose and formed one man, who might bear in himself the whole truth of this divine example (*documentum*) and show to all by his example (*exemplum*) how much true felicity and glory would follow a life held wretched and despised on earth, so long as it was undertaken not ungratefully or against the judgment of the mind but freely from God and on account of God' (58;88).

It therefore comes as a surprise when, after many pages in this vein, the whole approach changes: 'But by what means are we justified? . . . "by the redemption", he says, "which is in Christ Jesus". For Christ Jesus, when he was without any sin, was nevertheless punished as a sinner and made compensation, in order that the old sin should no longer be a charge against us . . . Jesus died, not for his own sins, but for ours; which death he freely took, so that, having appeased God by his sorrows and sufferings, we might escape death, the partner of sin. But why should Jesus do this? What reason moved him to bear such love towards us, such trouble and care for us? Because, he says, "God set him forth as a propitiation through faith in his blood". God himself, he says, not only determined to bestow on us his grace and friendship, but also added that by which we might merit it. For he gave us his Son, by whom he was appeased; and, having blotted out all memories of our former injuries against himself, reconciled the human race by him – something which in no way could be done by us. For if anyone took our death upon himself, even if someone gave himself up for all, and did it with the best intention and a godly will, yet he would be sprung from an infected race, and could hardly redeem his own guilt, let alone the salvation of others. And in this especially shines the greatness and majesty and glory of the most high God, who poured all this blessing of his upon us. And he showed himself not only as capable of being appeased but also as the sacrifice by which he is appeased, so that, the less the merit on our side, the more we should love his clemency, and goodness, and righteousness' (66–67; 102).

There is hardly anything for a Reformer to object to in this and much that he would approve. Christ crucified is definitely and clearly set forward as the Saviour of sinners. No man can save himself or others. All depends on the mercy and love of God. What more could be asked? Had Sadoleto stopped at this point, we should have done no more than raise our eyebrows at the use of the word 'merits'. But in his next sentences more than a little ambiguity creeps in: 'But granted that there is nothing worthy from us, nothing containing any power or reckoning of merit, yet it is necessary that something shall proceed from us which shall trust in the grace and righteousness of God – and that is not of a work but only of a good will towards God which can happen to us only by the faith of Christ. For faith is what trusts and commits itself wholly to God, and we determine both now and in the future to please God; and as for the past, we trust that every offence from our former sins is completely blotted out from the divine Mind' (67;102-3). 'It is necessary that something shall proceed from us' – *tamen aliquid a nobis proficiscatur necesse est.* This is not a work; it is a 'good will towards God'. But is not the movement of the will a "work". Yes, but Sadoleto believes this point is covered by the addition of 'which can happen to us only by the faith of Christ'.

He continues by relating the contrast of the earthly and the heavenly to the death of Christ. What is it to die with Christ? How do we use the death of Christ to our salvation? By dying to the earthly and setting our minds on the heavenly: 'And so we reconcile God to us in the blood of Christ if in that blood and death of Christ we also die with him by an assent of the mind and the will, that is, if we hold the enticements of the world and this life as nothing and set the sum of all good things in God. For those who act and determine this are dead with Christ to sins and raised afterwards with him to the fruit of eternal life' (67;103).

The same answer is given in a different form when he asks whether Christ did not make satisfaction for the sins of all men. 'Certainly. But that satisfaction must be understood more subtly. For the case is not the same as what may often happen in an army. If a cohort or a legion deserts its post or loses its standard, a few are punished, but all the rest get off free from punishment. Thus it happens in Christ that he himself was punished, but all the rest were freed. But they only are freed who wish to die with Christ. Thus it is necessary, if we wish to be saved through Christ that we suffer the same death that he suffered. I say that this is necessary – yet not in just the same manner. For Christ destroyed man's flesh on the Cross as the tinder of sin that he might annihilate the sin which totally boiled up out of the flesh, whereby we might have in that flesh of Christ our flesh also destroyed by faith and will, and might die to sins. But this can happen to none save to him who wills and has the faith of Christ Jesus' (68;105).

Therefore none can rise with Christ to the life of true righteousness in whom the flesh of sin has not previously been killed (68;105). And so he comes back again to the need for cutting off the love of the world and acquiring a love of heavenly things. 'For this', he says, 'is faith in God and the imitation of Christ, by which an entrance into heaven is opened for us, which Christ himself reveals and opens' (69;106).

How are we finally to assess Sadoleto's doctrine of justification as it appears in this exposition? It is not at all surprising that he has been interpreted in more than one way. Richard Simon writes him off without more ado as a Pelagian, a view apparently held also by the Roman theologians who censured his *Romans*. Martin Bucer, however, according to M. Bernard Roussel, regarded his doctrine as identical with that of Scripture and the Reformers. Roussel himself agrees. R.M. Douglas seems to me to have come closer to the truth and for this reason we will leave his explanation to the last. Bucer and Roussel may have the first word.

Bucer was more than half-way through writing his commentary when that by Sadoleto appeared. He read it with some enthusiasm, (possibly with less care than enthusiasm) as well as with pain and indignation at the accusations of insincerity and immorality levelled against the Reformers, and he wrote a reply which, since the chapters on justification were complete, he placed at the end of Chapter 8: *A peroration on being justified by the faith of Christ alone according to the Apostle up to this point, and a rejection of the calumnies written against our teaching by Ja. Sadoleto, Bishop of Carpentras'* (370^a-373^b). We must expound this little essay carefully, and above all recite Bucer's own words, for Roussel's article prefers to paraphrase, and I do not find it possible always to agree with his rendering.

The first four paragraphs contain a summary of the teaching of the Epistle on justification from Chapters 4–8 (370^{a-b}). 'This contains the chief part, good reader, of the Christian philosophy' (370^a). In paragraph 5 (370^b) he enters upon his reply: 'Jacobus Sadoletus, the bishop of Carpentras . . . recently published his *Three Books of Commentaries on the Epistle to the Romans*. It is learnedly and carefully written. He thought that he ought to scourge us without more ado, we who desire the restoration of the ruins of doctrine and life in the churches – restoration according to what Christ our God commanded. And that, also, on our treatment of faith (in which, however, he teaches throughout the same things (*in qua tamen idem per omnia docet*) which we, nay, which St Paul and the whole of Scripture [teach], and which the Parisians and others less learned in divine Scripture than in their own *quaestiones* have already (*pridem*) condemned – namely that, without doubt, no man can be justified before God save by the faith of Christ, and that it is the society and conjunction of faith and righteousness (which is greater than all human virtue) so that righteousness will always follow as the result of true faith. These are our own very words in sermons and books; this is what we emphasize uniquely' (370^b). Many people today acknowledge that this truth has dropped out of the teaching of the Church, replaced by the system of penance. Sadoleto lived for years among Popes and Cardinals at Rome and knows the truth of this (370^b–371^a).

'And so we censure this avowed defection from God and the Lord Christ, this most impudent mockery of Christ and God. We teach that we must acknowledge that our ungodliness is so terrible that it can be expiated by the satisfaction of Christ alone and not by any creature; and so we rest all our hope of salvation in the mercy of God alone and in the satisfaction of our Lord Jesus Christ' (371^a). Faith, 'as Sadoleto himself confesses, can never be without substantial and perpetual meditation and practice of true righteousness' (371^a). And so he strives to make quite clear that for the Reformers faith and righteousness, faith and good works must stand together. In all this there is much about the merit of Christ, nothing about the merit of man.

He takes up Sadoleto's exposition of our passage. 'Now look, Sadoleto; do the things become you which you write against us in the digression in the third chapter of your Romans and elsewhere? You contend that when we preach that it is by faith alone that we are justified before God and are saved, our preaching does not accord with that faith which is through Jesus Christ in one God. And to prove it you affirm that we trust in the world and that our preaching and our lives and manners are an indication of this' (371^{a-b}). They are guilty according to Sadoleto of all sorts of serious sins. But where does he get all this from? What evidence has he? Bucer then returns the charges upon the clergy high and low in Rome, among whom Sadoleto lived. He knows the truth of the matter. And so to a long passage, unconnected with the immediate question, of anti-Roman polemic and Protestant *apologia* (371^{b}-373^{b}). And when he has set out the Reformation position, 'See from all this, Sadoleto, whether you are just in treating our preaching, our life, and our general morals as an indication that we trust in the world, and that when, along with you, nay, with Paul and all Scripture, we proclaim that faith alone receives justification before God, and at the same time faith alone brings about all true righteousness, whether this our preaching does not accord with the faith which is by Christ Jesus in one God, which is faith of the heart, not only believes in God, but also trusts in him alone. All our books and sermons testify that we teach and preach no other faith. Nor do our lives, thanks to Christ, bear any contrary witness, although we all transgress in many things and fall, not just seven times a day, but seventy times seven' (373^{b}). And he concludes, 'I wanted, godly Reader, to reply to some extent to Sadoleto's calumnies, which were certainly most unworthy of a bishop and man of letters. May the Lord, who is truth, and will not be adored and worshipped save in truth, grant to that bishop and to us, that we consecrate ourselves wholly to the truth' (373^{b}).

I think that anyone must agree that the tone of this *Peroratio* is not so much eirenic as responsive – that is, that it sounds like a frank and often indignant reply by one who thinks himself and his cause unjustly slandered rather than a conciliatory acceptance of an olive branch. Nevertheless, M. Bernard Roussel, in an interesting essay of 1980, takes it in the other sense. The main thesis of his essay is that this *Peroratio* must be understood as a move in the complicated political game that was being played in the fifteen-thirties between France and the German Protestant princes. Bucer, as the leading spokesman for the free city of Strasbourg, regarded Sadoleto's treatment of justification in Romans as both Scriptural and reformed and therefore as offering an opportunity for the two sides to reach agreement on lesser matters as well. 'Relatively well informed about Sadoleto himself, a careful reader of his commentary on Romans, Bucer deserves to be taken seriously when he wishes to open (with this particular man and at this particular time) a theological discussion which might lead to a positive outcome. This is our thesis . . .' (516). Later in the essay, M. Roussel mars his case by indulging in open guess-work. It was necessary that the fragmentation of church and theology in France should be overcome. But around whom could unity be built? Guillaume Budé had shown himself a broken reed in practical matters, Guillaume du Bellay was merely 'an honest courtier'. Did not perhaps Bucer see Sadoleto as the man of the moment? 'This is only a suggestion' (523). And then, without any need, M. Roussel has to ask who gave Bucer Sadoleto's *Romans* – as if he were not capable of coming upon it for himself. There is, of course, no evidence one way or the other, but M. Roussel proposes 'in the absence of any indication, the name of John Sturm' (523).

These lapses from objective judgment make one cautious about his general thesis, even if we were not already doubtful at the interpretation of the *Peroratio*. Let me say at once, however, that there was a political dimension, either deliberate or unavoidable, in any theological writing during the Reformation, and that the position was particularly sensitive and delicate in the fifteen-thirties. It is also true that Bucer was a man always on the look-out for possibilities of reconciliation, and that he not infrequently went further in that direction than many of his reformed friends thought wise or desirable. But whether the *Peroratio* is to be read as a peace-offering intending to lead to dialogue and at last agreement seems very doubtful.

M. Roussel, in effect, relies on three statements in the *Peroratio* for his case. The first is the clause '*erudite ac accurate scriptos*', with which Bucer describes Sadoleto's *Romans*. This becomes, in Roussel's paraphrase, 'ces commentaires sont "fondées sur de solides connaissances" et à la compétence du "grammaticus" Sadoleto a joint la pertinence de son inter- prétation théologique' (513). 'These commentaries "are based on solid learning" and to the skill of a "grammarian" Sadoleto has added the relevance of this theological interpretation'. He takes this up again at greater length on p.521 and makes of it a positive commendation of Sadoleto's commentary as almost a commendation of what a commentary should be. But surely this is no more than a polite opening to an *apologia*. The words themselves simply amount to "learned and careful" – the opposite of something dashed off by someone who was an uneducated man. It was the sort of thing that any reply to an opponent might say.

The other two sentences are a different matter, however, especially as they are really one sentence said twice. It comes first near the beginning: 'idque etiam in tractatione fidei, in qua tamen idem per omnia docet quod nos, imo quod D. Paulus et tota scriptura, quodque Parrisiani et alii non tam divinae scripturae, quam suarum quaestionum consulti pridem damnarunt, istud nimirum, neminem hominum apud Deum nisi per fidem Christi posse iustificari' (370[b]). And in the last paragraph: 'eoque cum tecum, imo cum Paulo et omni scriptura praedicamus solam fidem iustificationem apud Deum percipere, simulque omnem veram iustitiam conciliare' (373[b]). These M. Roussel paraphrases as: 'Sadolet dit les mêmes choses que nous, mieux, que Saint Paul et l'Ecriture tout entière' (513 n.20) – 'Sadoleto says the same things as we – more, the same as St Paul and the whole of Scripture'. On this basis he can therefore go on to say, 'Here then is a partner fit for discussions (une rencontre) whose stake is the preparation of a general council' (513).

This is then broadened to a general agreement on this topic in the *Metaphrases* as a whole. In the *Metaphrases* 'Bucer declares that between him and Sadoleto there is no longer a difference on this fundamental problem. Although rooted in different terms, their theses, if made more specific, have the same sense. The one says, "It is by faith alone in Jesus Christ that we obtain being justified before God, and then being saved". The other writes, "We are saved by faith in the one God, faith which can only be by the mediation of Jesus Christ"' (514). These are translations of: 'sola nos fide in Iesum Christum iustificationem apud Deum consequi et omnem salutem' (*Met.*371[b]), and: we are saved 'ea fide quae est per Iesum Christum in unum Deum' (373[b]). The latter is, of course, Bucer's description of Sadoleto's formula. So far as it goes, it is fair, and certainly it is capable of being interpreted as 'sola nos fide in Iesum Christum iustificationem apud Deum consequi'. But this raises the question as to whether this is only Bucer's reading of Sadoleto or whether it is a correct interpretation. M. Roussel seems to think the latter and goes so far as to say that between the *Metaphrases* and the *Libri Tres* there is only a slight shift of emphasis, 'un léger déplacement d'accent' (517). And yet this slight shift of emphasis turns out to be, first, that for Bucer, Scripture (and therefore Romans) is clear, whereas for Sadoleto it is dark and a labyrinth (517), and secondly, on the effect of the Incarnation, 'for Bucer, the "revelation" is from the outset the demonstration of the power of the Spirit, who, since Christ's resurrection, possesses the elect called to ethical excellence. For Sadoleto, the "revelation" is the irruption in the world of shadows and worldly attachments of the perfect teaching of a doctor who convinces by the example he has given and triumphs because he has, by the Cross, removed the obstacle to the imitation of God by believers' (518). In other words, the clarity as opposed to the obscurity of Scripture, and the power of the Spirit as opposed to a Platonic and mystical educational scheme. One would have thought that this was what the Reformation was all about.

We saw in our exposition of Sadoleto's treatment of 3.20ff. that it was difficult to determine precisely his concept of faith.

M. Roussel has no difficulty in seeing it as identical with Bucer's: 'In brief, there is for each only one kind of faith, towards God and in God; faith "lively" and "formed" by love, dynamic faith, and therefore saving' (520). There are many places where this seems to be Sadoleto's view, but in the last resort I believe he was still thinking, however much he used the word *confido*, of "belief" as assent to propositions.

Nevertheless, the fact that M. Roussel can find this affinity is evidence of the ambiguity inherent in Sadoleto's book. And the ambiguity has been well-noted in R.M.Douglas' treatment of the subject. He points out Sadoleto's propensity for qualification by the use of *tamen*, and gives examples with references to several others. 'The force of the qualifying *tamen* here again is to set off man's part from God's and to reserve to human will the *bona voluntas* which, according to Sadoleto, is the beginning of salvation. Justification is God's work, and not man's, yet man begins what God completes' (84). And again: 'The *tamen* shows Sadoleto's "new course" to be a twisting path which veered far closer to Pelagius than to Augustine' (85).

So far as Bucer is concerned, however, his apparent acceptance of Sadoleto's teaching is satisfactorily explained if we take his remarks in the context of his reply to the accusation that the Reformers taught "faith alone" to give themselves licence to sin. 'Not so', he answers, 'we teach "faith alone" like St Paul and the rest of Scripture, and, indeed like you yourself'. If Bucer was going further than this and giving approval to Sadoleto's doctrine of faith, we must say either that he had not read him very carefully or that he had little theological acumen or that he was sacrificing theological truth to eirenicism.

Bucer

This part of Bucer's commentary comprises Sections IV & V of Book I (176ᵃ-207ᵇ), the content of which is given on our pp. 46-7.

He alone among the reformed commentators interprets "the works of the law" as referring to the ceremonies of the

Law: 'ceremonies, which are alone under discussion are here
called "the works of the law"' (177[a]); and, 'He calls the things
which the Law commands "the works of the law". And this
is what the Apostle here calls the ceremonies of the Law. He
does this by *autonomasia* or *synecdoche*, for they are a part of
the things of the Law' (179[a]). As his custom is, Bucer appeals
for support to what he claims is the practically unanimous
opinion of the Church fathers: 'Augustine alone contends that
by "the works of the law" are to be understood all the
precepts of the Law, even the Decalogue. . . But we agree
with the holy fathers that the Apostle meant by "the works of
the law" particularly to express ceremonies . . . For the
whole question is about ceremonies' (179[a-b]). It is for this
reason that he couples Romans with Galatians as dealing with
the same subject.

But this interpretation is far from determining his understanding of the passage. He does not go on from this point to
say that Romans teaches that although a man cannot be
justified by practising the ceremonies he can be justified by
doing the works of the Law other than ceremonies. On the
contrary, he insists throughout that, although the phrase used
means ceremonies, it is used only as *synecdoche*, a part for the
whole. Hence, whether, as he himself claims, he was being
faithful to the context, or whether, as we may suspect, he was
being led by the authority of the Church fathers, he came to
the same opinion in the end as the other reformed commentators, that Paul was saying that no works of the Law, whether
moral or ceremonial, justify.

He sees 3.20ff. as the positive conclusion of negative
premises (176[a]), as a proclaiming of 'the Gospel that all are
justified by faith in our Lord Jesus Christ' (176[a]). The
negative premises concerned the Law and sin, and here we
can straightway see how little practical force his identification
of *opera legis* with *ceremonia* actually had. To explain 'For
through the law is the knowledge of sin' (v.20b) he uses three
familiar lines of argument: 'The first from the whole to a
part. The works of the Law (that is, the precepts and keeping
of ceremonies) do not justify before God because the Law
itself does not justify before God. The second from a

contrary. The Law itself does not justify because it accuses and convicts of sin. The third from the cause. The Law accuses and convicts of sin because it makes it known' (180ᵃ). At this point Bucer refers the reader back to the previous section, to the Preface entitled 'What the Law was in Paul', and to the Conciliations subjoined to Section III, ch.2, in order to show how the Law condemns man by making him know his sin.

But in itself the Mosaic Law had also a positive purpose. It was intended to save and to give eternal life. 'The Law of Moses was given to bring life, and there was no precept in it which was not in its own way for salvation *(salutiferum)*' (176ᵃ). This needs explanation, however, and Bucer adds: 'but observed by faith and therefore also in that way which the Lord prescribed' (176ᵃ). Once again we notice that he is talking about "the Law" and not about ceremonies only. It is quite clear that that identification was not made in order to suggest that some works of the Law apart from ceremonies avail for justification; or, on the other hand, if these other works do avail for justification, yet for some reason the observance of the ceremonies must be excepted. What differentiates him from Haresche and Grimani is that whereas they place the saving activity of the Law in the future for Old Testament man, he gives it a so to say contemporaneous validity.

When he calls this passage 'a proclaiming of the Gospel', he is no doubt glancing back to 1.16; but he is also making the point that it is a declaration which is also a promise and which is therefore directed to faith: 'Moreover, he does not prove, but proclaims, that it is through Christ that men are justified before God – that is, they receive remission of sins' (178ᵃ). And this is the way of Scripture in general. First will come the simple promise and statement, without any proof, and this corresponds to the movement of faith as primary: 'For God has determined to save us by faith. . . Therefore he demands that we simply have faith in his promises; and what he demands he also bestows' (178ᵃ).

Verse 21 introduces a contrast between the Law and the Gospel. The phrase 'without the law the righteousness of

God is revealed' means that the Gospel is revealed (180[b]). But it is revealed in a different way, that is, 'through the hearing of faith' (180[b]).

At this point Bucer enters on an explanation of the word *iustitia*. His treatment is oblique, partly by cross-reference to his Section 5, Chapter 1, partly by reference to other writers, to Melanchthon, Ambrose, Origen, and Augustine. It is on Melanchthon and Ambrose that the emphasis falls. From Ambrose we learn that *iustitia* is 'God's mercy forgiving and pardoning sins' and that it is based on the concept of promise: 'For it is God's righteousness because what he has promised is delivered' (180[b]). Thus righteousness is here taken as faithfulness to what is right – *ius*. The reference to Melanchthon broadens the definition: 'Philip Melanchthon takes "the righteousness of God" here for the acceptance by which God accepts us. And this agrees with our understanding of it as the incomparable goodness of God exhibited in Christ, by which he forgives sins, imputes righteousness, and bestows eternal life; and this eternal life he begins by inbreathing new life and a desire for godliness' (180[b]). The reference appears to be a paraphrase of Melanchthon's comment on 3.24: 'The righteousness of God signifies the acceptance by which God accepts us'(56[v]).

The *pactum* (which we might translate here as the counterpart in an agreement) of the righteousness of God is itself revealed. It is faith: and 'Where there is faith in the Gospel, and so complete trust placed in Christ the Lord, there men begin to know and experience the righteousness of God justifying and blessing them' (181[a]). And the revelation of God's righteousness in the Gospel is addressed, according to v.22, to Jews and Gentiles alike. Following his understanding of the words 'For there is no distinction' as the forestalling of an objection, Bucer punctuates fairly heavily with a full-stop followed by a lower case letter, perhaps a little stronger than our modern colon. In other words, it is a self-contained clause, but it leads on to the next statement, that all men are sinners and are destitute of (Bucer's word) the glory of God. He defines *gloria dei* as 'the singular presence and dignity of God shining in a more divine life, that is a godly and innocent life. This is certainly the *summa dignitas* of man and is what Scripture calls כבוד ' (181[b]). But he then embarks on quite a long lexicographical study of the word in the rest of Scripture, ending with an apparent restricting of this verse to the Jews: 'And so the Apostle rightly says that the Jews lacked (*destitutos fuisse*) this glory. They had cast themselves into such wild and barbarous ungodliness that no reverence for God, no goodness whatsoever, was left in them' (182[b]).

Bullinger

In Bullinger's arrangement of the subject matter, 3.20 is the final verse of the section *On Sin*. The next part, of which v.21 is the commencement, is headed *Quod Fides Sit Iustitia – That Faith is Righteousness*, and the cursory *Argumentum* has: 'Hitherto of Sin, now of Righteousness' (32).

The exposition he offers is unremarkable; its chief interest lies in the polemic. Positively, he expresses and emphasizes the Reformation doctrine of justification by grace alone. God created man good, but, 'corrupted by his own fault, he hereafter seeks only himself and his own' (33). Thus, he lacks the glory of God, that is, the image of God in which he was created. Men therefore 'cannot glory in their righteousness before God' (33). But none is excluded from the righteousness and salvation of God. Justification is not 'repaid as an owed reward for observing the Mosaic or the natural Law, BUT IS GIVEN GRATIS by the divine beneficence' (33-34). The capitals reflect Bullinger's particular emphasis in the doctrine. It is grace that he opposes to the merit of works (34), and it is on this basis that he attacks the contemporary Romanists.

St Paul, he says, intends the word "works" to be taken comprehensively – 'of all the works which are done by a man in this life' (34). The Romanists, however, (and here he is too sweeping, as we have seen) contend that the Apostle was referring only to the ceremonial works of the Law. Why is it that no flesh shall be justified by the works of the Law? Because 'by the law is the knowledge of sin'. But (and here I expand his argument, which is terse and enigmatic) how can ceremonies be said to convey the knowledge of sin? It must therefore be taken also as the moral Law. 'Therefore we are justified freely and not of works, whether of ceremonies or of the moral Laws' (34).

Bullinger's subsequent criticism is more penetrating, however. He fastens on the distinction between works of the Law and works of grace, and calls it playing with words. The Romanists do not regard the works of the Law as such or our own works done in our own power meritorious. They ascribe righteousness to such works 'because they are done in faith, as if faith absorbed the flesh and transmuted man completely into spirit' (34). He cannot, in the end, see why, if righteousness is from the *works* of faith, glorying should be prohibited, or, indeed, how righteousness can be called the *gift* of God if it is won by works of faith (34).

Melanchthon

Melanchthon's treatment of the passage is characterized by a powerful awareness of the reality of justification. If Haresche's scholastic doctrine of justification meant more for him than a set of correct propositions, he concealed the fact well. In Melanchthon we encounter the dreadful reality of *Deus iratus*, of the tortures of conscience, of the impotence of man to satisfy, of the propitiating sacrifice of the Son, of the complete forgiveness of all sins and the bestowal of eternal life. We ought not to write all this off as merely an illustration of Melanchthon's insistence on the *beneficia Christi*, although he will expressly speak of the Gospel in these terms, '*de beneficio Christi*' (CVIII^v). On the contrary, that insistence itself stems from his manner of making theology. His theology is a theology of the heart, even though the form of the commentary is, in its own way, scholastic.

He divides the whole passage into two parts, the principal proposition and the entrance to the principal proposition. By calling the first part "the entrance", he is using language appropriate to his theological method. His aim is to discover the chief concept and argument. His method (μεθ'όδος – following a way or path) is, as it were, a path of discovery, and the path must have a beginning or an entrance and so be an entering upon the chief concept and argument itself. So

here. The entrance is to be found in v.20. That 'no flesh shall
be justified from the works of the law' is in effect a repetition
of v.19 'that every mouth should be shut and the whole
world guilty before God'. Both statements are "universals";
all men without any exception whatsoever are sinners. Those
who 'imagine that men merit remission of sins and are
righteous on account of *bona opera moralia*' (54ʳ;CVIᵛ) would
weaken the force of the universal and make it refer to all
except a very few good men. The Gentile mind might want
to say that, although most men in Rome are guilty, yet just a
few, like Scipio or Atticus, should be excepted. Or one might
except John and Peter from among the Jews. But not only
must the statement be taken as it stands, but it must also be
referred to the good works which men perform as well as to
their persons: 'here he expressly not only accuses persons but
also takes away justification from the actual good works
themselves' (54ᵛ;CVIIʳ). It follows, therefore, that man
cannot be justified by doing the *bona opera moralia* which the
Law commands.

But it might be objected: If this is so, what is the use of the
Law? why was it given? It is to meet this objection that Paul
adds the second part of v.20, 'For by the law is the knowledge
of sin'. The purpose of the Law is 'to show sin, not to take it
away' (55ʳ;CVIIᵛ). In the interests of public and private
morality Melanchthon now has to remind us what the
passage is talking about. All that he has said has to be read in
the light of the distinction between the different types of law
and the different uses of law.[9] Here Paul is not talking about
lex politicus, that is, the laws obtaining in society, which is a
'public coercion of carnal men' (55ᵛ;CVIIIʳ). Obedience to
this law is required by God; it does not merely give a
knowledge of sin, but restrains and deters from the commission of social crimes. The subject of this passage, however, is,
How are we reckoned righteous before God? How do we
attain remission of sins? How does the law contribute in this?
(55ᵛ;CVIIIʳ). In this context of God's judgment and man's
conscience, 'the Law shows sin and terrifies the heart; this is

[9] In 1532 this material forms a *locus*, *De Duplici Usu Legis*, which is
placed after the exposition of *Per legem enim agnitio* (55ᵛ-56ʳ).

the awareness (*agnitio*) spoken of here. For he does not intend
an idle speculation, but such a recognition (*agnitio*) in which
we are aware (*agnoscimus*) of the wrath of God against sin and
are really frightened by it . . . And when consciences are
terrified, they cannot be pacified by the Law, which accuses
us more and more and drives us to desperation' (CVIII^(r-v)).[10]

Thus Melanchthon has entered on the way to the "principal
proposition" and has, in fact, been led right up to it: 'Above,
he had made an entrance to the principal proposition. For he
had said that all men are guilty of sin and under the wrath of
God and cannot be set free from sin by the Law. Now
follows the principal proposition, which is that *status huius
controversiae* . . . this proposition contains the proper and
chief statement of the Gospel *de beneficio Christi* . . . and to
this *statum*, as to a head, all the arguments are to be referred'
(56^(r-v); CVIII^v).

The rest of Melanchthon's exposition of this passage may
be taken as an explanation and working out of this "principal
proposition" *de beneficio Christi*. It should be noted that he
does not say *de beneficiis Christi*, but *de beneficio*; he is not
talking about the blessings which Christ gives to his people,
but about the blessing which Christ himself is. Accordingly
we have definitions of *iustitia* and *fides*, statements on the true
nature and office of Christ, that he is not a new legislator but
the sacrifice for sin; and, above all, Melanchthon insists that
the Mediator must be "used"; that is, trusted and believed in,
not merely looked at or considered without relation to
oneself. (It would, I think, be unfair to apply Augustine's
distinction, taken up in Lombard's *Sententiae* I Dist.1,
between "enjoying" and "using" God, to Melanchthon here).

The *iusticia Dei* which is now manifested apart from the
Law is that with which he justifies us. It is '*acceptatio, vel
remissio peccatorum et imputatio iusticiae*' (56^v;CIX^r). By this
brief definition Melanchthon is summarizing, and needs to be

---

[10] 1532: 'Here the Law accuses consciences . . . So here, when he
says, "By the law is the knowledge of sin", knowledge is not
understood as idle knowledge but of those terrors of conscience. For the
Law is truly understood when it accuses, and we know our sins when
we are terrified; we know that God is offended' (55^v-56^r).

amplified. The *acceptatio* means that God does not reject the man but accepts him into his company and fellowship. Yet he does not accept the man who is of like mind with himself, but the man who is contrary to him. Therefore the *acceptatio* is both a correction and a supplying of a lack. It consists of the two parts of forgiveness and imputation. The holy and loving God accepts sinners by remitting their sin, so that they are no longer sinners, and by imputing or reckoning to them the righteousness of Jesus Christ. That 'we are justified freely' (v.24) is, 'we obtain remission of sins and are reckoned righteous, that is, accepted; and with this reckoning is joined the gift of the Holy Spirit and acceptation to eternal life' (CX^v).[11] This doctrine of justification he opposes expressly to the doctrine we have met in other writers: 'Although a new obedience begins in those who are justified, yet that new obedience or Law is not the reason why we attain remission of sins and are accounted righteous, or accepted; but these things are freely given because of Christ' (59^v-60^r; CX^r).

He also defines faith (under vv.27 & 28) in its relation to Christ, that is, to God's mercy towards the sinner on account of Christ, and to the promise of mercy. It is predominantly trust, *fiducia*: it signifies '*fiducia* in the mercy promised on account of Christ . . . it stands as correlative to promise and it is *fiducia* apprehending promised mercy' (CXIIII^v).[12] We shall see how Calvin also, perhaps borrowing from Melanchthon, makes use of the concept of correlation between faith and mercy. As he had opposed the Romanist doctrine of justification, so now also the Romanist doctrine of faith, which would, on the one hand, make faith into dependence on the natural law or the Decalogue or, on the other, understand it as only an historical knowledge (CXV^r). And again we have seen examples of this in our earlier commentaries.

[11] 1532: 'And so on account of these two causes, we join together three things – remission of sins, the imputation of righteousness, and the gift of new life' (59^r).

[12] 1532: 'by faith alone, that is, by trust in mercy alone, men are justified' (70^r). And: 'And so, even if faith is a certain quality within us, yet it does not justify in so far as it is our quality, our newness, but in so far as it apprehends mercy' (57^v).

The Christ on whose account God justifies the ungodly, and whose work is the foundation of man's faith, must be seen clearly in his office as Mediator. He is not a new Law-giver but the victim of sacrifice. And here Melanchthon is not opposing the Romanists but "the world" and Anabaptists. 'The world has *imaginationes politicas* about Christ and thinks he is a legislator, bringing in a new law, one that is considerably easier than Moses' Law in that it abolishes the ceremonies, which were not suitable for all nations, and one which also commands much about love. So they enumerate what laws Christ added to the Mosaic laws and fancy that by observing these laws men merit remission of sins and are righteous, and they interpret "without the law" as "without ceremonies" (CIX^r). Then again: 'And this verse is not only to be opposed to Anabaptists and their like, who imagine that the Gospel is a *novam politiam mundanam*, (a new earthly policy) but it is also to be held *in agone conscientiae*, (in the trial or contest of conscience), so that we may truly understand that the *beneficium Christi* is *gratuitum*' (CIX^v-CX^r).

On the contrary, Christ is that sacrificial victim for sin demanded by *Deus iratus*. For we have already learned from the "entrance to the principal proposition" the universal statement that 'all men are guilty of sin and under the wrath of God' (CVIII^v), and 'God could be placated by no sacrifice but the death of his Son' (CXI^r). Christ's sacrifice, therefore, is the effectual satisfaction for sin; the redemption is 'in Christ Jesus' (3.24). The glory of Christ consists in the uniqueness of his sacrifice and satisfaction. 'How great a blasphemy therefore is it, to transfer the glory of the Son of God to human works and to invent other sacrifices, like satisfactions, Masses, monk-hood, etc.' (CXI^r). But Melanchthon is well-aware, of course, that the issue between the Romanists and the Reformers does not turn on the straightforward choice between all Christ and no Christ, but on how much Christ; it is a matter of the place given to Christ in justification. And so we come to the "use" of the Mediator. The heading "Through faith [in his blood]" (v.25) calls forth the following attack on the Romanist doctrine: 'Our adversaries also confess that Christ is the Mediator and Propitiator.

But afterwards they change and corrupt this. For they say nothing about application and do not teach that Christ the Mediator is to be used. First, they say absolutely nothing about this faith, that is, about trust in the Mediator. They do not teach men to use Christ the Mediator. In fact, they tell them to doubt in their consciences. This doubting clearly clashes with the faith which Paul here requires. Secondly, they feign that Christ is only a propitiator in respect of giving an opportunity to merit . . . They ascribe to Christ only so much as that he earned for us this beginning and opportunity for meriting. Their own language is that Christ merited the first grace. Afterwards they bury him and make him idle, imagining that men merit remission of sins and are righteous on account of their own fulfilling of the Law etc. We, on the contrary, rightly understand that Christ always remains the Mediator and is to be applied by faith; that is, it is to be determined that we are pleasing to God, not on account of our *dignitas* or fulfilling of the Law, but on account of Christ' (64^v-65^r;CXI^v-CXII^r).

In agreement with his insistence on the completeness of the work of the Mediator in contrast to the teaching that the work is only potential or preliminary or initiatory, Melanchthon sees this passage as undercutting the medieval doctrine of penance, the restoration of those who have by subsequent sin lost the grace conferred in Baptism. The phrase in 3.25, 'of sins that are past', does not therefore refer to sins committed before the Incarnation (as Grimani and Haresche) but to sin in general, whether actual sins or original sin: 'They say that this clause is added to teach us that the Gospel does not give licence for sinning and that sins are remitted to those who do penance, in whom sin is mortified. But it does not follow from this that lapses after remission cannot again be pardoned if they again repent. . . This is therefore a description of present remission in general, not exclusively of subsequent remissions. To my mind the sentence is very simple, if we understand it as setting this clause against the Law. As if he said, "Sin reigned hitherto, and the Law did not abolish sin and death: but by this faith in Christ sin is now abolished, which hitherto existed or reigned"; for Paul speaks not only of actual sins but also of original sin' (CXIII^r). Original sin 'is abolished in two ways; that is, imputatively, in that the guilt is removed; and the thing itself begins to be abolished and mortified, that is, when in penitence there exist true terrors, true consolation, and the beginning of a new creature in the heart' (CXIII^{r-v}).

Pellicanus

Pellicanus' treatment of this passage is noticeable for a lack of any anti-Roman polemic – or rather, of anything overt of the sort, for his strong assertions may not unjustly be read as tacit polemic. He also seems in the main to be viewing it historically, as referring to the Jews and Gentiles of New Testament times; but a reference to "us" or a slipping into the present tense shows us that he is also expounding it universally.

He begins by placing the chapter in its context: 'In the first chapter and the beginning of the second he convicts the Jews and Gentiles that their lives and openly bad morals are alien from all righteousness. From this it follows that there was absolutely nothing in them, whether of law or of philosophy, to avert God's wrath and procure eternal life by justifying. But from the eighth verse [2.17(?); the verse divisions had not yet been devised] up to here he convicts the Jews by Scripture of ungodliness (since the Law had not brought righteousness, for none is justified through the Law) so that, deprived of trust in their own soul, in the Law, and in natural wisdom, they might of necessity be led to Christ, as the unique righteousness by whom all the elect may be saved. And here he returns and convicts them, from the Scripture, of such perversity' (39). Pellicanus is not saying anything at all original. He concentrates on the universality of sin in the Jews and Gentiles, and regards the Law whether written or natural, as a compulsion pressing men towards Christ. "Law" in this passage means not the ceremonies, but the whole Law; 'The works of the Law, not distinguished by Paul but only spoken of generally, I also prefer not to distinguish, with Augustine . . . who by the works of the law insisted should be understood all the precepts of the Law'

(42). And again, under 3.27: 'all glorying of merits is excluded; also excluded is any glorying of works. Of works, I say, of the whole Law, the Decalogue as well as ceremonies' (45). On this point, then, he has not followed Bucer. The reason why the Law does not justify lies in man's inability to perform perfectly the works demanded by the Law: 'there is absolutely no work of the Law which can justify men, since it is certain that it cannot be performed by any man as it should be' (42). What, then, is the purpose of the Law? Why was it given, if it does not make men better or more righteous? 'The use of the Law is not single but manifold' (43). It has a threatening aspect, a didactic, and an admonitory: 'Granted it does not justify, yet it accuses, convicts, and deters. It also teaches what things to beware of and what in us pleases God. It directs into the way of righteousness and equity, so that we may render to God what is his, and similarly to our neighbours, as we are admonished by the Lord our God', (42-43). But the threatening aspect of the Law has a positive purpose, for 'when we neglect it, it accuses our consciences and urges us to humility and to begging humbly for forgiveness' (43). Within the Law are contained also some consolations and promises by which it not only draws but also leads 'the human race to better things' (43).

Although Pellicanus makes the sacrifice of Christ on the Cross the unique and sufficient means of justification, what he concentrates on is, like Bullinger, the free-ness of salvation. Under 3.24, the word *gratis* gives him the opportunity both to state this and also (covertly as we said) to reject the sort of teaching on the place of the Cross in justification that we have seen in earlier writers: 'If here he had said only that we are justified by the grace of God, it would have expressed sufficiently that it was not by merits. And by "redeemed", he had again excluded our merit. But not content with these, he added also *gratis*, to impress upon believers that they are redeemed, restored, and saved by the grace of God alone and by the merit of Christ alone. For we do not merit justification because we have first done something or other, nor, having received it, do we compensate with any work' (44).

Again, what is emphasized in the saving work of Christ is that he was predestined to this end: 'The Apostle here explains the rationale (*quonam pacto*) of the redemption effected by Christ, and says that God determined it from the beginning. Long before he came in the flesh he had been destined to this; so that it was no novelty, but predestined before the ages' (44). Eternal election appears in Pellicanus, therefore, as the final and inevitable destruction of even the refined semi-Pelagianism of a Grimani. Man cannot merit justification. Not even his faith is meritorious: 'all works universally, even if good, avail nothing to propitiate God. Not even our faith justifies us by itself and formally, but only by the free and spontaneous benevolence and grace of God; and the merit of Christ and his righteousness pardons all our sins and merits eternal life for us. But we receive it by faith' (42).

Calvin

Calvin's exposition of this passage runs to only about two thousand words in the first edition. It is, indeed, among the shortest of those by Reformers and certainly matches his conception of a commentator's work as consisting in brevity and conciseness. We may ask, however, whether he has not succeeded too well, whether he has not sometimes sacrificed intelligibility in his pursuit of conciseness. His criticism that Bucer's prolixity and fecundity makes him impossible for the average reader is fair; but he himself often lays another kind of burden on the average reader, that of supplying missing steps in the argument. The older Calvin must himself have agreed with this criticism, or he would not have made his exposition half as long again in his revisions. It is, however, with the earlier and short form that we are concerned.

He divides the passage into four sections: (1) vv.19-20a; (2) vv. 20b-22a; (3) vv.22b-26; (4) vv.27-28.

The meaning of the expression 'the works of the law' is, he says, a matter of debate among scholars. Some extend it to cover the keeping of the whole Law. Others confine it to the ceremonies of the Law. A puzzling historical note, apparently at variance with Bucer, ascribes the former view to Chrysostom, Origen, and Jerome, who take the word "Law" in a strict sense so that it cannot be understood *de quibuslibet operibus*. The answer to the orginal point is that works are righteous before God in so far as we take care (*studemus*) to render worship and obedience to God through them. The more emphatically to divest works in general of the power to justify, Paul names those works which surely could justify, if any there were. If they could not justify, then none could. The connection between this statement and what follows is far from clear, and in fact needed the addition of a passage of ten lines in 1556 to make it intelligible. 'For the Law is that which has promises, apart from which our works are of no value before God. You see therefore for what reason Paul used the expression "the works of the law" – because a value is given to works through the Law' (66^{90-93}). The works of the Law have a value and receive a reward from the Lord not because of a claim that man can make on God on the basis of the value of his obedience to the Law (for in fact his obedience is always tarnished with disobedience) but because of the gracious promise with which God has invested the Law – that is, 'which if a man do, he shall live in them' (Lev.18.5). So the three steps in the argument are: (1) works are agreeable to God in so far as they are genuine acts of worship and obedience; (2) works in this passage are those which must be regarded as agreeable to God, in that they are works done in obedience to his Law; (3) for God has, in giving the law, promised that obedience to it will be rewarded. And this is why St Paul says that 'by the works of the law there shall no flesh be justified in his sight'. Why? The reason is deferred until Calvin has finished clearing up the exegetical point that "works of the law" is to be taken of the whole Law. The mention of circumcision (in vv.1 & 30) is not to be taken as restricting the use of the word Law to ceremonies. Nor should they (= those who say that "the works of the law" are ceremonies) base their argument on Galatians, for even there Paul is not speaking only of ceremonies but of the whole Law. In the present passage the thread of the argument is sufficient to show that Paul is contending for the whole Law. 'And therefore this is one of the most memorable of all his assertions, that none receives justification from observance of the Law' (67^{19-21}). And now comes the reason why by 'the works of the Law there shall no flesh be justified in his sight', notwithstanding that God himself has promised that the man who does them shall live in them: 'because all without exception are convicted of transgression and accused of unrighteousness by the Law' (67^{22-23}).

The office of the Law (under 'For by the law is the knowledge of sin' v.20) is considered with vv.21-22, no doubt to make it serve as a contrasting introduction. The Law does not bring us justification, because that is not its office, which is 'to convince us of sin and damnation' (67^{29-30}); 'for life and death do not flow from the same spring (67^{30}). Therefore 'you must understand that the unique effect of the Law is to show a man his sin' ($67^{n.31}$). Certainly, in itself it teaches and trains men to righteousness and life, but man's perversity (*vitiositas*) prevents it having this effect in practice. The emphasis is thus moved from the Law in itself to the observance, or rather the non-observance, of the Law, so that 'without the law' in v.21 is to be understood as 'without the help of the law', taking "Law" here as "works". God has not revealed and does not reveal righteousness in response to man's works of obedience to the Law, but out of his mercy: 'we see that he does not confuse works with God's mercy' (68^{55-56}). In other words, this verse teaches justification by faith alone. Those who accuse "us" of inserting the word "alone", which does not come in Scripture, are refuted by the verse. For if God's righteousness is revealed 'without the law' and if justification is "outside us" (*extra nos*), why is it not to be reckoned of God's mercy alone? But if it is of mercy alone, then also of faith alone, faith being the corollary of mercy. (We notice that the word "grace" does not occur at this place, and, in fact, comes only once in the exposition of 3.20-28; it is replaced by "mercy", no doubt used, not only in a forensic sense, but also with the common Old Testament connotation of loving-kindness.)

The word "now" can be understood either simply as an adverb or temporally. Calvin seems to prefer the latter sense, which leads him to a discussion of the relation between the old and new Covenants. If "now" means that the righteousness of faith is revealed in the preaching of the Gospel after Christ has been revealed in the flesh, it will not follow that that righteousness was hidden before his advent. The revelation is therefore twofold: in the old Covenant, consisting in Word and Sacraments; and in the new Covenant 'which contains the complement in Christ, apart from the ceremonies and promises' (70[13-15]). Paul had already said that the righteousness of faith did not need the help of the Law. He now goes further and gives the Law the secondary and confirmatory role of a witness, in contradiction to the scholastic view of it as primary and preparatory: 'if the Law bears witness to gratuitous righteousness, it is clear that it was not given in order to teach men to acquire righteousness for themselves by works. Therefore they pervert it who twist it to this purpose' (70[20-22]). Calvin proves this point by showing that in the Old Testament restoration for fallen man is placed in Christ alone, who is figured by the ceremonies and promised by the Prophets. For a more complete proof he directs the reader to the *Institutio* (1539 Cap.XI).

Verse 22 shows Calvin using the words *iustitia* and *iustificatio* almost interchangeably. Or perhaps we should say that he is conscious of the literal meaning of *iustificatio*, from *iustitia* and *facio*, "I make righteous"; in other words, the transmission or bestowal of *iustitia*. For on the clause *Iustitia inquam Dei* he begins his comments with a definition of *iustificatio*: 'He shows in a few words the nature of this justification (*qualis sit haec iustificatio*); that it resides in Christ and is apprehended by faith' (70[31-33]). He explains and expands this rather cryptic statement in an "order of procedure". The first step is to establish that we are here concerned with a judicial case – 'the case of our justification'. It is a case which is not heard before and judged by men, but which must be referred to the judgment of God. By his judgment, however, only 'perfect and absolute obedience to the Law' counts as righteousness. Therefore, if no man reaches 'such exact holiness', it follows that all men are destitute of righteousness in themselves. The second step is the step which Christ takes: 'Then Christ must appear on the scene'(70^{42}). The previous statement, that righteousness 'resides in Christ', now becomes 'he alone is righteous'. This sentence can only be understood if it is seen in terms of the union of Christ and the believer: 'as he alone is righteous, so by transferring his righteousness to us he makes us righteous' ($70^{42\text{-}43}$). By saying this, Calvin believes that he has made his next point: 'Now you see that the righteousness of faith is the righteousness of Christ' ($70^{43\text{-}44}$). That is to say, he has bound these two parts together to form complements: one cannot speak of the righteousness of Christ without at the same time speaking of the righteousness of faith, and conversely.

Calvin now expands what he has said by making use of the Aristotelian distinction of causes to bring out the unity and the absoluteness of each cause. In this immediate context we are given only three causes, the efficient, the material, and the instrumental: 'That we may be justified, therefore, the efficient cause is God's mercy; the material, Christ; the instrumental, the Word with faith' (70^{44}-71^{45}). Under v.24, *Iustificati gratis*, this becomes the usual four causes: 'he shows that the mercy of God is the efficient cause; that Christ, with his blood, is the material; that the formal, or instrumental, is faith conceived from the Word; and the final is the glory of the divine righteousness and goodness' ($72^{94\text{-}97}$). Thus, in this movement or change from unrighteous to righteous, the original and purposing cause is the free grace or mercy of God. To say that Christ, the sacrificed Christ ('Christ with his blood') is the material cause, means that Christ is not simply the instrument or means by which God wrought the change (this would be the formal cause) but is himself the agent of justification. The material cause is, then, the mediatorial work of Christ, the results of which (that is, the destruction of sin and the acquisition of righteousness) he communicates to the elect through the formal cause, faith in his Word. The final cause or ultimate purpose is that God's own righteousness or justice and his mercy in turning to man in Jesus Christ, may be justified in the event and therefore glorified.

It should also be noticed that at this point Calvin has a place for the reward of works. It is not only the person but also his activities, his works, which are reckoned righteous before God 'after we have become partakers of Christ' (71[47]), and the imperfections in the works of believers are 'obliterated by Christ's blood' (71[49-50]). For this reason they become perfect and are rewarded by God according to the promises conditional on good works (71[50-52]).

'There is no distinction. For all have sinned and lack the glory of God' (v.22b-23). Calvin follows and draws out the exclusiveness of these sentences. On the one hand there are not various ways of obtaining righteousness. All must be justified by faith, for the opposite of faith is glorying in works, and 'since all are sinners, they have not anything to glory of before God. Confusion and ignominy await all sinners before God's judgment seat' (71[67-70 & n.]). And on the other hand, the righteousness demanded by God is "perfect and absolute" (71[76]-72[77]) and not a "semi–righteousness" (*dimidia*) (72[77]), a hinted rejection of the current semi–Pelagian mingling of faith and works.

Calvin regards v.24 as 'perhaps the most remarkable place in the whole of Scripture for explaining and magnifying the force of this righteousness' (72[92-93]). The reason is that it contains all the four causes we have already spoken of. That the efficient cause is God's grace and mercy means that 'the whole is of God, and nothing of ours' (72[98]). 'The *materia* of our righteousness' (72[3]) is contained in the clause 'through the redemption which is in Christ Jesus', and it is so, 'because by his obedience Christ satisfied the judgment of the Father and by submitting in our place to the tyranny of death, by which he was held captive, he set us free' (72[3-5]).

Calvin has little of an expository nature to add to what he has already said when he comes to v.25. The first part is largely devoted to exegeses of the words *proponere* (προτίθεναι) and ἱλαστήριον. For the rest, he says that Paul's intention in this verse was to show that apart from Christ God is angry with us, and that we are reconciled through Christ when we receive his righteousness (continuing, in fact, the theme of *materia* and participation). It is not his own workmanship with which God is angry, but 'our uncleanness which extinguishes the light of his image. But when Christ the Lord cleanses it, God loves and embraces (*osculatur*) us as his pure work' ($73^{31-33 \& n.}$). And God's favour coincides with man's faith or trust, for Paul intended 'a propitiation through faith in his blood' to be taken as a single statement (*uno contextu*) – 'God is rendered favourable to us at the same time as we have our trust set in the blood of Christ; for by faith we come into possession of his benefit' (73^{35-37}) ("Blood" is to be taken broadly of the whole self-sacrificial work of Christ (73^{37-40}). We therefore receive righteousness by the remission of sins. But if remission is the gift of God, given purely out of his liberality, it follows that there can be no place for human merit. Certainly it must be added that remission does not serve as a licence to sin, for it is remission 'of sins that are past': 'the dispensation of the Gospel is to set the judgment and wrath of God before him who is going to sin in the future, but mercy before him who has sinned' (74^{67-69}).

This teaching was true at all times, but Paul with 'at this time' is here referring it to 'the day of Christ's showing' (75^{81-82}). The revelation of this righteousness had previously existed in the form of promises and sacraments. When Christ came, the promises and sacraments were realized in him. Calvin is here repeating what he had said earlier.

His comment on 'that he might be righteous' (v.26) is fairly short and again highly concentrated. God's righteousness is never rated highly enough until it alone is confessed to be worthy of honour, and he alone righteous. It must never be ascribed to men, who must be condemned universally of unrighteousness. But we then have to go on to say that his righteousness is one with his goodness and that 'the fullness of his righteousness and goodness' is shown by his pouring out the communication of his righteousness on men also. 'For all who are righteous are no otherwise justified than from the faith of Christ; otherwise all are ungodly. Therefore they are justified because they are reckoned righteous, even if they are not, when the obedience of Christ is imputed to them as righteousness' (75^{89-1n}).

We come to the 'splendid summary', the *egregium epiphonema* (76^{n5-9}) in which Paul triumphs over our vanity, which he has bruised and laid low with his arguments

(76^{n5-9}). Glorying is excluded (v.27), because we can bring forward nothing of our own that is worth God's approval or praise. Merit as the *materia* of glorying, whether it is the first stage of *meritum de congruo*, or the second of *meritum de condigno*, is here overturned. The glorying of works is removed by faith, and faith cannot be proclaimed in its purity without ascribing everything to God's mercy. And so man is despoiled of all praise $(76^{9-17 \& n})$. "Works", mentioned here without qualification, must be taken as the antithesis of faith. Glorying would not be excluded if righteousness were performing the works commanded in the Law. But if righteousness is of faith, which receives all things from God and brings nothing to him but a humble confession of poverty, then we have nothing to be proud of.

The "principal proposition", towards which Paul has been working, appears in v.28: 'Therefore we conclude, that a man is justified by faith without the works of the law'. Calvin's comments are practically confined to a refutation of the views of 'our present day adversaries', who 'mingle faith with merits of works' so that, although they confess that a man is justified by faith, yet they place the real power of justifying with love. The saying in James 2, that a man is not justified by faith alone but by works, must be taken in context, when it does not conflict with the present passage. But a fuller explanation, he says, will be found in my *Institutio* (1539 Cap. VI).

PART FIVE

CONCLUSION

Now that we have surveyed our authors and their books we must try to draw the separate studies together into something closer than an assembly of individuals. It is not possible to construct a single harmonious interpretation of the passages of Romans, or even two clearly opposed harmonious interpretations. In this respect, the best that can be done is to note agreements in general, agreements in intention and tendency. Nor would it be sensible to attempt to form doctrines out of expositions; this is always a hazardous undertaking, but with such short passages of commentary it would fail in almost every instance to do justice to the author. Therefore I do not propose to take up and argue either the idea of natural theology in the expositions on Rom.1.18–23 or the doctrine of justification from those on the other two passages.

We will first look at the circumstances of the commentaries, secondly at the methods used and their significance, and thirdly at the directions in which the expositions pointed.

What strikes us at once as we look at these books is the remarkable diversity of their authors. Three Italian cardinals: a German professor of Greek; two active members of the Paris Faculty of Theology; a provincial French diocesan director of studies and prison chaplain; the senior minister of the Reformed Church in Strasbourg, one day to become Regius Professor of Divinity in Cambridge; two Reformers from left-wing Zürich; and the man exiled from France, exiled from Geneva, the author of the *Institutio*. What is more important, however, is that the commentaries are not the product of Biblical schools. Jarrow, Laon, and St Victor have given place in the sixteenth century to individual commentators. The "Italy" of the three Italian cardinals was not a school. Paris could have been, with its great tradition and its

renewed interest in the Biblical languages; but in the event its
Biblical work at this period was vitiated by its obscurantism.
Geneva briefly became such a school, with the two Biblical
scholars of the first rank, Calvin and Beza, and the excellent
professors brought into the Academy – but that lies beyond
our period. Apart from Louvain, represented here by
Titelmann, Zürich was the nearest to the early medieval
schools, and Bullinger might be regarded as the counterpart
of Hugh of St Victor. But, apart from that one example, our
eleven commentators are eleven individuals with various
ecclesiastical, cultural, or personal relationships among themselves.

They are, however, drawn together into a group precisely
by their common concern with the Epistle to the Romans.
And it is a group with quite concrete inter-relationships.
Often, while studying them, one is driven to exclaim what a
small world it is, this world of the commentaries on Romans
in the fifteen-thirties. We see the circle around Bucer:
Guilliaud and Pellicanus, who copied from him; Sadoleto, to
whom he wrote a reply; Calvin, who wrote or revised much
of his own commentary while in almost daily converse with
him. Or, as we read Bullinger, Bucer, and Calvin, we are led
time and again back to Melanchthon, whether in method or
in doctrine; while from Melanchthon to Sadoleto is the link
forged by Erasmus. Or we may take Guilliaud, borrowing
from Bucer and Caietan, and also a fellow-member of the
Paris Faculty with Gagney and Haresche and, indeed, a
former class-mate of Gagney.

Yet from their relations we swing back again to their
individuality. They all expound the same verses; they all
expound the same text, for the variants are minimal; in the
main those commenting on the Vulgate have only occasionally a version markedly different in meaning from the original,
and these places their knowledge of Greek can cope with well
enough. And yet each exposition is so different from the
other, if not in substance yet in presentation and expression.
Each author has his own personal understanding of the
passage; perhaps it has been borrowed, but it is still what he
thinks the passage means. Each has his own way of

expressing that understanding; even when they have a common method of exposition, the individuals use it in their own way. So we get Haresche's scholastic St Paul, Sadoleto's Platonic St Paul, Bucer's Ciceronian St Paul, Caietan's literal St Paul. Even Bucer's satellites manage to present the material with some appearance of freshness.

Nor had their common task been undertaken with a common mind and in a common spirit. Nothing is more startling than the contrast between their initial sentiments on the Epistle. For Calvin, as for Luther before him, it is more 'useful' than his words can express (5^{2-4}); anyone who really understands it 'has the doors opened to all the profoundest treasures of Scripture' (5^{7-11}); no commentator could do better than expound Romans, for 'when anyone understands it, he has an entrance laid open into the understanding of the whole of Scripture' (2^{38-41}). For Bucer, in the Pauline Epistles 'absolutely everything is filled to the full with divine and most efficacious wisdom for all comfort of the soul, for the whole duty of life; so that the reading of the Apostle ought to stand for us in place of the oracles and the faculty of divining which once existed among the people of God' (iiii^r). In general, all the Reformers approached the book with this joyful sense of discovery.

For the other side Romans is a difficult book. We may excuse Gagney's prolonged grumble ('this one to the Romans is much the most difficult' of all Paul's Epistles – 3^v) as the rumbling of Parisian theological indigestion, but the attitude itself is shared by his fellow-Romanists. Even to Sadoleto, who could write with the excitement of one who had discovered what Romans really meant, the Epistle was a suitable hiding place for the new heretics because of the conciseness and obscurity with which it expressed sublime thoughts and God's secret counsels: 'a book so full of divine thoughts that it seems scarcely possible for the human mind to enter into its understanding' (10;7). Should one censure the temerity or praise the courage of a man who, in the face of such difficulty and danger, persisted in his intention of explaining Romans? (Perhaps Caietan was an exception. Since he neither expresses enthusiasm nor bemoans the difficulties, it is hard to say what his sentiments were.) There was also no common motive or purpose. For some of them it would not be unjust to say that they wrote less out of a desire to expound the teaching of St Paul than to claim St Paul's support for what they themselves believed. We must at once exempt from this charge Guilliaud and Pellicanus, both of whom seem to have been sincerely attempting to help the clergy in their task of preaching.

What we have already suggested of Caietan is also true of others. The "Lutherans" were preaching justification by faith alone as the genuine message of the Bible. Their opponents had only two bases of defence. They could have opposed the teaching of the Bible with "the teaching of the Church". Plainly this was an untenable position as here stated; but its weakness was at least masked by certain adjustments – for one, the existence of an oral tradition from the Apostles which had been developed and incorporated into "the teaching of the Church"; for another, that the understanding and interpretation of Scripture had been bestowed into the keeping of the Papacy. This latter adjustment lies behind much of the frustration and anger of Sadoleto and Haresche: Scripture had been interpreted, plausibly enough, in a sense contrary to the beliefs of later medieval Romanists. The other base of defence was to prove that Holy Scripture itself supported the Romanist position, and for this purpose, what could be bolder and more sensible than to show that the Epistle to the Romans itself refuted the novel teaching of justification by faith alone, as understood by the heretics? Caietan must stand supreme on the Romanist side in this respect for the calm and measured way in which he expounded the literal sense with the help of such rather meagre "modern" scholarship as he possessed.

Sadoleto seems to have embarked on his commentary for other reasons, and I am unable to take so favourable a view of him as M. Bernard Roussel does. When we have peeled off the humanist style and the Platonic discourse method, we are left with very ordinary ideas by a man who was temperamentally and artistically on the side of the humanists and therefore opposed to the obscurantists among his co-religious, but who had insufficient knowledge of theology to undertake the explanation of a theological work. We shall probably be not far from the truth if we ascribe his *Romans* to a combination of literary ambition and muddled ecclesiastical loyalty – unless perhaps unconsciously he wrote it to find out what he believed.

The Reformers were, on the face of it, in an easier situation, in that they were not setting out to defend a threatened interpretation, but were free to give themselves single-mindedly to the clarifying of St Paul's teaching. Moreover, they seem to have been more aware of what they were trying to do, altogether more sophisticated in their methodology. But perhaps their freedom from alien constraints is partly illusory. There was a pressure on them to show that the "novel" teaching was, as they claimed, the genuine Gospel, the teaching of God himself in his Word. And again, there was the secondary pressure of demonstrating (as Bucer set out to demonstrate) that their interpretation of Romans was faithful to that of earlier and purer centuries. Of course, they did not claim that their minds were free of dogmatic presuppositions. On the contrary, it was a part of their principle of interpretation that Scripture was to be understood in the light of its own presuppositions, according to its essential message. The message might be expressed in different terms – for example, it was for Bullinger the Covenant, for Calvin the sum of the Faith – but these different terms and concepts stood for a common central truth. This principle of interpretation was a continual guide in the process of exposition and as such was a presupposition already contained in the passage to be expounded.

We see, then, that our eleven commentators did not approach their task in a common spirit, with a common mind, from a common motive. The same must be said of their formal methods. Here the outstanding difference is between those who "rhetoricize" and those who do not. This needs explanation. Everyone who reads a piece of writing understands it, consciously or unconsciously, by the rules of rhetoric; there is no other way to understand. But when Bullinger says that the Reformers were accused of "rhetoricizing", what he means is that they were accused of interpreting the Bible by the canons of classical rhetoric. We have seen that Melanchthon was the first of our authors to adopt this method and that he was followed by Bullinger, Bucer, and Calvin (and no doubt by Pellicanus as well). Melanchthon himself, however, uses rhetoric more strictly and extensively than the others, and his rhetoric sometimes, in fact, becomes dialectic and concerns the logical structure of Romans. We have also seen that there was some difference among them on the purpose and scope of rhetoric in exposition, that, whereas Melanchthon, Bullinger, and Bucer employed it more as a literary tool, that is, in first understanding and then explaining the document, Calvin integrated it into the substance and argument of at least the earlier part of the Epistle as forensic rhetoric.

Those who do not use the rhetorical method of exposition are Caietan, Gagney, Grimani, and Sadoleto. Thus we see that it is the Reformers who "rhetoricize" on Romans, the Romanists who do not. This is a fact more easily noticed than explained. It cannot be because these four Reformers happened all to be men of the new learning and therefore used the tools of the new learning, for Sadoleto and Grimani were both humanists and yet did not "rhetoricize". It may be that commentaries on other Biblical books show a different grouping; but the fact that Melanchthon found I Corinthians less adapted to the rhetorical method than Romans was merely because 'The First Epistle to the Corinthians is not a coherent perpetual (una perpetua) disputatio' (C.R.XV.1065). Plainly, then, Reformation commentaries were not dependent on rhetoric; it was thought the proper method for Romans. The question to ask, it would seem, is not why the Reformers used the method, but why the Romanists did not. Perhaps it was merely a matter of loyalty to a tradition. Beside the ecclesiastical division, however, we ought also to observe that what we are witnessing here is a skirmish in the long warfare between rhetoric and dialectic.

Finally we come to the directions of the expositions on 2.13-16 and 3.20-28. There is, first, considerable diversity of outlook. In Haresche, his thinking ordered by the medieval

sacramental theology, we seem to be in another world from
Melanchthon's presentation of the wrestlings of the Christian
soul or from Caietan's intellectual, sober enquiries into the
literal meaning of each verse. Different from all these is
Calvin's solemn eschatological spectacle of man arraigned
before his Judge. Different, again, Bucer's comprehensive
survey of the landscape and heaven-scape of righteousness.
Different, Sadoleto's precarious efforts to plant his foot-steps
in the sea of Pelagianism while at the same time riding upon
the storm of Augustinianism.

Certain things they had in common. It would have been
strange if eleven men could expound the same passages and
not talk about the same thing. Rom.2.13-16 and 3.20-28
speak of the Law, righteousness, faith, works, grace,
justification, God, Jesus Christ and his death, sin, forgiveness, redemption. We shall expect to find all these mentioned, if not explained, in the expositions. And, in varying
degrees and with varying emphases, we do so find them. All
the writers dealt with the concepts set before them and in
general used the terminology they had been given.

We may go further. Their agreements, even on the
doctrine of justification, were greater than books on the
history of doctrines often tell us. They all held that man needs
to be justified, for he is in himself unrighteous and,
moreover, cannot justify himself. Secondly, as justification
involves man's relationship with God, so it is God who
effects the justification. Thirdly, the basis for justification is
the saving work of Christ. Fourthly, justification is of God's
grace. Fifthly, it is, on man's side, by faith. Sixthly, this faith
must be genuine faith. All these aspects of the doctrine will be
found in each of our authors, even if in a rather muted form
sometimes.

Are their disagreements, then, merely in terminology?
Certainly we can see some of the words – notably *grace* and
faith – bear different or additional meanings for the Romanists
than for the Reformers, and that among those on both sides
words are not given uniform weight. Does *faith* mean the
same thing to Haresche, Caietan, and Sadoleto? – that is to
say, does each lay the emphasis on the same aspect of faith?

Were Caietan and Grimani using *grace* in the same sense when
the one denied and the other affirmed that justification was by
grace alone? And were Melanchthon and Calvin saying
something quite different from them when they preferred
mercy as a synonym for *grace*?

It is when we ask about the consistent direction in which
each commentary points that the oppositions appear. If our
authors are measured by the six points of agreement, it
becomes clear that whereas the Reformers take them strictly
and consistently, the Romanists introduce qualifications into
all except the first and last. On these two there is agreement.
Man is unrighteous and cannot justify himself: faith must be
genuine and not spurious. But on the others the agreement is
limited. It is God who justifies: yes, but at a certain point
co-operation is demanded of man. The basis of justification is
the redemption wrought by Christ: yes, the *basis* on which
man, by the prompting and help of the Spirit, must build.
Justification is of God's grace: yes, understanding grace as the
initial work of the Spirit or as God's love in giving Christ to
die and rise again and so provide the basis. Justification is by
faith: yes, but not by faith only; man must co-operate; and
faith itself must be understood properly as a meritorious
virtue.

Caietan, Grimani, and perhaps Sadoleto, in their expositions on Romans, were all moderate men, what Calvin was
to call in later editions of his commentary 'our modern
moderators'. But even such eirenic persons as Bucer and
Melanchthon could not be satisfied with the "semi-
remission", "semi-righteousness" which they taught. The
objection of the Reformers was that this failed to do justice to
the Biblical view, which gives the complete glory in all things
to God in Christ.

As a last word, we must not lose sight of a momentous
fact. These opposites were engaged in a common task. For
whatever reason, whether from a desire to teach or from
reforming zeal or from a concern to defend an old and
threatened faith, they had all turned to a final court of appeal,
Holy Scripture. Merely by undertaking this particular task
and at this particular time they were confessing their belief in

Scripture as the final court of appeal. The fact that some of them qualified that confession by saying that only the Church under the Pope could properly understand and faithfully expound Scripture does not alter the confession itself; nor does even the adding of tradition to Scripture alter the confession – for in both cases it was what Paul wrote in Romans that has to be seen as agreeing with a commentary on Romans. Whatever qualifications and disclaimers they might make, our six Romanists, like our five Reformers, were, so to say, voting for the Bible with their pens.

Was there not here a foundation for agreement? Calvin certainly thought that acceptance of the authority of Scripture would mean the solution of the great controversy: 'If the Papists admitted that obedience to God is more than all sacrifices (1 Sam.15.22), we could easily come to an agreement. They might go on to argue over individual articles, but agreement would be reached if they would subscribe simply and unreservedly to the Word of God'.

BIBLIOGRAPHY

1. The Commentaries

Bonadus

Divi Pav=/li Apostoli Gentivm, Ac / Christi Iesu Ecclesiae doctoris Euangelici Epistolae di/uinae ad Orphicam lyram traductae Fran/cisco Bonado Angeriae / presbytero para-/ phraste. / Cap.16 Ad Rhomanos 1 / Ca.16 ca.13 Ad Corinthios 2 / Cap. 6 Ad Galathas 1 / Cap. 6 Ad Ephesios 1 / Cap. 4 Ad Philippenses 1 / Cap. 4 Ad Colossenses 1 / Cap. 5 ca. 3 Ad Thessalonicenses 2 / Ca. 6 ca. 4 Ad Timotheum. 2 / Cap. 3 Ad Titum 1 / Cap. 1 Ad Philonem 1 / Cap. 13 Ad Hebraeos 1 / Basileae, Anno / M.D.XXXVII.
Colophon: Apvd Bartholom. VVest=/ heme. Anno M.D.XXXVII. Romans, pp.15-59.

In/Testamenti/ Novi Maiorem Partem, Hoc/ est, in Euange-lia & Epistolas Pauli om-/nes, poemata carmine disertissimo à ua=/rijs & doctis, cum pręteriti tum no/ stri temporis Poëtis, in gra-/tiam studiosorum poëti/cae artis, collecta et aedita./ Quorum nomina uersa pagella / indicabit./Basileae.
No colophon, but: Bartholomaeus Wertheme/rus Phorzensis candido lectori. (Basileae M.D.XLII).
This collection contains six authors on various subjects or books. Bonadus' *Romans*, without introductory matter, forms pp.267-309.

Bucer

Metaphrases Et / Enarrationes Perpetvae Epistolarvm/ D. Pauli Apostoli, quibus singulatim Apostoli omnia,/ cum argumenta, tum sententiae & verba, ad autori-/ tatem D. scripturae, fidemq₃. Ecclesiae Catho-/licae tam priscae quam praesentis, religiose/ ac paolo fusius excutiuntur./ Dissiden-tivm in speciem locorvm Scri-/pturae, & primarum hodie in religionis doctrina con-/trouersiarum conciliationes & de-

210

cisiones. XLII./ Omnia citra dentem & ad communem
Ecclesiarum restituendam/ concordiam modis omnibus
accommodata./ Tomvs Primvs./ Continens Metaphrasim et
Enarrationem/ in Epistolam ad Romanos, in qua ut Apostolus praecipuos totius Theologiae / locos tractauit, quam
exactissime & plenissime, ita est hoc Tomo maxima / pars
totius non tam Paulinae, q̄ uniuerse S. Philosophię explicata./
Per Martinvm Bvcervm./ Argentorati per VVendelinvm /
Rihelium. Mense Martio. Anno / M.D.XXXVI.

Colophon: Excvsvm Argentorati Apvd VVende-/linum Rihelium, Mense Martio. Anno M.D. XXXVI.
pp. 1-507.

Bullinger

In Omnes Aposto=/licas Epistolas, Divi Videlicet / Pavli
XIIII. Et VII. Canonicas, Commentarii / Heinrychi Bulling-
eri, ab ipso iam recogniti, & / nonnullis in locis aucti./
Accessit operi Index copiosus, accesserunt ad finem quosq̊ /
duo libelli, alter de Testamento dei unico & aeterno, alter
uero / de Vtraq̊ in Christo natura./ [Device] / Iesvs./ Hic est
filius meus dilectus in quo placata est anima / mea, ipsum
audite./ Matthaei 17./ Tigvri Apvd Christophorvm Fros-
chove-/rum, Mense Martio. Anno M.D. XXXVII.
No colophon
pp.1-731, 1-195. Romans, pp. 3-121.

Caietan

Epistolae/ Pavli et Aliorvm Aposto=/lorum ad Gręcam
veritatem castigatę et per Re=/uerendissimum Dominū
Dominum Thomam de /Vio, Caetanum, Cardinalem sancti
Xisti, iuxta sen/sum literalem enarratae. Recens in lucem
editę./ [Device] Iehan Roigny:/ Apud Iod. Badium Ascen-
sium. & Ioan. Paruum./ & Ioannem Roigny. M.D.XXXII.
Colophon (at end of Jude): Caietę die. xvii. Augusti.
M.D.XXIX. aetatis autē proprię sexagesimo primo...
℃ Commentariorum Thomae de Vio Caietani Cardinalis
sancti Xisti in epistolas / omnes Pauli & canonicas, per
Ioannem Danielis. S.D.N. p̄p̄. poeniten=/tiarium & authoris

operis familiarem summo studio reco=/gnitorum: finis. Laus
uni & trino./ Sub prelo Ascensiano, mense Maio, Anno
domini / M.D.XXXII.
Romans, fo. I–XLVIII.

R.R.D.D./ Thomae de Vio / Caietani / Titvli S.Xisti
Presbyteri / Cardinalis Eminentissimi / in Omnes D. Pavli et
Aliorvm / Apostolorvm Epistolas / Commentarii, nunc
denuo recogniti.../Tomvs Qvintvs. / [Device]/ Lvgdvni,/
Sumptibus Iacobi & Petri Prost./ M.DC.XXXIX.
Romans, pp.1–84.

Ientacv=/la noui testamenti Cardi./nalis sancti Xisti./ℭ
Reuerendissimi domini Thomę de Vio ca/ietani Cardinalis
sancti Xisti preclarissima/ sexagintaquattuor notabilium sen-
tentiarum / noui testamenti literalis expositio, in/ duodecim
capita distincta: que toti /dē Ientacula noui testamen=/ti
ratione operis initio / reddita inscribūtur./ [Device]/ Colonie,
Anno domini M.D.XXVI./ Mense Iulio.
Colophon: Finis Ientaculorum noui testamenti per / R.D.D.
Caietanum Cardinal. S. Xisti / & cetera. Anno M.D. XXVI./
iiij Iulii.

Calvin
Ioannis / Calvini Commenta=/rij in Epistolam Pauli / ad
Romanos./ [Device] / Argentorati per Vuendelinum /Rihe-
lium./
Colophon: Argentorati per Vuendelinum / Rihelium./ Mense
Martio./ Anno M.D.XL.

Iohannis Calvini Commentarius in Epistolam Pauli ad
Romanos. Edidit T.H.L. Parker. Leiden, 1981

Gagney
Epitome / Paraphrastica / enarrationum Ioannis Ga-/gnaeii
Parisini doctoris / Theologi, in epistolā / diui Pauli apostoli /
ad Romanos./ Parisiis./ Apvd Michaelem Vasco-/sanvm, Via
Ad Divvm / Iacobvm, Svb Si-/gno Fontis./M.D.XXXIII.
No Colophon

Divi Pav/li Apostoli / Epistolae, Bre=/uissimis & facillimis scho/lijs per Ioannē Gagnęiū / Parisinum Theologum / Christianissimi Francorū / regis Ecclesiasten & do=/ctorem illustratae./ Parisiis / Apud Simonē Colinaeū,/ & Galliotum à Prato./ 1538 / Cum priuilegio ad triennium.
Colophon: Parisiis Apvd Simonem / Colinaevm Et Galiotvm À / Prato Anno Domini Mil=/lesimo Qvingentesi=/mo XXXVIII Men=/se Martio.
Romans, fo. l^r − 26^r.

Grimani
Commentarii In Epistolas / Pavli, Ad Romanos,/ Et Ad Galatas./ [Device] /Venetiis. M.D. XLII.
Colophon: Apvd Aldi Filios./ Venetiis. M.D.XLII./ Mense Martio.
Fo. 1–173.

Guilliaud
Collatio / In Omnes Divi / Pavli Aposto-/li Episto-/las,/ Iuxta eruditorum sententiam facta, per s. Theo=/logiae Doctorem Claudium Guillaudum Belli=/iocensem, apud insignem Eduorum ecclesiam / Praepositum, & Canonicum ecclesiasten./ Omnia iudicio Eccle=/siae submissa/ sunto. / [Device] / Lvgdvni Apvd Seb./ Gryphivm./ M.D.XLII.
Colophon: Omnia Ivdicio / Ecclesiae Svbmis-/sa svnto. pp. 1-465.
Romans, pp. 1-107.

Collatio/In Omnes Divi / Pavli Aposto=/li Episto-/las . . . Lvgdvni Apvd Seb./Gryphivm,/M.D.XLIIII.

In/Omnes Divi / Pavli Apostoli Epi-/stolas, Collatio./ . . . / Parisiis,/ Apud Audoënum Paruum, via ad / diuum Iacobum, sub Lilio aureo./ 1548.

Haresche
Expositio / Tvm Dilvcida, Tvm Bre=/vis Epistolae Divi Pavli Ad / Romanos cum definitionibus vocum diffici=/ liorum, & diuersarum acceptionum adnota=/tione, ex veteri

testamento authoritates, siue / septuaginta interpretum, siue hebraicę verita=/tis, quas interdum sequitur Apostolus ita pla=/num facieris: vt nemo sit qui non ex ea fru=/ ctum capere possit vberrimum. Authore / Fratre Philiberto Haresche Augu=/stinianę familię Doctore Theo=/logo facultate, origine, &/ conuentu Parisi=/ensi./ Cum indice copiosissimo./ ℂ Parisiis./ Vęnit apud Ioannem Paruum & / Poncetum le Preu [effaced by ULC bookmark] in vico Iacobęo./ 1536./ ℂ Cum priuilegio.

Colophon: Absolutum est in alma Parisiorum/ academia opus hoc expositionis epi=/stolę ad Romanos Fr. Philiberti Ha=/resche Heremitanę Augustinianę fa=/milię doctoris Theologi facultate, o=/rigine, & conuentu Parisieñ. Anno a / Christo nato sesquimiliesimo trige=/simo sexto mense Iulio. Fo. i – cccxxxvii.

Lonicer

Vetęris Cv-/iuspiam Theologi Graeci / Svccincta In D. Pavli Ad Romanos Episto-/lam Exegesis, ex Graecis Sacrae Scripturae/ interpretibus desumpta: nimirum ex / Theodoreto / Gennadio / Isidoro / Ioanne Chrysostomo / Cyrillo / Oecumenio / Seueriano/ Gregorio Nazanzeno / Photino / Basilio / Tito aduersum Manichaeos / Methodio, in concione de Resurre-/ctione / Dyonisio Alexandriense./ Ioanne Lonicero interprete./ Cum gratia & priuilegio Imperiali / ad quintum quennium./ Basileae./ 1537.

Colophon: Basileae, In Officina / Roberti Winter./ Anno a Christo nato / M.D.XXXVII./ Mense Septembri.

Melanchthon

Com/mentarii In Episto/lam Pavli Ad / Romanos, Re=/cens scripti a Philippo Melan./ Anno./ 1.5.3.2.
Colophon: Impressvm Vitebergae / In Edibvs Iosephi Clvg. fo. 1 – 264.

Com=/mentarii In Epi=/stolam Pavli / ad Romanos, hoc anno / M.D.XL. recogni=/ti, & locuple=/tati./ Autore Philippo Melanthone./ Vitebergae. Anno. M.D.XL.

Colophon: Impressvm Viteber/gae per Iosephum Clug./ Anno./ M.D.XLI.
fo. I – CCLXXVIII.

Pellicanus

In Omnes Aposto=/licas Epistolas, Pavli, Petri, Iaco=/bi, Ioannis Et Ivdae D. Chvonradi Pellicani / Tigurinae ecclesiae ministri Commentarij, ad collationem opti=/morum quorumqȝ interpretum conscripti & aediti,/ in usum theologiae apostolicae / studiosorum./ [Device] / Psal. XIX./ In omnem terram exivit sonus eorum, & in fines orbis / terrarum verba illorum./ Tigvri In Officina Froscho=/uiana Mense Augusto, Anno / M.D.XXXIX.
No Colophon.
pp. 1 – 795
Romans, pp. 1 – 176.

Sadoleto

The copy of which I saw a photocopy lacked the title: Lyons, Sebast. Gryphius, 1535.

Iacobi Sadole=/ti Episcopi Car/pentoractis In Pav=/li Epistolam Ad Roma/nos Commentario/rvm Libri / Tres./ Ad Lectorem./ Exeunt iterum a nobis, Lector, Iacobi Sadoleti Commentarij, multa / diligentia ab autore nunc demum recogniti, & locis quamplurimis ab / eodem tum aucti, tum immutati. Tu uiri tam integri, & religiosi tam san/ctis religiosisqȝ lucubrationibus fruere, & nostram tibi deditam operam / atqȝ laborem ama./ [Device] / Sebastianvs Gryphivs / Germanvs Excvde/bat Lvgdvni,/ Anno / M.D.XXXVI.
No Colophon.
pp. 1 – 231

Jacobi Sadoleti / Cardinalis Et Episcopi / Carpentoractensis / Viri Disertissimi,/ Opera quae exstant omnia./ Quorum plura sparsim vagabantur,/ Quaedam doctorum virorum cura nunc/ primum prodeunt./ Veronae / Ex Typographia Joannis Alberi Tumermani./ M.DCC.XXXVII./ Superiorum Permissu Ac Privilegio. (vols. 2-4 1738).

Titelmann

Colla/tiones Qvinqve Svper/ Epistolam ad Romanos beati Pauli Apostoli, qui=/bus loca eius Epistolae difficiliora, ea potissimum / quae ex Graecis aliquid habere uidentur difficultatis / diligentissime tractantur atq₃ explicantur, ita ut e=/am a graece nescientibus facile capi ualeat empha/sis graecarum dictionum, simul & Ecclesiastica no=/ui Testamenti latina aeditio rationabiliter defendi=/tur. Idq₃ ex authoritate ueterum interpretū, caetero/rumq₃ probatissimorum patrum, latinorū pariter / atq₃ graecorum. Per Fratrē Franciscū Titelmannum / Hasselēsem, ordinis Fratrū minorū, sanctarū scri/pturarū apud Louanienses Praelectorem./ Antuerpiae apud Guilielmum Vorstermannum./ Anno. M.CCCC.XXIX. Mense Maio./ Cum Gratia & Priuilegio. *Colophon*: Antverpiae, Apvd Gvilielmvm / Vorstermannvm, Anno. M./CCCCC.XXIX. Mense/Maio.

Fo. 1 – 308, with 4 fo. concluding matter.

Elvci=/datio In Omnes / Epistolas Apostolicas,/ quatuordecim Paulinas, & Canonicas septem,/ vna cum textu ad marginem adiecto, & ita com/mode distributo, vt vnaquaeq₃ textus particula / suae elucidationi exaduerso respondeat, iuxta ve=/ritatem veteris & vulgatae aeditionis, additis ar/gumentis, quae & Epitomatū vice esse possint,/ totam Epistolarum substantiam, iuxta ordinem / singulorum capitum, summatim complecten=/tibus, Per fratrem Franciscum Titelmannum / Hasselensem, ordinis Fratrum Minorum,/ sacrarum scripturarum apud Loua=/nienses Praelectorem: ex ipsa/authoris recognitione,/ iam tertio typis / exusa./ Antuerpiae apud Michaelem Hillenium,/ Anno Dñi. 1532. Mense Maio.

No Colophon.

Romans, sig. A8ᵛ – F6ʳ.

In Omnes / Epistolas Apostoli-/cas F. Francisci Titelmanni Or/dinis Minoritorum, publici sacrarum litera-/rum apud Louanienses quondam Lectoris / Elucidatio, una cum Textu suo loco ad mar/ginem trāslato, & argumentis miro / compendio capitis cuiusq₃ ma-/teriam complectentibus./ Ex

autoris recognitio/ne iam cultius quam /antehac unquam / renata sunt/omnia. ¶ Multa hic inuenies Lector eruta, quae hacte- / nus attigit nemo, multa explicata, quae / in hunc diem usq; obscuriora / sunt uisa. / ¶ Paulus. Ephe. 5./ ¶ Si spiritu uiuimus, spiritu & ambulemus./ ¶ Antvverpiae / ¶ Apud Ioannem Steelsium sub / scuto Burgundię. Anno/ M.D.XL.
Romans, fol. 9^r – 50^r.

2. Other commentaries
Ambrose
Divi Ambrosii Epi/scopi Mediolanensis Opervm To-/mus Quartus, continens explanationes, hoc est ea / quae faciunt ad interpretationem diuina-/rum scripturarum, ueteris testa/menti, deniq; noui./
Colophon: Basileae Apvd Ioannem Frobenivm/ Mense Avgv-sto An-/no M.D.XXVII.

Divi Ambrosii Epi/scopi Mediolanensis Omnia Ope=/ra, per eruditos viros ex accurata diuersorum codicum / col-latione emēdata, Graecis quę vel aberāt, vel erāt / corruptissi-ma, plerisq; ī locis feliciter restitutis,/ in quatuor ordines digesta: quorū prim^9 ha=/ bet mores: secūdus pugnas aduersus hae=-/reticos: terti^9 oratiōes, epistolas, & cō=/ ciones ad populum: quartus expla=/nationes voluminum veteris & noui testamenti:/ Cui supra Frobenianam editionē accessit nusquā hacte=/nus impressa elegans & erudita eiusdem authoris / in duodecim Davidicos psalmos enarra-tio./ Inspice lector, & comperies alium Ambro=/sium q̄ antehac habuisti./ .../ Parisijs ex officina Claudij Cheuallonij sub / Sole aureo in via Iacobaea./ 1529.
Colophon: Lvtetię Parisiorvm Apvd / Clavdivm Chevalo-nivm / Mense Febrvario M.D.XXIX.

Qvintvs Tomvs /Divi Ambrosii Epi/scopi Mediolanensis Opervm Complectens Scho-/liorum seu Commentariorum in Euangelium Lucae libros x./ tum Commentarios in omnes Pauli epistolas, excepta / ad Hebraeos./ .../ Basileae / Anno MD.XXXVIII.

Colophon: Basileae Apvd Hieronymvm Frobenivm, Et /
Nicolavm Episcopivm. Mense Martio / Anno M.D.XXXVIII.

Thomas Aquinas
Commētaria San/cti Thome Aquinatis in epistolas Pauli/
...1529/ ℭ Venundantur Parisijs in vico sancti Iacobi./ Apud
Iohannem Pettit. Sub Lilio aureo.

Diui Thome aquinatis / ... in beati Pau-/li apostoli epistolas /
commentaria...Parisijs./ ℭ Veneunt in via Iacobea sub sole
aureo./ M.D. xxxij.

Diui Thomae Aquinatis, ... in omnes beati / Pauli Apostoli
epistolas commenta/ria... Parisiis./ Ex officina...Ambrosij
Girault Pellicani via ad / Diuum Iacobum ante S. Yuonem
1541.

Peter Lombard
Petri Longobardi...in omnes / D. Pauli Apost. Epistolas
Collectanea,/ ex DD. Augustino, Ambrosio, Hieronymo,
aliisque / nonnullis S. scripturae primariis Interpretibus,
sum-/ma arte diligentiaꝗ contexta... Pro Haeredibus Iod.
Badii Ascensii / MDXXXV, Mense Decembri.

Petri Longo/bardi, ... In Om=/nes D. Pauli Apost. Epistolas
Collecta-/nea, ex DD. Augustino, Ambrosis, Hiero-/nymo,
aliisque nonnullis S.scripturae prima-/tiaꝗ contexta ...Parisiis /
Apud Ambrosium Girault, in via Iacobea, sub intersignio /
Pellicani./M.D.XXXVII.
Colophon: ... Mense Septembri. M.D.XXXVI.

Primasius
Primasii / Vticensis...In Omnes / D. Pauli epistolas commen-
tarij...Coloniae,/ Excudebat Ioannes Gymnicus, Anno /
M.D. XXXVIII.

Theophylact
Theophy/lacti...in omnes D. Pau/li epistolas enarrationes,/
diligentèr re=/cognitae./ Christophoro Porsena Romano /

interprete./ .../ Eucharius Ceruicornus excudebat,/ Anno M.D.XXVIII.
Colophon: Coloniae impensis honesti uiri Godefridi / Hytor-pij pridie calendas Martij.

Theophy/lacti... in omnes D. Pavli / epistolas enarrationes, di=/ligenter recognitae./ Christophoro Porse/na Romano interprete./.../Coloniae, ex officina Eucharij Ceruicorni,/ Anno M.D.XXXII./ mense Martio.
Colophon: ... pridie calendas Ianuarij.

Theophy/lacti...in omnes D. Pauli episto/las enarrationes, diligenter / recognitae./ Christophoro Porse/na Romano interprete./.../Coloniae, ex officina Melchioris Noueli=/ani, M.D. XXXVII.

Theophylacti Bulgariae in omnes diui Pauli Apostoli Episto-las enarrationes, iam recens ex uetustissimo archetypo Graeco per D. Ioannem Lonicerum fidelissime in Latinum conuersae. 1540.

3. Bibles and New Testaments
Colinaeus

Η ΚΑΙΝΗ ΔΙΑΘΗΚΗ ... Εν λευκετία τών Παρησιων, Παρα Σίμωνι τῷ Κολιναίῳ [1534]

Complutensis
Nouum testamentum grece & latine in academia complutensi nouiter impressum [1522]

Erasmus
(1) Novvm Instrumentū omne, diligenter ab Erasmo Roter-odamo recognitum & emendatum... una cum Annotationi-bus...[Froben, Basel, 1516]

(2) Novvm Testamentvm omne, mvlto qvam antehac diligentius ab Erasmo Roterodamo recognitū, emēdatum ac translatum... [Froben, Basel, 1519]

(3) Novvm Testamentvm omne, tertio iam ac diligentius ab Erasmo Roterodamo recognitum...[Froben, Basel, 1522]

(4) En Novvm Testamentvm, ex Erasmi Roterodami Recognitione, iam quartum damus studiose lector, adiecta uulgata translatione...[Froben, Basel, 1527]

(5) Novvm Testamentvm iam qvintvm accvratissima cura recognitum a Des. Erasmo Roter....[Froben, Basel, 1535]

Stephanus
Biblia..Parisiis Ex officina Roberti Stephani...M.D.XXVIII.

Biblia Breves in eadem annotationes, ex doctiss. interpretationibus, & Hebraeorum commentariis...Ex officina Roberti Stephani. M.D. XXXII.

4. Other books mentioned

Bale, John: Select Works (Parker Society, Cambridge, 1849).

Baudrier, J.: Bibliographie Lyonnaise (Lyons & Paris, 1908).

Bizer, E.: Theologie der Verheissung. Studien zur theologischen Entwicklung des jungen Melanchthon (1519-1524) (Neukirchen, 1964).

Bucer: Common Places of Martin Bucer. Tr. and ed. by D. F. Wright (Abingdon, 1972).

Bullinger: Heinrich Bullingers Diarium (Annales Vitae) der Jahre 1504-1574...herausgegeben von E. Egli (Basel, 1904).

...Heinrici Bvllingeri...Ratio Stvdiorvm, sive De institutione eorum, qui studia literarum sequuntur...Tiguri, excudebat Iohannes VVolphius, 1594.

De Scripturae Sanctae Praestantia...dissertatio...Tigvri Excvdebat Christ. Frosch.M.D.LXXI.

Caietan: Epistola Theologorvm Parisiensium, ad Cardinalem Coetanum reprehensoria. Vitebergae 1534. [Excudebat Nicolaus Schirlentz].

Calvin: Ioannis Calvini Opera Quae Supersunt Omnia, tom. XL. Ed. E.Reuss, A.Erichson, G.Baldensperger (Brunswick, 1889).

Dictionnaire de Biographie Chrétienne, ed. F. X. de Feller et F. Pérennès (Paris, 1851).

Douglas, R. M. : Jacopo Sadoleto (1477-1547), Humanist & Reformer (Cambridge, Mass., 1959).

Eells, H.: Martin Bucer (New Haven and London, 1931).

Erasmus: Opus Epistolarum Des. Erasmi Roterodami Denuo Recognitum et Auctum Per P. S. Allen et H. M. Allen Tom. VIII (1529-1530). (Oxford, 1934). Tom. IX-XI (1530-1536) Per H. M. Allen et H. W. Garrod (Oxford, 1938, 1941, 1947).

Farge, J. K.: Biographical Register of Paris Doctors of Theology 1500-1536 (Toronto, 1980).

Feret,P.: La Faculté de Théologie de Paris et ses Docteurs les plus Célèbres. Tome Second. XVIe Siècle (Paris, 1901).

Gilbert, N. W. : Renaissance Concepts of Method (New York, 1960).

Girardin, B.: Rhétorique et Théologique. Calvin. Le Commentaire de l'Épitre aux Romains (Théologie Historique 54. Paris, 1979).

Hagen, K.: Hebrews Commenting from Erasmus to Bèze 1516-1598 (Tübingen, 1981).

Jenkins, R.C.: Pre-Tridentine Doctrine. A review of the Commentary on the Scriptures of Thomas de Vio, Cardinal of St. Xystus, commonly called Cardinal Cajetan (London, 1891).

Joachimsen, P.: Loci Communes. Eine Untersuchung zur Geistesgeschichte des Humanismus und der Reformation (Luther-Jahrbuch 1926. Re-printed Amsterdam, 1966).

Joly, A.: Etudes sur J. Sadolet (1477-1547) (Caen, 1856; reprinted Geneva, 1970).

Melanchthon: Philippi Melanthonis Opera Quae Supersunt Omnia edidit C.G. Bretschneider, tom. XIII-XV (Halle, 1846, 1847, 1848).

Oldoinus, A.:Vitae, Et Gestae Pontificvm Romanorvm Et S.R.E. Cardinalivm ... Alphonsi Ciaconii .. descriptae ... Ab Avgvstino Oldoino ... recognitae ... Romae, MDCLXXVII.

Athenaevm .. Stvdio Avgvstini Oldoini ... Erectvm ... Pervsiae M.DC.LXXVI.

Original Letters Relative to the English Reformation. Ed. H. Robinson (Parker Society, Cambridge, 1847).

Parker, T.H.L.: Calvin's New Testament Commentaries (London, 1971).

Pollet, J.V.: Martin Bucer Etudes sur la correspondance avec de nombreux textes inédits. 2 vols. (Paris, 1958, 1962).

Potter, G.R.: Zwingli (Cambridge, 1976).

Roussel, B.: Martin Bucer et Jacques Sadolet: la concorde possible (Bulletin de la Société de l'histoire de protestantisme français, 1976, pp. 525-550. Paris, 1976).

Sadoleto: Jacobi Sadoleti S.R.E. Cardinalis Epistolae Qvotqvot Extant Proprio Nomine Scriptae Nunc Primum Duplo Auctiores In Lucem Editae. Pars Secunda Romae, MDCCLX. Excudebat Generosus Salomonius Praesidum Facultate.

Schiess, T.: Briefwechsel der Brüder Ambrosius und Thomas Blaurer 1509-68 (Freiburg, 1908ff.).

Simon, Richard: Histoire critique des principaux Commentateurs du Nouveau Testament... A Rotterdam, chez Reinier Leers, MDCXCIII.

Walch: Io. Georgii Walchii Bibliotheca Theologica Selecta Litterariis Adnotationibus Instructa. Tomus Quartus ...Ienae Sumtu Viduae Croeckerianae MDCCLXV.

Zürcher, C.: Konrad Pellikans Wirken in Zürich 1526-1556 (Zürcher Beiträge zur Reformationsgeschichte Bd. 4. Zürich, 1975).

INDEX

Adrian VI 26
Agricola, R. 1, 19
Albert, Archbp of
    Brandenburg 4
Amerbach 6, 27
Ambrose 14, 24, 25, 28, 33,
    77, 145, 153, 183, 217-8
Anabaptists 189
Aquinas 7, 8, 14, 16, 77, 160,
    218
Arbenz 36 n.23
Aristotle 1, 16, 109f., 197
Atticus 140, 186
Augsburg, Bp of 6
Augsburg, Diet of vii
Augustine 6, 15, 24, 28, 31,
    33, 34, 139, 143, 145, 151,
    180, 181, 183, 187, 191f.,
    207

Badia 28
Bale 11, 220
Basil 33, 65
Baudrier 80 n.45, 220
Bede 15
Bembo 26
Beza 71, 90 n.1, 202
Bibliander 69
Bizer 1 n.1, 220
Blaurer 35 n.22
Bonadus 65 & n.32, 210

Bucer v, vii, viii, x, 7, 22, 25,
    29, 34-61, 70, 71, 72, 73ff.,
    82, 83, 85, 86, 89, 91, 96,
    107-111, 113, 114, 115, 116,
    117, 122, 123, 124, 125,
    129, 137-8, 143, 144, 145,
    146, 147, 148, 149f., 151,
    152, 155, 156, 160, 166,
    174-180, 180-184, 192, 193,
    202, 203, 205, 206, 207,
    208, 210-11, 220
Budé, G. 177
Bullinger v, vi, viii, x, 14-23,
    35, 65, 69, 70, 71, 73, 74,
    76, 84, 85, 86, 87, 90, 92,
    104-6, 113, 129, 138f., 141,
    142, 144, 145, 146, 147,
    148, 150, 151, 153, 184-5,
    192, 202, 205, 206, 211-12,
    220

Caietan v, vi, vii, viii, x, 7-11,
    76, 82, 84, 85, 86, 87, 88,
    89, 90, 91, 92, 93, 99-104,
    125, 126, 127, 129-31, 132,
    138, 142, 146, 147, 148,
    151, 152, 154f., 155,
    156-60, 202, 203, 204, 206,
    207, 208, 211-12, 220
Calvin v, vi, vii, viii, x, 4, 7,
    10, 15, 22, 23, 35, 37, 71-

77, 82, 84f., 86, 87, 88, 90, 91,
    92, 93, 94, 95, 96, 116-20,
    125, 126, 129, 140-1, 142f.,
    144, 145, 146, 147, 148,
    151, 152, 153, 154, 155,
    156, 159 n.8, 193-200, 201,
    202, 203, 205, 206, 207,
    208, 209, 212, 220
Capreolus 28
Carrensis 16
Catharinus vii, 10
Chrysostom 14, 24, 27, 28,
    33, 65, 70 n.38, 86, 143,
    151, 193f.
Cicero 1, 22
    de nat. deorum 109, 114f.,
    119, 203
Clement VII 26
Clug 4
Colinaeus x, 82, 84, 87, 88,
    219
Complutensis x, 82, 84, 87,
    88, 91, 92, 126, 127, 128,
    142, 146, 147, 149, 150,
    154, 155, 219
Contarini 32, 34
Cranmer 36, 159 n.8
Crozet 81
Cyril 65

Danès 23
Darwell and Moule 79f.
De Bujanda 81 n.46
de la Porte 79f.
de Lorraine 66
Demosthenes 22
Dionysius 65
Douglas 28f., 29 n.15, 174,
    180, 221
du Bellay 177
du Moulin 24
Duns Scotus 16
Durandus 28

Eells 36 n.23, 221
Epicurus 98 n.5

Erasmus 1, 6, 8, 10, 11, 12,
    18, 21, 24, 27, 29, 77, 78,
    82, 120, 202, 221
    Annotations 34, 82-3, 84,
        86, 87, 89f., 92, 93f.,
        125, 127, 148, 149, 150,
        151, 153, 154, 156
    Editions ix, 18, 20, 34,
        82-3, 84, 87, 88, 91, 92,
        125, 126, 127, 142,
        144, 146, 147, 149,
        150, 154, 155, 156,
        219-20
    Version ix, x, 84, 87, 88,
        90, 91, 92, 93, 125,
        126, 127, 128, 142,
        144, 147, 148, 149,
        150, 154, 155, 156
    Vulgate x, 84, 87, 88, 91,
        93, 125, 127, 128, 142,
        144, 147, 149, 150f.,
        154, 155
Estienne, see Stephanus
Euthymius 33

Faber, see Lefèvre
Fabius 141
Farge 23 n.13, 62 nn.29, 30,
    63 n.31, 79, 81 n.46, 221
Feller 79 n.44, 221
Feret 221
Francis I 23, 29
Froben 27
Froschauer 67

Gagney v, vi, x, 23-5, 62, 65,
    66-7, 70, 87, 89, 90, 202,
    203, 206, 212-13
Galen 99
Gellius 144
Gennadius 65
Giberti 26
Gilbert 2 n.2, 221
Girardin 76, 221
Glossa interlinearia 64
Glossa ordinaria 68, 80 n.45

Gratian 14, 15
Gregory Nazianzen 65
Grimani, Domenico 78
Grimani, Giovanni 78
Grimani, Marino v, vi, x, 4,
    77–8, 82, 85, 86, 87, 89,
    120–22, 125, 129, 132–3,
    143, 144, 146, 148, 152,
    153, 155, 163–6, 190, 193,
    206, 208, 213
Grynée 71f.
Gryphius 27
Guilliaud v, vi, viii, x, 4, 62,
    79–82, 89, 122–4, 129,
    131–2, 155, 160–1, 202, 204,
    213

Hagen 65 n.32, 221
Haller 15, 23
Haresche v, vi, vii, x, 62–5,
    86, 91, 111–3, 126, 129,
    133–6, 143f., 145, 147, 153,
    155, 156, 161–3, 185, 190,
    202, 203, 204, 206f., 213–4
Haugubinus, see Pagninus
Higman 81 n.46
Hugh of St. Victor 90, 123
Hurault 79, 80, 81

Isidore 65

Jenkins 10f., 11 n.8, 159 n.8,
    221
Jerome 15, 24, 142, 194
Joachimsen 2 n.2, 221
Joly 221

Lefèvre 1, 8, 10, 12
Leo X 26
Lewis and Short 92
Liddell and Scott 109 n.6
Littré 80 n.45
Lombard, see Peter of
    Lombard
Lonicer 65, 214
Luther v, 1, 7, 8, 10, 15, 21,

    26, 37, 64, 203
Lyra, see Nicolas of Lyra

Melanchthon v, vi, vii, viii, x,
    1–7, 15, 19, 22, 27, 70, 73,
    74, 77, 85, 86, 87, 88, 96–9,
    116, 117, 125, 126, 129,
    139–40, 141, 142, 145, 146,
    148, 150, 152, 153f., 183,
    185–91, 202, 206, 207, 208,
    214–5, 221
Methodius 65
Mexia 12
Myconius 70 n.38

Nicolas of Lyra 16
Novatians 154

Occam 28
Oecumenius 65
Oldoinus 78, 221–2
Origen 6, 14, 24, 90, 110, 142,
    145, 151, 183, 194

Pagninus 80 n.45
Parker, T.H.L. 222
Paul III 78
Pelagianism 31, 33, 129, 137,
    160, 168, 174, 180, 193, 207
Pellicanus v, vi, vii, x, 18f.,
    67–70, 86, 87, 89, 113–6,
    129, 140, 142, 143, 144,
    151, 191–3, 202, 204, 206,
    215
Pérennès 79 n.44, 221
Peter of Lombard 7, 14, 15,
    16, 34, 65, 69, 187, 218
Philip of Hesse 4
Photinus 65
Plato 31, 119, 179, 203, 204
Pollet 35 nn.19, 20, 71, 222
Potter 67 n.35, 222
Primasius 24, 65, 70, 77, 218

Quintilian 96

Rabanus Maurus 15
Regensburg, Conference at vii
Reuchlin 78
Reuss v
Roussel 25, 29 n.15, 174,
    177ff., 204, 222

Sadoleto, Jacopo v, vi, vii, x,
    6, 8, 25-34, 82, 136-7, 142,
    144, 166-80, 202, 203, 204,
    206, 207, 208, 215, 222
Sadoleto, Julius 31, 32, 144,
    167, 171
Schiess 35 n.22, 222
Scipio 140, 186
Scotus, see Duns Scotus
Seneca 71, 105
Septuagint 63
Servetus 79f., 80 n.45
Severianus 65
Simon, Richard v, 8 n.5, 10,
    25, 174, 222
Soto vi
Stephanus, R. 23, 220
    Vulgate ix, x, 84, 87, 88,
        91, 93, 125, 126, 127,
        128, 142, 144, 147,
        148, 149, 150, 154,
        155, 156
Steuchus 78

Stoic theology 108ff., 118,
    121, 123
Sturm 177

Theodoret 65
Theophylact 14, 24, 33. 65,
    151, 156, 219
Titelmann v, vi, 11-14, 24, 77,
    202, 216-7
Titus of Bostra 65
Trent, Council of vi, vii, 7,
    71, 83

Valla 12
Venetus 63
Villeneuve, see Servetus
Virgil 23
Vulgarius 156
Vulgate vii, x, 9, 10, 11, 13,
    63, 70, 78, 82f., 88, 89, 90,
    93, 148, 151, 153, 202
    see also Erasmus Vulgate
    and Stephanus Vulgate

Walch 10, 222
Wartmann 36 n.23
Wright 35 n.16

Zürcher 67 n.34, 69, 222
Zwingli 14, 69